Effective Teaching Strategies That Accommodate Diverse Learners

Third Edition

Michael D. Coyne
University of Connecticut

Edward J. Kame'enui
University of Oregon

Douglas W. Carnine
University of Oregon

PEARSON

Merrill
Prentice Hall

Upper Saddle River, New Jersey
Columbus, Ohio

Library of Congress Cataloging-in-Publication Data

Coyne, Michael D.

    Effective teaching strategies that accommodate diverse learners/Michael D. Coyne, Edward J. Kame'enui, Douglas W. Carnine. —3rd ed.

        p. cm.

    Rev. ed. of: Effective teaching strategies that accommodate diverse learners/Edward J. Kame'enui . . . [et al.]. 2nd ed. c2002.

    Includes bibliographical references and index.

    ISBN 0-13-172022-8

    1. Teaching—United States.   2. Multicultural education—United States.   3. Minorities—Education—United States. 4. Curriculum change—United States.   I. Kameenui, Edward J.   II. Carnine, Douglas.   III. Effective teaching strategies that accommodate diverse learners.   IV. Title.

LB1025.3.E36 2007

371.102—dc22

2006010704

Vice President and Executive Publisher: Jeffery W. Johnston
Executive Editor: Ann Castel Davis
Editorial Assistant: Penny Burleson
Senior Production Editor: Linda Hillis Bayma
Production Coordination: Mary Tindle, Carlisle Editorial Services
Design Coordinator: Diane C. Lorenzo
Cover Designer: Thomas Borah
Cover Image: Getty One
Production Manager: Laura Messerly
Director of Marketing: David Gesell
Marketing Manager: Autumn Purdy
Marketing Coordinator: Brian Mounts

This book was set in Garamond by Carlisle Publishing Services. It was printed and bound by R.R. Donnelley & Sons Company. The cover was printed by R.R. Donnelley & Sons Company.

Pearson Education Ltd.
Pearson Education Singapore Pte. Ltd.
Pearson Education Canada, Ltd.
Pearson Education—Japan
Pearson Education Australia Pty. Limited
Pearson Education North Asia Ltd.
Pearson Educatión de Mexico, S.A. de C.V.
Pearson Education Malaysia Pte. Ltd.

10 9 8 7 6 5
ISBN: 0-13-172022-8

PREFACE

Like the first two editions of this book, this edition is about diverse learners—students who, by virtue of their instructional, experiential, cultural, socioeconomic, linguistic, cognitive, and physiological backgrounds, bring different and oftentimes additional requirements to instruction and curriculum. What are these different and additional instructional and curricular requirements? Why are they different? Why are additional instructional and curricular requirements necessary for these learners? What is it about diverse learners that requires teachers, publishers, and developers of educational materials (e.g., textbooks, basal reading programs), as well as school administrators, legislators, and others, to consider these additional burdens? Will a teacher's effective response to these additional instructional and curricular requirements help the average and high-performing learners?

Although this book is about diverse learners, it would be of little value if it focused exclusively on them and their learning and behavioral characteristics, because as we see it, they are not the issue. Instead, they are *our challenge* and *our promise*. Thus, in the interest of full and accurate disclosure, this book is about the teaching, instruction, and curricula required to give diverse learners a fighting chance in today's classrooms as well as outside the classroom.

We offer in this text a synthesis of our critical examination of pedagogical and curricular requirements in schools. What is demanded explicitly or implicitly of students with diverse learning and curricular needs by typical school tasks and materials in grades K–8? Based on these analyses, we have developed a core of six architectural principles for developing, selecting, or modifying the instruction and curriculum for diverse learners. These six principles are the core of this text and serve to frame our analysis and recommendations in teaching beginning reading (Chapter 3), reading comprehension (Chapter 4), writing (Chapter 5), mathematics (Chapter 6), science (Chapter 7), social studies (Chapter 8), and also teaching English language learners (Chapter 9).

The text consists of nine chapters—an introductory chapter, a chapter on the characteristics of diverse learners, and seven content-specific chapters that influence curriculum change and reform. But at the heart of the text are the six principles—**big ideas, conspicuous strategies, mediated scaffolding, primed background knowledge, strategic integration,** and **judicious review**—and the application of these principles across very different and sometimes unwieldy knowledge structures and skills in reading and writing, science, social studies, and mathematics. We assert that these six principles serve as the organic basis, if not the DNA, for the design of instruction and curriculum for diverse learners.

We believe these principles represent the minimum instructional and curricular elements necessary for the adequate design of school materials. However, architectural principles for designing instruction and principled curricular and instructional analyses are necessary but insufficient to ensure that diverse learners succeed in the classroom. As most practitioners know, the harsh reality is that the day-to-day success of teachers and children resides in the instructional and curricular details—in the examples teachers use to teach a concept such as proportion in mathematics; in the strategies used to make visible and clear how best to work with concepts efficiently, effectively, broadly, and deeply; in the integration of concepts across topics; and in the decisions made to schedule further review and practice that students may need to ensure that critical concepts or big ideas are not forgotten or confused with other highly similar concepts or ideas.

In this text, we offer guidelines for determining the curricular and instructional priorities in teaching diverse learners, who are typically behind their school-age peers in academic performance and knowledge of content. In addition, we describe concrete examples of how key concepts (big ideas) in reading, mathematics, science, social studies, and writing are taught, scaffolded, integrated, and supported. What the reader will discover is surprising conceptual and technical coherence and generality of the six principles as they are applied across the content areas. For students with diverse learning and curricular needs, there is no time to waste and little room for error and reckless experimentation. These students are deserving of our best thinking and our best instructional and curricular efforts.

Acknowledgments

We would like to thank the reviewers of this edition: Jill Allor, Louisiana State University; Judy L. Bell, Furman College; Judy Davison, Emporia State University; Susan Gately, Rivier College; Jamie Hodge, Clemson University; and Sheldeen G. Osborne, John F. Kennedy University.

DISCOVER THE MERRILL RESOURCES FOR SPECIAL EDUCATION WEBSITE

Technology is a constantly growing and changing aspect of our field that is creating a need for new content and resources. To address this emerging need, Merrill Education has developed an online learning environment for students, teachers, and professors alike to complement our products—the *Merrill Resources for Special Education Website*. This content-rich website provides additional resources specific to this book's topic and will help you—professors, classroom teachers, and students—augment your teaching, learning, and professional development.

Our goal is to build on and enhance what our products already offer. For this reason, the content for our user-friendly website is organized by topic and provides teachers, professors, and students with a variety of meaningful resources all in one location. With this website, we bring together the best of what Merrill has to offer: text resources, video clips, web links, tutorials, and a wide variety of information on topics of interest to general and special educators alike. Rich content, applications, and competencies further enhance the learning process.

The *Merrill Resources for Special Education* Website includes:

- Video clips specific to each topic, with questions to help you evaluate the content and make crucial theory-to-practice connections.
- Thought-provoking critical analysis questions that students can answer and turn in for evaluation or that can serve as a basis for class discussions and lectures.
- Access to a wide variety of resources related to classroom strategies and methods, including lesson planning and classroom management.
- Information on all the most current relevant topics related to special and general education, including CEC and Praxis standards, IEPs, portfolios, and professional development.
- Extensive Web resources and overviews on each topic addressed on the website.
- A search feature to help access specific information quickly.

To take advantage of these and other resources, please visit the *Merrill Resources for Special Education* Website at

http://www.prenhall.com/coyne

TEACHER PREP

**MERRILL
PRENTICE HALL**

Teacher Preparation Classroom

See a demo at
www.prenhall.com/teacherprep/demo

Your Class. Their Careers. Our Future. Will your students be prepared?

We invite you to explore our new, innovative and engaging website and all that it has to offer you, your course, and tomorrow's educators! Organized around the major courses pre-service teachers take, the Teacher Preparation site provides media, student/teacher artifacts, strategies, research articles, and other resources to equip your students with the quality tools needed to excel in their courses and prepare them for their first classroom.

    This ultimate on-line education resource is available at no cost, when packaged with a Merrill text, and will provide you and your students access to:

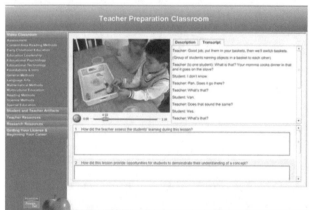

Online Video Library. More than 150 video clips—each tied to a course topic and framed by learning goals and Praxis-type questions—capture real teachers and students working in real classrooms, as well as in-depth interviews with both students and educators.

Student and Teacher Artifacts. More than 200 student and teacher classroom artifacts—each tied to a course topic and framed by learning goals and application questions—provide a wealth of materials and experiences to help make your study to become a professional teacher more concrete and hands-on.

Research Articles. Over 500 articles from ASCD's renowned journal *Educational Leadership.* The site also includes Research Navigator, a searchable database of additional educational journals.

Teaching Strategies. Over 500 strategies and lesson plans for you to use when you become a practicing professional.

Licensure and Career Tools. Resources devoted to helping you pass your licensure exam; learn standards, law, and public policies; plan a teaching portfolio; and succeed in your first year of teaching.

How to ORDER *Teacher Prep* for you and your students:

For students to receive a *Teacher Prep* Access Code with this text, instructors must provide a special value pack ISBN number on their textbook order form. To receive this special ISBN, please email: **Merrill.marketing@pearsoned.com** and provide the following information:

- Name and Affiliation
- Author/Title/Edition of Merrill text

Upon ordering *Teacher Prep* for their students, instructors will be given a lifetime *Teacher Prep* Access Code.

CONTENTS

1

Introduction   *1*

2

Characteristics of Students with Diverse Learning and Curricular Needs   *23*

3

Effective Strategies for Teaching Beginning Reading 45

4

Effective Strategies for Teaching Reading Comprehension 79

5

Effective Strategies for Teaching Writing   *111*

6

Effective Strategies for Teaching Mathematics   *139*

7

Effective Strategies for Teaching Science   171

8

Effective Strategies for Teaching Social Studies   *203*

9

Modulating Instruction for English Language Learners   *231*

Note: Every effort has been made to provide accurate and current Internet information in this book. However, the Internet and information posted on it are constantly changing, so it is inevitable that some of the Internet addresses listed in this textbook will change.

CHAPTER 1

Introduction

Edward J. Kame'enui
University of Oregon

Douglas W. Carnine
University of Oregon

Robert C. Dixon
J/P Associates

STUDENTS WITH DIVERSE learning and curricular needs, primarily children of poverty, children identified with disabilities, and children with limited English-speaking skills, face numerous forces—cultural, familial, sociological, political, and educational—that place them at increasing social and educational risk. For example, the cultural, familial, sociological, and political forces that influence the lives of children *outside* of school appear to affect in subtle but profound and insidious ways how children learn about their world and themselves when *inside* school. More than a decade ago, Hodgkinson (1991), noted that these forces were responsible for the "spectacular changes that have occurred in the nature of the children who come to school" (p. 10). He further asserted that some children were almost "destined for school failure because of poverty, neglect, sickness-handicapping condition, and lack of adult protection and nurturance" (p. 10).

At the beginning of the 21st century, the risk factors that plagued children with diverse learning and curricular needs a decade ago have not diminished. In fact, it could be argued that the risks that students with diverse learning and curricular needs face are more intense now at the beginning of a new millennium than they were a decade ago. For example, the Information Age and the global economy will be unforgiving to workers with poor reading and literacy skills (National Center for Educational Statistics, 2005). Eight of the 10 fastest growing jobs in this decade will require either a college education or moderate- to long-term postsecondary training (U.S. Department of Labor, 1997). Students unable to negotiate the "new basic skills" (Murnane & Levy, 1996) will be left behind in the new economy of the 21st century. The reality of the new economy is made particularly chilling when the most recent reports from the National Assessment of Educational Progress (NAEP) are considered. In 2005, two in five fourth-grade children could not read at a basic level, which means they could not comprehend or make simple inferences about fourth-grade material (National Center for Educational Statistics, 2005). The gravity of this outcome is particularly profound when examined in the context of three current demographic trends that will shape: (a) as the U.S. population ages, the younger cohorts decline in relative size and increase in minority composition, which means that the U.S. workforce is becoming increasingly minority in composition; (b) by 2010, there will be 10 million more jobs than workers; and (c) 42 percent of all U.S. jobs by 2010 will require a vocational certificate, associate degree, bachelor's degree, or a higher degree (Carlson, 2004). Thus, while educational requirements of workers are increasing, the educational attainment of the U.S. workforce is declining. These changing demographics portend how critically important it is to address the needs of diverse learners, immediately and for the long term (Carlson, 2004).

Concurrent with the cultural, familial, and sociological changes that place diverse learners at risk, and the demands of the new global economy of the 21st century, educational leaders are requiring more from *all* students. Students and teachers alike are asked to move beyond the mere acquisition of basic knowledge and skills and to integrate thinking and content-area knowledge in authentic problem-solving activities. At the beginning of the 20th century, the challenge of integrating thinking and content area knowledge was considered formidable, even in the education of the elite. As Resnick (1987) stated two decades ago, "Although it is not new to include thinking, problem solving, and reasoning in *someone's* school curriculum, it is new to include it in *everyone's* curriculum" (p. 7). "Everyone" at the beginning of the 21st century included more than 53 million children who attended nearly 94,000 pre-K–12 public schools (U.S. Department of Education, 2003). By all indications, the number of children that will be included in the curriculum of the 21st century will continue to increase well into the year 2020 (U.S. Department of Education, 1999). As noted previously, what is particularly noteworthy is that children of the 21st century (and the U.S. workforce) will be more diverse culturally, linguistically, socioeconomically, and developmentally.

The increased expectations of educational leaders for diverse learners are manifested in *curriculum standards*—that is, goals that indicate what students should have learned upon completion of their public school education. These standards have been developed and promoted by a range of professional organizations, each calling for curriculum changes for *all* children.

- For example, the Standards 2000 Project of the National Council of Teachers of Mathematics (NCTM) reinforces the Curriculum and Evaluation Standards for School Mathematics, which were released in 1989: "We believe that *all* students can benefit from an opportunity to study the core curriculum specified in the *Standards*" (p. 259).
- The National Standards for History Basic Edition (1996) also reinforce the previous standards: "A reformed social studies curriculum should be required of *all* students in common, regardless of their 'track' or further vocational and educational plans" (Crabtree, Nash, Gagnon, & Waugh, 1992, p. 9).
- Likewise, the development of the National Science Education Standards (1996) were guided by the premise that "Science is for all students." The standards assert that "All students, regardless of age, sex, cultural, or ethnic background, disabilities, aspirations, or interest and motivation in science should have the opportunity to attain high levels of scientific literacy" (p. 20).
- Finally, the Standards Projects for English Language Arts of the International Reading Association and National Council of Teachers of English (1996) called for promoting "equality of educational opportunity and higher academic achievement for *all* students" (p. 2).

Although the development of curriculum standards is an important task for achieving improved student-learning outcomes, without effective strategies and programs for teaching and managing students with diverse learning and curricular needs, such standards set the stage for angst and doubt in teachers and administrators alike, leading to lower personal and professional efficacy (Smylie, 1988), and most seriously, continued failure for students most at risk. Moreover, in contrast to middle- and upper-middle-class students, who receive substantial support for academic pursuits outside of school, diverse learners, especially children from low-income families, are more dependent on schools for their academic development and educational achievement (Alexander & Entwisle, 1996; Snow, Barnes, Chandler, Goodman, & Hemphill, 1991, as cited in Goldenberg, 2001). In the final analysis, they are dependent on effective programs and strategies that consider their learning characteristics (e.g., lack of background knowledge, delayed language development) in the design and delivery of the curriculum content.

The clear commitment to help an increasingly diverse population of learners meet emerging curriculum standards requires a closer scrutiny of instructional innovations, particularly instructional methods, strategies, interventions, and programs. Early innovations in curriculum and instruction grew out of objections to an overly narrow curriculum and teacher-dominant instructional methods. Innovations in the scope of the curriculum—that is, what is deemed important and should be taught— are to some extent independent of innovations in instructional methods—how students are actually taught what is deemed important. Innovations in the scope of the curriculum are important in that reasonable expectations must be set for diverse learners. However, innovations in instructional methods that do not accommodate the unique learning and curricular needs of diverse learners can place these students at greater educational risk.

A RETROSPECTIVE OF EDUCATIONAL INNOVATIONS

In this section we review past curriculum and instruction innovations in reading, mathematics, social studies, and science. By looking back at these innovations, we gain a perspective and an appreciation for the challenges involved in bringing about educational change that is sustainable and beneficial to all learners. What this retrospective suggests is that, in the context of systemic educational change, care must be taken in meeting the needs of diverse learners. Family and social support for schooling available to more-advantaged students makes them less dependent on the quality of schooling for initiating and sustaining success in school. However, just the opposite is true for diverse learners, who are often greatly dependent on the quality of schooling if they are to break the pernicious cycles of illiteracy, innumeracy, and invisibility.

Reading Innovations

Endemic to the cycles of educational innovations is the age-old debate about beginning reading (Adams, 1990; National Research Council, 1998; National Reading Panel, 2000). As Adams states, "The question of how best to teach beginning reading may be the most politicized topic in the field of education" (p. 13). According to Stanovich (cited in Kame'enui, 1993), the debates about beginning reading are more than 100 years old. These debates were characterized simplistically by Rudolph Flesch (1955) almost 50 years ago as phonics versus "look-say" and for all practical purposes, this "vulgar dichotomy" (Kame'enui, 2004) continues to haunt the field today, although in a less shrill and rancorous manner. For example, the innovations associated with the "look-say" side of the debate were labeled "whole language," "meaning construction," "constructivism," "authentic literature," and "social constructivism," to name a few. On the other side, the innovations associated with the phonics approach were labeled "phonological and linguistic awareness," "phonetic coding," "phonological processing," "systematic and explicit decoding," "explicit beginning reading instruction," and so forth.

While the debate about beginning reading is not new, what is new is the seemingly unequivocal convergence of the various programs of research. In the last 20 years, our understanding of the cognitive, auditory, visual, psychological, neurophysiological, and pedagogical dimensions of beginning reading have advanced significantly (Adams, 1990; National Research Council, 1998; National Reading Panel, 2000; Shaywitz, 2003). What these research reports suggest is that beginning readers' knowledge of the alphabetic writing system and the sounds of one's language are essential to the successful processing of written and oral communications. Consequently, instructional approaches that enhance a beginning reader's awareness of sounds and experiences with spelling–sound relations, spelling patterns, and individual words should be embraced. However, the challenge facing practitioners concerned with giving beginning readers—especially diverse learners—a successful start is to move beyond the current debate about how best to teach beginning reading and engage in a constructive analysis of the current evidence.

Mathematics Innovations

The history of innovation in mathematics is not unlike the historical landscape of reform in reading. For example, Rappaport (1976) identifies three distinct periods of reform in math education between 1900 and 1975, which included transitions from traditional mathematics (1900–1935) to meaningful mathematics (1935–1958), and to the new math (1958–1970). These periods were witness to a range of instructional approaches that included, for example, self-discovery (Macarow, 1970), back-to-basics and consumer math (Offner, 1978), and approaches that emphasized "insight and comprehension, not meaningless manipulation and reciting by rote" (Cowle, 1974, p. 71).

In 1989, yet another era of reform in mathematics was initiated when the National Council of Teachers of Mathematics (NCTM) published a document entitled *Curriculum and Evaluation Standards for School Mathematics,* which is generally referred to as the standards. These standards de-emphasized computation and fractions, instead stressing problem solving and communication. The 2000 revision of the standards swung back to a more balanced position that emphasizes basic skills as well as problem solving. A new initiative with a paper called "Reaching for Common Ground in K–12 Mathematics Education" comes from mathematicians and math educators. It clarifies how mathematics should be taught to ensure students are well prepared for advanced courses as they proceed through school (Ball et al., 2005).

The 1989 standards state, "We believe that all students can benefit from an opportunity to study the core curriculum . . . This can be accomplished by expanding and enriching the curriculum to meet the needs of each individual student, including the gifted and those of lesser capabilities and interests" (p. 253).

Insisting that all students can benefit from studying the core curriculum is one thing, but "expanding and enriching the curriculum" to meet the needs of those with "lesser capabilities and interests," as called for by the NCTM, is another more profound matter. The challenges to meet these standards are enormous. For example, how do teachers expand and enrich the curriculum to respond to language-minority children? How should we expand and enrich the curriculum for students identified as learning disabled, whose language and reading deficits contribute indirectly to their difficulties in solving verbal mathematics problems? How do we expand and enrich the curriculum for students whose knowledge base is already in serious jeopardy? What mathematics knowledge do we expand and enrich? The challenges are indeed enormous and the need for valid, research-based approaches to mathematics instruction is equally great.

Social Studies Innovations

For nearly 100 years the field of social studies has suffered from unresolved disagreements about its content. Prior to the early 20th century the content was restricted to the study of history. During the 1920s and 1930s the study of history was replaced by the idea of "social studies" with the aim of promoting "good citizenship" and "the skills and attitudes necessary to fit into the social order" (Ravitch, 2000, p. 127). Particularly important was to provide immigrants with a curriculum that would "inculcate in them democratic traditions and values to prepare them to function as American citizens" (Brophy, 1990, p. 356).

The late 1970s and 1980s ushered in a return to conservatism and the "basics." Social studies was criticized for placing too much emphasis on process and individual issues of personal adjustment and morality. A significant effort was made to restore history and geography to the core of social studies (cf. Ravitch & Finn, 1987). The content of social studies instruction continues to wobble between the goals of disciplinary content, such as history and geography, on the one hand, and inculcation in the values of citizenship and civic involvement, on the other hand. For example, a 2001 critique of the 1994 National Council for the Social Studies Curriculum Standards argued that the standards give "too much emphasis to the social sciences" and "they do not give sufficient attention to (1) controversial issues, (2) higher level intellectual processes, such as critical thinking and decision making, and (3) citizenship participation and social action" (Ochoa-Becker, 2001, p. 165). Meanwhile, others argue against "this use of social studies as a vehicle for promoting social change . . . [because it] has deflected social studies leaders' attention away from the important role of developing students' understandings of important subject matter in history, geography, economics, and civics" (Leming, 2003, p. 124).

Currently the content of social studies is dictated by the various state standards that specify what needs to be taught at each grade level in some detail. The balance between the competing aims of social studies instruction has been decided at the state level. The results are arguably highly uneven, with some states designing and promoting effective standards and others developing standards that arguably undermine teachers' ability to teach effectively (Stern, 2003). As Kauffman et al. (2002) assert, "The standards and accountability environment created a sense of urgency for these teachers but did not provide them with the support they needed" (p. 273).

In contrast to the ongoing battles over content in the social studies, the methods of teaching social studies have continued to reflect the ideas of the 1950s and 1960s, "new social studies" programs that emphasized inductive teaching, discovery learning, and student-selected content. These programs were not a great success in the classroom, as they required impractical materials or tasks, and, according to Hertzberg (1981, as cited in Brophy, 1990), "emphasized the brightest students without much consideration of other students" (p. 356). The ideal social studies classroom still advocates "hands-on" group learning activities, project-based instruction, field trips, experiential learning, and other forms of discovery learning to the exclusion of any alternatives (Schug, 2003). Seldom in evidence in social studies classrooms are the recommendations from the large body of research from the 1970s and 1980s on the use of teaching techniques effective for diverse learners that documented the power of explicit instruction with active, teacher-led focus on academic tasks (Rosenshine, 1997). This exclusive reliance in social studies on outdated, ineffective teaching methods has a potentially serious impact on the ability of diverse learners to learn the social studies content.

Science Education Innovations

Historically, two instructional perspectives have dominated science education: traditional and process approaches. *Traditional approaches* stress the learning of scientific knowledge (i.e., facts, concepts, laws, theories) as a major classroom focus and use laboratory (or hands-on) activities as applications to expand understanding of concepts taught in class. In comparison, *process approaches* stress the use of hands-on activities and/or laboratory experiments to develop an understanding of the mechanics of how scientists gain knowledge that, in turn, serve as a framework for student learning about science through experience (Shymansky, Kyle, & Alport, 1983). In recent years, many science educators have enhanced both approaches through the use of inquiry strategies that focus on the interaction between teacher and students.

Beginning with the years following the launch of *Sputnik* through the present time, there have been several evolving waves of reform in science education. In addition to the emphasis on inquiry, two other notable themes have occurred. One of these is the evolution from addressing the process of science as a set of specific skills to a broader emphasis on the nature of science as representing the means through which scientific knowledge evolves. The second of these is the recognition that meaningful learning requires rich instructional environments within which students actively construct knowledge by integrating prior learning with present learning in a fashion that is conceptually coherent (Stavy & Berkovitz, 1980). Both of the above perspectives also have enhanced traditional and process approaches.

In recent years, a series of interdisciplinary and research findings are suggestive of significant clarification and integration of virtually all popular instructional perspectives within science education. These findings encompass both the traditional and process approaches and their enhancements. Perhaps the most useful view of these developments is a general cognitive-science perspective offered by Bransford et al. 2000 in a well-recognized book, "How People Learn." In their book, Bransford et al. approach the development and organization of conceptual knowledge as a form of "expertise" that is readily interpretable in light of the standards that a science curriculum must satisfy if meaningful learning is to occur (e.g., conceptual, coherent, articulated). Falling within this curriculum-oriented view, other complementary research initiatives (e.g., basic research on the underlying dynamics of meaningful learning, models for representing the dynamics of successful meaningful learners, models for the design of effective classroom instruction) are suggestive of substantial educational implications for how teachers are able to best approach the cumulative and meaningful learning of science by their students within regular classroom settings. The strategies for effective teaching of science presented in this textbook involve the integration and translation of previously established and newly evolving instructional perspectives into a form in which they can be applied by teachers to enrich instruction in regular classroom settings in order to enhance meaningful student learning of science for students with diverse learning and curricular needs.

THE PURPOSE OF THIS BOOK

The brief history of innovations in instructional methods reflects swings between approaches to instruction that are almost exclusively teacher-directed to those that are principally child-directed. Similarly, content goals swing from a predominant emphasis on basics to ambitious goals emphasizing advanced applications and higher order thinking. The consequences for diverse learners of such dichotomous thinking have not been positive.

For example, if diverse learners receive all or almost all of their instruction through teacher direction, they are unlikely to become independent, self-regulated learners. At the opposite extreme, the effects of purely child-centered discovery approaches have ranged in the past from ineffective to detrimental (Corno & Snow, 1986, p. 620; Cronbach & Snow, 1977; Snow, 1982; Jeynes & Littell, 2000). As in most things, moderation serves diverse learners the best: teacher direction can be very helpful during the initial phases of learning new content, but students should be purposefully weaned from teacher direction to ensure that they become self-directed. Similarly, diverse learners have the right to a full complement of academic experiences, including rigorous higher order thinking; however, to our knowledge, no serious theory of cognition contends that such thinking emerges from the ether.

The principal premise of this book is that synthesizing teacher-directed and student-directed learning and incorporating the basics in the quest for higher order thinking can contribute to improved learning for widely disparate groups of students. Without such syntheses, educational reform will most likely not make the transition from rhetoric to reality, particularly for diverse learners (Kame'enui, 1998).

Specifically, this book presents effective and validated instructional strategies for teaching students with diverse learning and curricular needs. That information is directed to professionals with a particular interest in the problems attendant to serving diverse learners: teachers, school administrators, curriculum specialists, developers, and publishers. Much research in the field of curriculum design and instruction has been conducted in the last 40 years. Numerous studies and investigations have identified the characteristics or features of high-quality educational tools (textbooks, electronic media, computer software) that are effective with students with diverse learning and curricular needs. We aspire to present those essential features in a manner that educators with similar goals but different responsibilities will find practical as aids in fulfilling those responsibilities. The research base for these features is not presented in detail in the chapters that follow but is bsed on extensive reviews of the literature conducted by researchers at the National Center to Improve the Tools of Educators (NCITE, 2001).

Before considering specific design features of educational tools, it is important to clarify what the tools are and their potential value for teachers and curriculum supervisors. As used here, an educational tool is any identifiable component of instruction used to accomplish a set of specifiable student performance outcomes. Thus, educational tools represent *means for accomplishing student achievement.* Common categories of educational tools include textbooks, media, software, and teacher/student activities. The connotation of the term is that some particular tool is of value to the degree to which its use results in desired student outcomes. Although it is most convenient to think of tools as specific "things" to be used within a more comprehensive instructional program, the instructional program, if properly developed and validated, can itself be considered a tool (with respect to a set of outcomes). By linking design features and the definition of tools to their effectiveness, a perspective that considers good tools to be those that work and bad tools' to be those that are less effective (all other things being equal) is very natural within a context of instructional improvement.

Cognizant of our own responsibilities and challenges, we focus on just those validated instructional design features that benefit diverse learners and their peers alike. If teachers typically teach writing, reading, social studies, math, and science three times a day—one time each for low-, medium-, and high-performing groups of students—we could focus on different curricula that might be optimal for each group. Obviously, teachers have no such luxury, and there are compelling reasons for not segmenting instruction in such a manner. The instructional features we identify and illustrate here accommodate the full range of student diversity that teachers are likely to routinely encounter. Nothing presented here suggests a "watering down" of curricula for high performing students as a means of accommodating lower performing students.

FEATURES OF HIGH-QUALITY EDUCATIONAL TOOLS

Most of the chapters in this book have been developed around six major features of effective educational tools (see Figure 1–1). Each feature is described thoroughly in the content chapters, including extensive examples of how a given feature can be applied to a specific content area. However, following is an overview of each feature.

Big Ideas

Highly selected concepts, principles, rules, strategies, or heuristics that facilitate the most efficient and broadest acquisition of knowledge.

Conspicuous Strategies

Sequence of teaching events and teacher actions that make explicit the steps in learning. They are made conspicuous by the use of visual maps or models, verbal directions, full and clear explanations, and so forth.

Mediated Scaffolding

Temporary support for students to learn new material. Scaffolding is faded over time.

Strategic Integration

Planful consideration and sequencing of instruction in ways that show the commonalities and differences between old and new knowledge.

Primed Background Knowledge

Related knowledge, placed effectively in sequence, that students must already possess in order to learn new knowledge.

Judicious Review

Sequence and schedule of opportunities learners have to apply and develop facility with new knowledge. The review must be adequate, distributed, cumulative, and varied.

FIGURE 1–1
Six Major Principles of Effective Instructional Tools

Big Ideas

In recent years, schools have faced an explosive proliferation of learning objectives. In the recent past, a school district typically established a committee whose purpose was to develop or align a set of district objectives with the curriculum objectives of the state. The committee typically considered the objectives addressed in tests, published materials, and in lists of objectives established by other districts or the state. Publishers and test developers, in turn, were pressured to conform to the objectives established by states, in order to ensure that instructional materials were not excluded from adoptions because of some missing objectives. As a consequence of such an intertwined influence, lists of objectives became longer and longer.

This proliferation of objectives has tended to affect instruction in one of two ways, neither of which benefits diverse learners. At one extreme, instruction may aspire to cover so much material that teachers are essentially forced to teach "for exposure." Only the highest-performing students are likely to learn, understand, and subsequently apply knowledge to which they are simply "exposed." At the opposite extreme, objectives or other forms of specific learning outcomes are abandoned in favor of an approach that assumes a rich learning environment will result in learning, even if no particular knowledge or set of skills is the target of instruction. Again, this approach favors the highest-performing students. Little evidence suggests that either approach serves the goal of empowering all students with the knowledge required to solve complex problems.

A focus on the big ideas of a content area is one promising means of striking a reasonable balance between an unending list of objectives and no objectives at all. Big ideas are highly selected concepts, principles, rules, strategies, or heuristics that facilitate the most efficient and broadest acquisition of knowledge. Big ideas serve to link several different little ideas together within a domain such as science, reading, social studies, and so on. They are the keys that unlock a content area for a broad range of diverse learners and are best demonstrated through examples, instead of a definition.

Some of the big ideas identified in the content chapters of this book will be familiar, such as the idea that a good piece of writing is usually the result of repeatedly planning, drafting, revising, changing plans, modifying drafts, and editing. Likewise, no scientist will be surprised to learn that the processes of scientific inquiry are central to an understanding of science. In other cases, the reader may be surprised by the articulation of certain big ideas, such as some of those identified in the chapter on social studies or in the content knowledge section of the chapter on science.

An illustration of a big idea in science may help to clarify the nature of big ideas why they are a unique architectural feature of content-area teaching. The principle of convection in science represents a dynamic natural phenomenon in several domains, such as geology, oceanography, and meteorology that are usually associated with earth science. Convection represents a big idea because it reveals for the learner how concepts that appear to be very different (e.g., solids, liquids, gases), operate in similar ways across different domains (e.g., geology, oceanography). In simple terms, the principle of convection refers to a specific pattern of cause-and-effect relations involving phenomena that range from a pot of boiling water to ocean currents to earthquakes. Convection is a big idea because it reveals how these different natural phenomena all follow the same flow of matter or energy in a manner that represents a rectangular figure (see Figure 8–2 in Chapter 8). The convection principle can be used to demonstrate how complex concepts (e.g., density, heating and cooling, force, pressure) across very different domains such as geology and meteorology, operate in the same or similar ways.

In reading comprehension, a big idea is story grammar, which refers to the specific architectural elements that form the overall structure of stories. These story grammar elements include, for example, characters, a conflict or problem, attempts to resolve the problem, and a theme. Story grammar is a big idea because no matter how greatly different the stories are, the story grammar elements are the same in each story. Teaching students to attend to each of these story grammar elements can enhance comprehension of each story.

There is something for everyone in the realm of big ideas. It almost goes without saying that students, from the brightest to the most challenged, are likely to benefit from thorough knowledge of the most important aspects of a given content area. In addition, publishers and developers might very well find some liberation in an approach that permits them to reallocate their resources to the most important topics within a content area (e.g., see California Reading/Language Arts Framework, Grades

Kindergarten to Grade 12, 1999). Teachers, certainly, would prefer to focus their precious instructional time on thorough experiences for students with important material. Finally, policy makers might very well appreciate being freed from an assessment system that places as much value on recalling Roman numerals as it does on solving authentic problems. A focus upon instruction based on big ideas opens the door to straightforward assessment of the most important learning outcomes.

Conspicuous Strategies

People who are accomplished at various complex tasks apply strategies to solve problems. Good writers have strategies for applying their craft. People with solid mathematics knowledge use strategies for understanding the role of "luck" or chance in predicting random events and making important decisions. People with a deep understanding of history use strategies for interpreting current events in relationship to their historical predecessors.

In many cases, experts are hard pressed to articulate the strategies they use to solve problems. For the most part, if one's strategies work well, one has little need to articulate them. This has led some educators to the conclusion that strategies should not be articulated for students. Their well-founded fear is that students might simply memorize the steps in an explicitly taught strategy, without developing the understanding required for actually using a strategy in many varied and challenging situations. On the other hand, there is a certain intuitive appeal to the notion of letting students in on the "trade secrets" that knowledgeable people know (albeit unconsciously) and employ. Few can deny the personal gratification inherent in discovering an effective strategy for solving problems on one's own, or the terrible frustration inherent in the failure to discover such strategies.

A conspicuous strategy for the big idea of the principle of convection would involve the use of a concrete visual map or model (e.g., concepts maps, pictures, diagrammatic sketches) to represent and illustrate, for example, the movement of air currents in a room in a rectangular pattern. Another visual map or scheme could be used to illustrate the movement of water in a heated pan. These maps make distinct and obvious the connections that are important to the big ideas. Of course, conspicuous strategies also involve words that the teacher uses to label or to call attention to the different features of the big ideas. For example, when introducing the big idea of story grammar, a teacher could offer the following directions to students to make obvious the important elements of story grammar: "You're going to learn a strategy that will help you understand stories. When you read a story, you will read about characters, their problems, and how they solve their problems" (Carnine, Silbert, & Kame'enui, 1997, p. 278).

Extensive empirical evidence suggests strongly that all students in general, and diverse learners in particular, benefit from having good strategies made conspicuous for them, as long as great care is taken to ensure that the strategies are designed to result in widely transferable knowledge of their application. For higher performing students, conspicuous strategies may be primarily the difference between learning strategies in a timely fashion or not. For many students with diverse learning needs and for many students who are normally achieving, conspicuous strategies are quite likely the difference between learning and not learning enough in a timely manner and at a high criterion level of performance.

Mediated Scaffolding

Ideally, the designers of instruction would accommodate the needs of each child as if each child were their own. One way most of us typically help our own children manage complex challenges is by providing scaffolding; that is, temporary support of one sort or another. It is common, for example, to see a caring parent going to great lengths to support a toddler learning to use a piece of playground equipment in a park. The parent has not read the vast literature on scaffolding, but nonetheless admirably supports the child as he or she learns. At first, the toddler learning to use the slide might get extensive support: The parent follows her up the ladder, then sits behind her on the way down the slide. The caring parent goes to great lengths to help the child be successful, and to avoid painful falls along the road to success. Gradually, as the child acquires more experience and confidence, the parent provides less support, right up to that thrilling moment when the toddler can say, "I did it myself!"

The content chapters in this book discuss a variety of means by which instructional materials may be every bit as supportive of students as loving parents are of their own children. This support comes in various forms. For example, the use of concept maps or graphic displays not only serves to make connections between ideas more conspicuous (i.e., conspicuous strategies), but they also support the learner in bridging familiar, well-established concepts with unfamiliar, new, complex concepts. Other scaffolds can be very different from that of a concept map or picture, such as how a teacher places examples of a particular concept in a specific sequence that makes the introduction of examples early in the sequence easier to understand than examples that come later in the sequence. Thus, the way a teacher places examples of a new concept in a sequence of a lesson represents another kind of scaffold designed to support the learner's acquisition of a new big idea.

Strategic Integration

The concept of integrating stores of knowledge as a means of promoting higher level cognition is universally endorsed. Yet in recent years, for some, integration has become more an end than a means. That is, curricula that is integrated is deemed "good," regardless of how or whether that integration actually facilitates complex cognition.

The term "integration" is vague in that it can refer to relationships that are either like compounds or simple mixtures. In compounds, of course, two or more elements integrate to form a new substance. Nothing new results from a mixture; elements retain their properties but occur in proximity to one another, rather than separately. In some cases, a mixture is little more than a mess. Similarly, knowledge integration should result in a "compound": a new and more complex knowledge structure. One cannot will elements into a compound. Rather, some elements (knowledge) interrelate naturally. It is incumbent upon those who design and develop instructional tools to identify such naturally occurring relationships, whether within a discipline (e.g., integrated language arts) or across disciplines. We can juxtapose long division and the Articles of Confederation, but such integration will not create meaningful relationships where none exist.

In designing a teaching sequence for the big idea of convection in earth science, there are several concepts that must be integrated, such as the concepts of density, heat, and pressure. Because these are complex concepts, the integration of each concept with the other must be designed and executed with care in which a new concept is introduced, scaffolded, practiced, and assessed before the next new concept is introduced and eventually integrated. For example, the concept of density may be taught first, then scaffolding is removed, and unscaffolded practice using the concept of density is provided in the context of teaching about the effects of heat on density. Likewise, when the concept of pressure is introduced, unscaffolded practice with the previously taught concepts of heat and density are provided in the context of learning the interaction of heat, density, and static and dynamic pressure. Finally, all of these concepts are further reviewed when integrated in the basic convection strategy.

The content chapters in this book illustrate the meaningful integration of strategies and other knowledge as a means of achieving higher level thinking: cognitive compounds. Those chapters do not address integration in the sense of mixing knowledge purely for the sake of the mixing. Strategic integration, then, is the careful and systematic combining of essential information in ways that result in new and more complex knowledge.

Primed Background Knowledge

Primed background knowledge is perhaps the most transparent of the six features of high-quality educational tools. Unlike big ideas, strategic integration, and mediated scaffolding, which are complex in design, background knowledge is rather straightforward and refers to the related knowledge students must know in order to learn a new concept, strategy, system, or big idea. For example, in order to learn the big idea of the convection cell model in earth science, a student must have background knowledge of heat, density, pressure, and other concepts related to the particular domain (e.g., oceanography, geology).

If an instructional program is like the blueprint for a complex building (as Baker, Kame'enui, Simmons, & Simonsen suggest in Chapter 2), then background knowledge could be thought of as those inviolable pieces of a design that support major structures. A common big idea (and a novel one) in Roman architecture was the dome. Many Roman domes failed relatively soon after their construction, due to lack of understanding among designers of the extent and directions of forces created by domes.

It is common knowledge now that someone who knows a lot about sailboats comprehends a passage on sailboats far more readily than someone who lacks such content-specific knowledge. In practice, however, many instructional tools have failed to capitalize upon that observation in ways that are meaningful to students.

The challenge of dealing with the relationships between new and previously acquired knowledge may be illustrated with an example from childhood: Should a child learn the concept of "intentional" before the concept of "accidental"? Clearly, there is no "should" involved. A child who knows neither concept is unlikely to learn both at the same time, although we commonly define one with the other, saying, "Oh, that was just an accident. It wasn't intentional." Occasionally, we see instructional tools make this type of slip-up: using a "defining" concept that is as foreign to the learner as the concept being defined.

A child who knows either the concept "intentional" or "accidental," and who has known one of those concepts for a period of time, is in a good position to learn the other concept relatively easily. The child who knows both concepts is in a good position to learn a superordinate concept, such as "motivation." Most young children will learn both "intentional" and "accidental" incidentally over time, and in either order. They will seem "smart" when they quickly acquire a new concept like "motivation." In contrast, the students who, for whatever reason, simply don't learn one or the other of the subordinate concepts will appear relatively "dull," in spite of the fact that their "disability" is merely a lack of opportunity to gain sufficient experiences with the new, yet-to-be-taught concepts.

With anything new—particularly big ideas—the means by which instructional tools accommodate background knowledge can be crucial to learning. Even very brief and informal assessments can yield useful information on the extent to which students have the background knowledge that instruction assumes they have. For students who lack such knowledge in any particular instance, an effective instructional tool would not only provide instruction on the background knowledge, but would place or sequence that instruction where it is likely to do the most good: neither too close to new instruction, nor so far back that students lose their facility with it before it is needed.

Judicious Review

Judicious review is defined as the process of repeatedly considering material but in sensible and well-advised ways. Review is like the proverbial machine that cannot put out anything of higher quality than what is put in. If we teach students something relatively trivial, and then religiously apply the empirically validated principles of effective review, the outcome will likely be very good acquisition and retention of something trivial.

Most teachers will corroborate the extensive research on the characteristics of diverse learners (see Chapter 2), perhaps the most ubiquitous of which is memory difficulty of one type or another. On the one hand, good review contributes principally to enhanced memory and closely related goals, such as fluency. But on the other hand, review should be the proverbial icing on the cake of improved memory. Well-organized knowledge, such as that created by good, conspicuous strategies designed to teach big ideas, should be the first and foremost means of accommodating students' memory needs (see Chapter 2). Next, a system of gradually dismantled scaffolding contributes significantly to improved memory. Then, assuming instructional tools contain those major characteristics, judiciously planned review takes on an importance far greater than the drill-and-practice so often employed in the extensive review of relatively trivial knowledge.

Carnine, Dixon, & Kame'enui (1994) identify four critical dimensions of judicious review:

1. The review must be sufficient to enable a student to perform the task without hesitation.
2. It must be distributed over time.
3. It must be cumulative, with information integrated into more complex tasks.
4. It must be varied, so as to illustrate the wide application of a student's understanding of the information.

These dimensions of judicious review reveal what is required to ensure that new information will be remembered and recalled. Specifically, in order for new, unfamiliar information to be remembered effortlessly and accurately, it must be presented frequently and on numerous different occasions (i.e., distributed over time). Moreover, the review must snowball strategically into an integrated form, in which familiar information establishes the groundwork for new information, and both new and old information are melded over time. Finally, in order for new information to really "stick," it must be applied and practiced in different ways (i.e., it must be varied).

These four dimensions serve as the basic elements for the design of judicious review. Each of the four dimensions of judicious review are described and applied to selected big ideas in the content chapters of this book.

BENEFITS OF INSTRUCTION BASED ON QUALITY DESIGN TOOLS

The assertion put forth in this book is that if quality design features are embedded in educational tools, better understanding and problem solving will result for all learners. Most importantly, educational tools so designed also can provide the effective learning opportunities for diverse learners, not just college-bound students, to acquire usable and important knowledge in content areas and reasoning. As argued here, such opportunity for diverse learners requires more than simply placing such students in a content class, such as science, typically earmarked for university-bound students, and adding a few teaching tips for making the contents accessible to diverse learners (Parmar & Cawley, 1993).

If the only methods (or tools) used in instruction are those that seldom work for diverse learners, the opportunity to learn is simply denied. In contrast, considerate, student-supportive instruction in the big ideas of a content area is the approach most likely to open the doors to future learning and understanding of important concepts. Although initial understanding of big ideas by diverse (or general population) learners is not at the same level of understanding as an individual with advanced understanding, both can learn the same big ideas. Thus, using the example from science, instruction in the big idea of convection certainly can result in students being able to explain such things as why mountains form or why seasons change, and in a manner that is acceptable to scientists (Muthukrishna, Carnine, Grossen, & Miller, 1993). In addition, key aspects of well-designed tools and instructional approaches that make science accessible to less able students also can make science accessible to more able students by accelerating their rate of learning across time. In such circumstances, the role of more supportive elements (e.g., scaffolding) of well-designed instruction may be reduced (or eliminated) for higher-ability students. In contrast, however, a nonoptimal approach that works only for more able students is far more difficult to augment so that less able students can also learn, because the teacher must design and create, rather than selectively eliminate, all necessary elements. Unfortunately, this is the task faced by many teachers who are forced to augment or otherwise adapt poorly designed existing tools in order to accommodate diverse learners.

The Application of Instructional Design Principles

Each of the content chapters in this book includes a section like this that focuses on developing, selecting, and modifying instructional tools. Educational reform efforts have focused primarily on the *goals* of teaching and instruction and less on *how* the proposed curriculum standards will be attained (Cuban, 1990). Unless careful attention is given to developing, selecting, modifying, and publishing validated and effective instructional tools and approaches, the higher expectations of the curriculum outcome standards may actually increase learning failure among diverse learners. Giving careful attention to validated and effective approaches has implications for educators, as well as for publishers who create, design, develop, and publish the tools used by classroom teachers. Table 1–1 provides a framework for evaluating how and who can use the information in this book.

TABLE 1–1
Information Use

How This Information Can Be Used	Who Can Most Realistically Use This Information
Developing New Instructional Tools	• School/District Curriculum Committees • Publishers/Developers
Supplementing or Modifying Existing Tools	• Curriculum Specialists • School/District Curriculum Committees • Teachers • Publishers/Developers
Evaluating and Selecting Instructional Tools	• School Administrators • Adoption Committees • Teachers

Developing Effective Instructional Tools

Ideally, developers and publishers would construct tools that enable the teacher to accommodate the entire range of students for whom a program is appropriate. It would not be realistic to expect an instructional tool for sixth graders to be appropriate for students performing at a third-grade level. However, it would be fair to say that the tool should be appropriate for all students who pass a pretest for the sixth-grade level program. The tool should contribute to a supportive instructional environment for diverse learners while not holding back the development of higher performing students. A key element in meeting this difficult objective is to organize the tool around big ideas. When incorporated with the other aspects of curriculum design (i.e., the conspicuous strategies, mediated scaffolding, sensitivity to differences in prior knowledge, and the effectiveness of review), teaching big ideas gives the teacher a means of establishing a strong knowledge base for all students.

We must strongly emphasize, however, that while the inclusion of the six instructional features discussed throughout this book on instructional tools would quite likely improve the effectiveness of those tools, a set of validated instructional *practices* does not necessarily add up to a validated instructional *program* (Slavin, 1989). This implies that publishers and developers should create "beta versions" of their tools, as software developers often do, and should field-test them prior to publication. On the one hand, we recognize that this practice imposes a burden upon publishers and developers in terms of both cost and time. We empathize with the pressures publishers face to get their product out into a quickly changing and often fickle market. On the other hand, the costs of publishing untested instructional tools are high and varied, with the highest cost exacted upon the learner who cannot easily recapture a school year or two lost to fashionable but unsuccessful experimentation. A reasonable middle ground might be to design validated instructional features into the beta version of an instructional tool, in order to dramatically improve the odds of ending up with an effective tool, and then to test that tool. Such an approach promises publishers and developers a relatively quick and successful field test, while offering teachers the promise of an effective tool that can be used for all learners.

As the expectations for student performance increase, the number of diverse learners grows larger. Meeting these new expectations in today's classrooms is a formidable challenge, one that will not be met without acknowledging that teachers of diverse learners need and deserve high-quality educational tools. Even as the specific recommendations presented in this book might be debated, effective tools must be made available to teachers. Moreover, teachers deserve ample professional development support to ensure that they will be able to use these tools successfully.

Selecting Instructional Tools

Teachers select materials to provide students with a beneficial instructional milieu designed to increase the odds that specific academic outcomes are likely to be attained. A critical aspect of an instructional program is its approach to big ideas and strategies, especially in preparing students for higher-order thinking. An educational tool that does not deal with big ideas but does use time efficiently to present individual concepts and strategies in a clear manner, with appropriate scaffolding and practice and review, can provide students with a benign educational milieu and thereby increase their probability of success. However, as students approach the middle-school level with its more difficult content, the lack of big ideas may result in less success, particularly for diverse learners. Furthermore, tools organized around big ideas also enrich the learning of higher-performing students.

Persons entrusted with the responsibility of selecting materials should examine how big ideas are developed throughout grade levels. For example, big ideas might be apparent in grades 3 and 4 as the foundation for how more complex concepts are established. One could note how the teaching of lower-order concepts prepares students for more complex tasks. Whenever possible, new strategies should build on what has been taught earlier. After noting the overall structure of how concepts are taught, one would examine the other aspects of the program, including, for example, the presentation of strategies, scaffolding, sensitivity to differences in prior knowledge, and the effectiveness of judicious review.

Modifying Instructional Tools

Teachers confront the reality of selecting available instructional tools and using them in a manner that results in effective and efficient instruction. Teachers can modify programs, for example, by supplementing existing lessons with more practice and with clear strategies and scaffolds. The modification process, though, depends on the organization of the content around big ideas. If a tool is not organized around big ideas, the modifications may support higher levels of success, but will not provide a clear and viable vehicle for helping all students develop deeper understanding and problem-solving proficiency.

SUMMARY

Validated and effective instructional approaches are characterized by the six curriculum design features that serve as the conceptual framework for the majority of the chapters in this book. However, the social, cultural, economic, educational, and demographic contexts in which such curricular and instructional strategies and tools are used are also critical.

The six features identified herein are critical to the design of effective strategies and tools for students with diverse learning and curricular needs, especially when one considers the pervasive academic failure of these learners, and the typical lack of attention to this knowledge base in the development of educational tools and standards. Most of the chapters in this book apply the six features to content areas: reading, language arts, mathematics, science, and social studies. This analysis is incomplete for one large segment of our student population: students who are limited- and non-English-speaking.

Consequently, a chapter is devoted to this important population. Finally, the context in which quality instructional tools are selected and used has a pervasive influence on what students learn. The next chapter examines these contexts and describes the changing demographics of students with diverse learning and curricular needs.

REFERENCES

ADAMS, M. J. (1990). *Beginning to read: Thinking and learning about print.* Cambridge, MA: MIT Press.

ALEXANDER, K., & ENTWISLE, D. (1996). Schools and children at risk. In A. Booth & J. Dunn (Eds.), *Family and school links: How do they affect educational outcomes?* (pp. 67–88). Mahwah, NJ: Erlbaum.

BALL, D. L., FERRINI-MUNDY, J., KILPATRICK, J., MILGRAM, J., SCHMID, W., & SCHAAR, R. (2005). Reaching for common ground in K–12 mathematics education. *Notices of the American Mathematical Society, 52* (9), 1055–1058.

BRANSFORD, J. D. (2000). *How people learn: Bridging research and practice.* Washington, DC: National Academy Press.

BROPHY, J. (1990). Teaching social studies for understanding and higher-order applications. *The Elementary School Journal, 90* (4), 351–417.

CALIFORNIA DEPARTMENT OF EDUCATION. (1999). *Reading/language arts framework for California Public Schools: Kindergarten through grade twelve.* Sacramento, CA: California Department of Education.

CARLSON, B. (2004). The economic imperative behind No Child Left Behind. Office of Vocational and Adult Education. Retrieved September 28, 2005 from http://www.acrnetwork.org/Documents/acrnconf04/opening_bcarlson.ppt

CARNINE, D. W., DIXON, R., & KAME'ENUI, E. J. (1994). Math curriculum guidelines for diverse learners. *Curriculum/Technology Quarterly, 3* (3), 1–3.

CARNINE, D. W., SILBERT, J., & KAME'ENUI, E. J. (1997). *Direct instruction reading* (3rd ed.). Upper Saddle River, NJ: Merrill/Prentice Hall.

CORNO, L., & SNOW, R. E. (1986). Adapting teaching to individual differences among learners. In M. E. Wittrock (Ed.), *Handbook of research on teaching* (3rd ed., pp. 605–629). Upper Saddle River, NJ: Prentice Hall.

COWLE, I. M. (1974). Is the "new math" really better? *The Arithmetic Teacher, 21* (1), 68–73.

CRABTREE, C., NASH, G. B., GAGNON, P., & WAUGH, S. (Eds.) (1992). *Lessons from history: Essential understandings and historical perspectives students should acquire.* Los Angeles: The National Center for History in the Schools, University of California.

CRONBACH, L. J., & SNOW, R. E. (Eds.) (1977). *Aptitudes and instructional methods.* New York: Irvington/Naiburg.

CUBAN, L. (1990). Reforming again, again, and again. *Educational Researcher, 19* (1), 3–13.

FLESCH, R. (1955). *Why Johnny can't read.* New York: Harper & Row.

GOLDENBERG, C. (2001). Making schools work for low-income families in the 21st century. In S. Neuman & D. Dickinson (Eds.), *Handbook of early literacy research.* New York: Guilford.

HODGKINSON, H. (1991). Reform versus reality. *Phi Delta Kappan, 73,* 9–16.

INTERNATIONAL READING ASSOCIATION AND NATIONAL COUNCIL OF TEACHERS OF ENGLISH. (1996). *The standards projects for English language arts.*

JEYNES, W. H., & LITTELL, S. W. (2000). A meta-analysis of the studies examining the effect of whole language instruction on the literacy of low-SES students. *The Elementary School Journal, 101* (1), 21–33.

KAME'ENUI, E. J. (1993). Diverse learners and the tyranny of time: Don't fix blame; fix the leaky roof. *The Reading Teacher, 46* (5), 376–383.

KAME'ENUI, E. J. (1998). The rhetoric of all, the reality of some, and the unmistakable smell of mortality. In J. Osborn & F. Lehr (Eds.), *Literacy for all: Issues in teaching and learning* (pp. 319–338). New York: Guilford.

KAME'ENUI, E. J. (2004). *The teaching of reading: Beyond vulgar dichotomies to the science of causality.* Speech presented at the Conference on Preparing Tomorrow's Teachers, Washington, DC.

KAUFFMAN, D., JOHNSON, S. M., KARDOS, S. M., LIU, E., & PESKE, H. G. (2002). "Lost at Sea": New teachers' experiences with curriculum and assessment. *Teachers College Record, 104* (2), 273–300.

LEMING, J. S. (2003). Ignorant activists: Social change, "higher order thinking," and the failure of social studies. In J. S. Leming, L. Ellington, & K. Porter (Eds.), *Where did social studies go wrong?* (pp. 124–142). Washington, DC: Thomas B. Fordham Foundation.

MACAROW, L. (1970). New math. *School Science and Mathematics, 70* (5), 395–397.

MURNANE, R. J., & LEVY, F. (1996). *Teaching the new basic skills.* New York: Free Press.

MUTHUKRISHNA, A., CARNINE, D., GROSSEN, B., & MILLER, S. (1993). Children's alternative framework: Should they be directly addressed in science instruction? *Journal of Research in Science Teaching, 30* (3), 233–248.

NATIONAL CENTER FOR EDUCATION STATISTICS (2005). *The nation's report card: Reading 2005.* Washington, DC: U.S. Department of Education.

NATIONAL CENTER TO IMPROVE THE TOOLS OF EDUCATORS. (2001). [On-line]. Available: idea. uoregon.edu/~ncite/

NATIONAL COUNCIL OF TEACHERS OF MATHEMATICS. (2000). *Principles and standards for school mathematics.* Reston, VA: Author.

NATIONAL COUNCIL OF TEACHERS OF MATHEMATICS. (1989). *Curriculum and evaluation standards for school mathematics.* Reston, VA: Author.

NATIONAL READING PANEL. (2000). *Teaching children to read: An evidence-based assessment of the scientific research literature on reading and its implications for reading instruction: Reports of the subgroups.* Bethesda, MD: National Institute of Child Health and Human Development.

NATIONAL RESEARCH COUNCIL. (1998). *Preventing reading difficulties in young children.* Washington, DC: National Academy Press.

NATIONAL RESEARCH COUNCIL. (1995). *National science education standards.* Washington, DC: National Academy Press.

OCHOA-BECKER, A. S. (2001). A critique of the NCSS curriculum standards. *Social Education, 65* (3), 165–168.

OFFNER, C. D. (1978, March). Back to basics in mathematics: An educational fraud. *The Mathematics Teacher, 71* (3), 211–217.

PARMAR, R. S., & CAWLEY, J. F. (1993). Analysis of science textbook recommendations provided for students with disabilities. *Exceptional Children, 59* (6), 518–531.

RAPPAPORT, D. (1976). The new math and its aftermath. *School Science and Mathematics, 76* (7), 563–570.

RAVITCH, D. (2000). *Left back: A century of failed school reforms.* New York: Simon & Schuster.

RAVITCH, D., & FINN, C. (1987). *What do our 17-year-olds know?* New York: Harper & Row.

RESNICK, L. B. (1987). *Education and learning to think.* Report of the Committee on Mathematics, Science, and Technology Education, Commission on Behavioral and Social Sciences and Education, National Research Council. Washington, DC: National Academy Press.

ROSENSHINE, B. (1997). Advances in research on instruction. In J. W. Lloyd, E. J. Kame'enui, & D. Chard (Eds.), *Issues in educating students with disabilities* (pp. 197–220). Mahwah, NJ: Erlbaum.

SCHUG, M. C. (2003). Teacher-centered instruction: The Rodney Dangerfield of social studies. In J. S. Leming, L. Ellington, & K. Porter (Eds.), *Where did social studies go wrong?* (pp. 94–111). Washington, DC: Thomas B. Fordham Foundation.

SHAYWITZ, S. (2003). *Overcoming dyslexia: A new and complete science-based program for reading problems at any level.* New York: Knopf.

SHYMANSKY, J., KYLE, W., & ALPORT, J. (1983). The effects of new science curricula on student performance. *Journal of Research in Science Teaching, 20* (5), 387–404.

SLAVIN, R. (1989). PET and the pendulum: Faddism in education and how to stop it. *Phi Delta Kappan, 90,* 750–758.

SMYLIE, M. A. (1988). The enhancement function of staff development: Organizational and psychological antecedents to individual teacher change. *American Educational Research Journal, 25,* 1–30.

SNOW, R. E. [IN COLLABORATION WITH E. YALOW] (1982). Education and intelligence. In R. J. Sternberg (Ed.), *Handbook of human intelligence* (pp. 493–586). London: Cambridge University Press.

STAVY, R., & BERKOVITZ, B. (1980). Cognitive conflict as a basis for teaching quantitative aspects of the concept of temperature. *Science Education, 64* (5), 679–692.

STERN, S. M. (2003) *Effective State Standards for U.S. History: A 2003 Report Card.* Fordham Foundation. [On-line]. Available: http://www.edexcellence.net/institute/publication/publication.cf m?id=320#940

U.S. DEPARTMENT OF EDUCATION. (2003). *Projections of education statistics to 2013.* (NCES 1999-038). Washington, DC: National Center for Education Statistics. Retrieved March 15, 2006 from http://nces.ed.gov/programs/projections

U.S. DEPARTMENT OF EDUCATION. (1999). *Overview of public elementary and secondary schools and districts: School year 1997-98.* (NCES 1999-322). Washington, DC: Superintendent of Documents. Retrieved September 28, 2005 from http://nces.ed.gov/pubs99/1999322.pdf

U.S. DEPARTMENT OF LABOR (1997). *The occupational outlook handbook* (1996–1997 ed.). Washington DC: Author.

CHAPTER 2

Characteristics of Students with Diverse Learning and Curricular Needs

Scott K. Baker
Pacific Institutes for Research and University of Oregon

Edward J. Kame'enui
University of Oregon

Deborah C. Simmons
Texas A&M University

Brandi Simonsen
University of Connecticut

THE FOCUS OF this chapter is students with diverse learning and curricular needs, who, by virtue of their instructional, experiential, cultural, socioeconomic, linguistic, and biological backgrounds, bring different and often unique requirements to instruction and curriculum. The first part of this chapter briefly discusses some of the recent changes that have occurred in achievement outcomes for students overall, as well as for diverse learners. Learning outcomes then are briefly discussed in the context of shifting demographic conditions in the United States that are increasing the number of students who have diverse learning and curricular needs. The second part of this chapter describes important characteristics of students with diverse learning and curricular needs, to help clarify the challenge educators face in designing and delivering high-quality educational programs that work for *all* students (Carnine & Kame'enui, 1992).

In responding to the serious problems in American education in the early 1990s, the U.S. Department of Education called for a "dramatic overhaul of our nation's public school system" (U.S. Department of Education, 1991, p. 1). That overhaul has begun and there are signs that improvements are taking place. Over the past few years, highly publicized improvements in large states such as California and Texas have paralleled reports from many other states. On close inspection, however, the positive changes that have occurred for large numbers of students overall, have not occurred to the same degree for large numbers of diverse learners.

Changes in California are interesting to consider in this context. In the 1980s whole-language reading methods were prescribed in California's Language Arts Framework, and explicit phonics instruction was banned (Mathes & Torgesen, 2000). By 1992 California's reading scores had plummeted; by 1994 their scores were among the lowest in the nation (Mathes & Torgesen, 2000; National Center for Educational Statistics, 1996). In a state used to being among the leaders in reform efforts and student achievement, this dramatic drop in performance was shocking (Staples, 2000).

To its credit, California responded by making fundamental changes in the way they expected students to be taught in school, particularly in the area of beginning reading (see Reading/Language Arts Framework for California Public Schools, Kindergarten Through Grade Twelve, California Department of Education, 1999). Data from the California Department of Education (2000a) indicates that reading scores went up after the change was made and are continuing to improve. From 1998 to 1999, the increase in the percentage of students scoring at or above the 50th percentile in reading increased at nearly every grade tested. Similar increases occurred in mathematics, language, and content area subjects such as science and social studies. From 1999 to 2000, the increase in the percentage of students scoring at or above the 50th percentile increased again over the previous year's performance. And once again, the pattern was similar in mathematics, language, and content area subjects.

During that same two-year period, improvements were also reported for English-language learners as a group. As they are in many other states across the nation, English language learners are California's largest, and most rapidly expanding, group of diverse learners (California Department of Education News Release, 2000a). In all academic areas assessed, English language learners scoring at or above the 50th percentile increased from 1998 to 1999 and from 1999 to 2000.

It is important, however, to look closely at the performance of English language learners. In absolute terms, their performance as a group is still woefully inadequate. The percentage of students scoring at or above the 50th percentile in reading, for example, still hovers around 10.2 percent, prompting Hakuta (Steinberg, 2000) to suggest that the reason English language learners were "posting such sizable gains, in part, [was] because their previous scores had been so abysmally low" (p. A13). The reality is that the performance of English language learners throughout the nation has remained far below the performance of other students in the country for many decades (Hoff, 2000).

The situation appears to be even worse for African American students, who throughout the 1970s and 1980s made consistent progress in narrowing the achievement gap between themselves and European American students. The gains African Americans made during these decades appear to be slipping away, and the gap is growing faster in higher level skills than in basic skills areas (Hoff, 2000).

The initial academic success overall of the standards-based reform movement, considered especially in the context of achievement levels historically, is even more troublesome for another group of diverse learners: students with disabilities. In many respects these students have been left out altogether in the high-stakes testing that is helping to define current changes taking place in education. The problematic nature standardized testing presents for students with disabilities has not been seriously addressed as a part of the ongoing development of a new generation of assessments, as it should have been from the beginning (National Center on Educational Outcomes, 1999; Thurlow, 2000; Tindal, Heath, Hollenbeck, Almond, & Harniss, 1998).

All special educators know, for example, that for a large number of students with disabilities, standardized tests, and the conditions under which standardized tests are administered, must be altered if students with disabilities are to have a fair opportunity to demonstrate what they have learned in school. The way these accommodations are implemented—so they are fair for all students and still valid for students with disabilities—is an extremely challenging problem and is beginning to be considered in earnest by state departments of education, well after most of them have the major components of their testing programs in place (Gersten & Baker, 2000; Thurlow, 2000; Tindal et al., 1998).

Large numbers of students with disabilities have been simply excluded from state assessments, and consequently accountability for how well states are educating these students is easily ignored. The federal government—via No Child Left Behind—has reiterated the expectation that (a) *all* students, regardless of disability, participate in state and districtwide assessments and (b) *all* scores are included in the state and district reports (34 CFR 200). Because many new (and traditional) standardized tests are not valid for students with disabilities (Messick, 1989), their performance is very low when these students are included in state level tests (Ysseldyke et al., 1998). To address this concern, No Child Left Behind includes provisions for either *accommodations* to typical assessments or *alternate performance assessments* to facilitate the participation of all students in accountability measures.

The challenge is to do a better job ensuring that the positive changes that have recently occurred overall in student learning extend to greater numbers of diverse learners. In many ways, the impetus for these changes began with Goals 2000: Educate America Act, which was designed to "dramatically reform our schools by establishing high academic and occupational standards and providing support to states and communities to help them reach those standards" (p. 1). No Child Left Behind continued the momentum with "three critical elements—academic content standards, academic achievement standards, and assessments aligned to those standards—[that] provide the foundation for an accountability system ensuring that students with disabilities reach high standards" (34 CFR 200).

A PORTRAIT OF DEMOGRAPHIC DIVERSITY

Sweeping changes in the demography of the United States make diverse learners a larger part of our classrooms than ever before. One of the toughest challenges facing educators is how to accomplish positive changes for all students in a population that is becoming increasingly diverse. For example, increases in population of European Americans is the lowest of any ethnic group in the country (Hodgkinson, 1992). The growth of African Americans is approximately double the growth of European Americans, and the growth of Hispanic Americans exceeded the growth of European Americans by an astounding 53 percent during the 1980s (Hodgkinson, 1992), a rate that largely continued during the 1990s. In fact, three states—California, Texas, and Florida—accounted for over half of the nation's growth during the 1980s; by 2010, over 50 percent of the youth population in each of these states will be minorities (Hodgkinson, 1992). Minorities now comprise 25 percent of the total U.S. population (U.S. Census Bureau, 2004a) and constitute the majority in many areas. The pattern of these changes is expected to continue throughout the 21st century.

Evidence suggests that poverty is the greatest risk associated with increases in the number of students with diverse learning and curricular needs, and poverty is associated with negative outcomes for students. Specifically, prior poverty status was found to predict lower scores in reading and math and higher ratings of antisocial behavior (Dubow & Ippolito, 1994). Nearly one child in five lives in poverty (i.e., 18 percent of children fall below the federal poverty level; U.S. Census Bureau, 2004b). Millions of children who are poor, but do not meet the official government definition of poverty, also are exposed to the multitude of educational risks associated with poverty.

The relationship between poverty and children's educational achievement seems to be mediated by parents' level of education. In general, the more educated parents are, the more likely it is they will raise children who do well in school. The connection is relatively straightforward. Educated parents actively prepare their children for the kinds of experiences that will help them do well in school (National Research Council, 1998). Also, well-educated parents are better able to help their children overcome the effects of poor or insufficient instruction than less-well-educated parents (Feitclson, as cited in Samuels, 1995). Less educated parents are frequently unaware of the connection between home experiences and school success, and even when they are, they frequently lack the knowledge and opportunities to provide positive school-related experiences to their children. Considering that 16 percent of the population over 25 has less than a high school diploma, this relationship merits consideration.

A report issued by the Educational Testing Service (ETS) (cited in Hodgkinson, 1993) highlights the powerful influence poverty and parents' education played in the performance of 9-year-old school children in specific academic areas. When tested for reading skills, only 16.6 percent of the children could search for specific information, relate ideas, and make generalizations. European American children performed better than Hispanic American children, who in turn performed slightly better than African American children. The most dramatic differences, however, were related to parents' level of education. Twenty-two percent of children whose parents had some college experience read at the intermediate level versus 6 percent of children whose parents were high school dropouts.

The performance of children in relation to issues of ethnicity and race were strongly mediated by parents' level of education (Hodgkinson, 1993). That is, when parents' education was controlled statistically, European American, Hispanic American, and African American children performed similarly on the reading test. The same kind of results in the ETS study were found in math and science. In math, 29 percent of children whose parents had a college degree performed at the intermediate level, compared to 6 percent of children whose parents were high school dropouts. In science, 36 percent of children whose parents graduated from college could apply basic scientific information, compared to only 9 percent of children whose parents were high school dropouts.

Unfortunately, understanding the connection between home experiences and school success seems to have little to do with developing effective policies to help students most in need. We have known for a long time that school achievement could be explained more by home conditions and social class than by school factors (Coleman et al., 1966). However, the impetus to develop stronger public policy initiatives to systematically provide more academic experiences to students in the home *seems slim,* given the current trend of decreased government involvement in domestic programs.

It is important to reiterate that poverty does not play a direct causal role in achievement. Rather, factors associated with differences between home and school "cultures" are critical (Bloom, 1982). In other words, a child growing up in an impoverished environment typically does well in school if the culture of the child's home closely matches the culture of the child's school.

Nonetheless, the implications are clear. The number of children in the country who can be classified as diverse learners because of the special circumstances they bring to public education is growing at a pace that currently outstrips educators' abilities to keep up. Significant educational changes must continue to be made in response to the dramatic changes occurring in classrooms throughout the country, especially the development and use of instructional strategies that address the needs of diverse learners.

LEARNER CHARACTERISTICS

Effective instructional strategies for diverse learners must be constructed with relevant learner characteristics in mind. In the remainder of this chapter, four important characteristics of diverse learners are discussed: *retaining information, learning strategies, vocabulary knowledge,* and *language coding,* especially as it is related to early literacy development. Important differences between diverse learners and average achievers are presented as well as the relationships among these characteristics.

Many other characteristics could be described that represent well established differences between diverse learners and average achievers. Some of these characteristics represent large, multicomponent constructs such as intelligence, achievement, or motivation. Important elements of constructs such as intelligence are partly subsumed in the four characteristics of diverse learners. For example, vocabulary knowledge is typically the subtest on measures of intelligence that most closely predicts an individual's overall IQ score. Constructs such as achievement motivation are highly influenced by previous achievement success. The effective implementation of instructional strategies to help students achieve greater academic success should have a noticeable effect on students' motivation to do well in school.

Other learning differences between diverse learners and average achievers seem to be the clear result of more fundamental underlying differences. The area of reading contains several well-known examples. Eye-movement differences between good and poor readers have led to interventions to address reading difficulties. However, these eye-movement differences appear to be caused *by* reading skill differences rather than being the cause *of* reading skill differences. Therefore, the remediation of reading problems through eye-movement training has been misguided (Stanovich, 1986).

It is also clear that good and poor readers use context cues differently during reading. In contrast to initial expectations, however, researchers found that poor readers use context *more* than good readers do, not less. This unexpected finding was attributed to a more fundamental underlying difference: Poor readers use context cues as a word-recognition strategy, whereas good readers use context cues as a reading-comprehension strategy.

The four characteristics presented in this chapter are important in fundamental ways. First, the characteristics represent some aspect of language use, which most researchers agree is the most crucial area differentiating diverse learners from average achievers. Second, the characteristics seem to play a causal role in the differences in language use between diverse learners and average achievers. Third, the characteristics represent alterable rather than unalterable variables. In other words, diverse learners can improve on these characteristics, and educators can facilitate improvement by using high-quality instructional strategies. An empirically validated framework of effective strategies is described throughout this book.

Retaining Information

Retaining information is based on how learners receive, organize, and retrieve information to which they have been exposed (Swanson & Cooney, 1991). Important learning and instructional considerations related to diverse learners' retention of information is presented in Table 2–1.

For the vast majority of diverse learners, being able to retain information does not appear jeopardized at the point of receiving information from the environment (i.e., the sensory input stage). Problems at this stage are likely attributable to deficits in attention, but these do not appear to seriously impair performance on memory tasks (Swanson & Cooney, 1991). Numerous differences between diverse learners and average achievers have been found in how information is organized in working memory and retrieved from storage in long-term memory (Mann & Brady, 1988; Torgesen, 1985).

Working memory functions in two important ways. First, it organizes information by integrating new information with existing information (e.g., when sorting items into categories or updating the details and meaning of a story as new information is presented). Second, it temporarily stores information for the learner's use (e.g., when repeating a list of items or summarizing the story line of a television show just seen). The degree to which diverse learners' problems with working memory can be attributed to difficulties at the organizational and storage levels is unclear (Swanson & Cooney, 1991).

TABLE 2–1

Learning and Instructional Considerations in Addressing Memory Skills of Diverse Learners

Important Considerations for Diverse Learners	Instructional Implications for Diverse Learners
• Normal reception of information from the environment • Problems with working memory skills (rehearsing and categorizing information) • Problems with long-term memory (storing information on permanent basis) • Differences compared to average achievers in naming common objects, recalling or recognizing items, and repeating sentences • Perform as well as average achievers on tasks with nonverbal components, such as recognizing and recalling abstract figures	• Explicit instruction in effective use of rehearsal and categorization strategies • Emphasize long-term retention of underlying meaning of important content • Have learners actively use new information • Emphasize connections between pieces of information • Connect new learning to learner's experiences • Systematically monitor retention of information and knowledge over time

In terms of organizing information, researchers have always been aware that teaching students when to use what they have learned can be as important as teaching specific content or learning strategies (Gersten, Baker, & Pugach, 2001). Studies have consistently indicated that diverse learners do not spontaneously organize unfamiliar material the way other students do. They tend to ask themselves fewer questions when they read hard-to-understand material, for example, and they have difficulties transferring approaches or strategies to novel situations unless they are explicitly taught to do so (Brown, 1978; Kolligian & Sternberg, 1987; Miller, 1985; Torgesen, 1977; Swanson, 1987; Wong, 1991). These types of fundamental differences in the way diverse learners organize information and work to understand complex information affect how well they are able to retain information over time.

At one of the first stages of retaining information, learners must organize information in working memory primarily through rehearsal and categorization strategies. According to Swanson and Cooney (1991), rehearsal "refers to the conscious repetition of information, either subvocally or orally, to recall information at a later date" (p. 108). Categorization involves organizing incoming information (e.g., ordering and classifying) in a way that is meaningful for the learner. Significant differences in how learners rehearse information (e.g., memorizing a phone number) and categorize information (e.g., arranging things by group membership-animals, furniture, foods, etc.) in working memory have been found between diverse learners and average achievers (Swanson & Cooney, 1991; Torgesen, 1985).

Long-term memory is where information is stored on a permanent basis. Information in working memory is transferred to long-term memory if it is used sufficiently. One's name, date of birth, capitals of selected states, and other such knowledge is stored in long-term memory. Information is stored in long-term memory through a complex series of linkages, associations, and organizational patterns (Swanson & Cooney, 1991). The reason some information in long-term memory seems to be accessible one day and not the next stems from the strength of the connections to a particular piece of information. Individual differences on tasks related to long-term memory can be attributed to the way information is connected in memory and the strategies learners use to retrieve information.

Performance on tasks that tap working memory and long-term memory skills has been the primary means of identifying memory problems in diverse learners (Mann & Brady, 1988). For example, one of the most pervasive long-term memory tasks requires learners to name common objects (e.g., dog, house, car, flower) as quickly as possible. On these kinds of tasks, diverse learners consistently name objects less quickly than average achievers (Torgesen, 1985; Wagner & Torgesen, 1987). On related tasks requiring the verbal recall of recently *presented* items—tasks that tap working memory skills—diverse learners consistently respond less quickly and accurately than average achievers (Mann & Brady, 1988). Other working memory tasks on which diverse learners perform more poorly than average achievers include the repetition of sentences (Mann & Brady, 1988) and the recall of strings of digits or objects (Torgesen, Wagner, Simmons, & Laughon, 1990).

Diverse learners do not do poorly on all memory tasks. Numerous studies have documented that the memory problems associated with diverse learners are related specifically to tasks with a verbal component. When memory tasks involve nonverbal information, differences between diverse learners and average achievers are not readily apparent (Mann & Brady, 1988; Liberman & Liberman, 1990; Torgesen, 1985; Wagner & Torgesen, 1987). For example, tasks employing stimuli that cannot easily be named, such as abstract visual figures, typically do not produce reliable differences between diverse learners and average achievers (Torgesen, 1985). Likewise, diverse learners demonstrate performance equal to that of average achievers on tasks that require memory for nonsense shapes or photographs of unfamiliar faces (Liberman & Liberman, 1990). Torgesen and Houck (1980) gave diverse learners and average achievers a recall task in which items were either nonsense syllables or familiar patterns such as words and digits. These researchers found that diverse learners could recall the sequences of nonsense syllables almost as well as average achievers, although their recall of words and digits was severely impaired.

Learning Strategies

Daneman (1991) noted that learners can absorb new information only in relation to what they already know. For example, an individual who knows nothing about baseball would have trouble understanding a "sacrifice bunt." However, an individual who understands chess and the strategy of sacrificing a pawn to improve board position could gain an understanding of a sacrifice bunt as a strategy for improving the chances of scoring a run. To make this analogy, the learner engages in a strategy to compare the two situations. A strategy can be thought of as a reasonably efficient and intentional routine that leads to the acquisition and utilization of knowledge (Prawat, 1989). It is possible that two people with the same advanced knowledge of chess but minimal knowledge of baseball might acquire knowledge about a sacrifice bunt differentially because of differences in how they use knowledge.

Important learning and instructional considerations regarding diverse learners' knowledge and use of strategies are presented in Table 2–2.

The use of learning strategies occurs in many different school-related contexts, including solving math verbal problems by creating diagrams of known and unknown quantities; grouping items into discrete categories (e.g., food, clothing, furniture); writing stories by integrating awareness of story grammar, background knowledge, and the intended audience; and studying for a test using a combination of note-taking, rehearsal, and summarization techniques. In general, research has found that diverse learners do not use these and other types of learning strategies as effectively as average achievers (Wong, 1991).

Strategy use in the classroom is critical to educational success. Palincsar and Klenk (1992) provided a framework for understanding the importance of learning strategies. They suggested that learning demands placed on students in the home are fundamentally different than the learning demands placed on students in school. Home experiences provide multiple opportunities for incidental learning to occur. In incidental learning, knowledge is a natural by-product of everyday experiences. Learning environments are unstructured, and it is generally assumed that a child's natural curiosity is the only condition necessary for

TABLE 2–2
*Learning and Instructional Considerations in Addressing Diverse Learners'
Strategy Knowledge and Use*

Important Considerations for Diverse Learners	Instructional Implications for Diverse Learners
• Inactive learners—difficulty monitoring learning and adjusting to tasks demands and learning outcomes • Difficulty adjusting to structure of intentional learning environments— i.e., being focused and goal directed • Uses similar strategies as average achievers, but uses them less efficiently • May use different strategies than average achievers to compensate for difficulties with fundamental aspects of problem • Difficulty giving up basic, successful strategies for more powerful ones	• Ensure that necessary skills underlying efficient use of target strategy are firm • Provide multiple examples of when to use and not use particular strategy • Make each step in new strategy explicit; have learners demonstrate proficiency using each step as well as combining steps to use whole strategy

important outcomes to occur. In school, however, learning opportunities are organized so that intentional learning occurs. In contrast to incidental learning, intentional learning opportunities are characterized by structure, stated expectations, and time constraints. Learners are encouraged to be purposeful, goal directed, self-regulated, and actively engaged.

According to Palincsar, David, Winn, and Stevens (1991), learners who most effectively respond to the intentional learning demands of school classrooms are those students who use conspicuous learning strategies, actively monitor task demands in relation to their own learning, and adjust their learning strategies on the basis of their own learning outcomes. A similar model is provided by Johnston and Winograd (1985), who referred to students who monitor their own learning outcomes as "active learners." Active learners use strategic, goal-directed behaviors to plan, monitor, and evaluate their learning. Palincsar and Klenk (1992) observed that these active or intentional learning behaviors are problematic for diverse learners across a number of academic domains.

Researchers have attempted to determine whether the use of different strategies or the less efficient use of similar strategies distinguishes diverse learners from average achievers. Although it appears that both instances do occur, the general finding is that diverse learners and average achievers use similar strategies but differ in how efficiently they use them. For example, Griswold, Gelzheiser, and Shepherd (1987) investigated whether diverse learners and average achievers used the same strategies for memorizing the definitions of vocabulary terms. They found that although average achievers learned more unknown words than diverse learners, the groups did not differ in the kind of strategies they used, nor in the time they spent studying the vocabulary words.

Diverse learners also may be reluctant to give up strategies that are useful in the initial stages of learning, but which over time should be replaced with more efficient strategies. For example, a high level of automaticity in basic fact math problems is needed to solve higher-level math problems (Silbert, Carnine, & Stein, 1990). Initially, most students learn to solve basic fact problems by invoking some type of counting strategy. Not only do diverse learners take more time than average achievers to master counting strategies, but they also take longer to master automaticity of basic facts. For example, students may learn initially to solve division problem "50/5" the long way. After some practice, students should not need a paper and pencil to work the problem out, but should know the answer "automatically." An overreliance on counting strategies to solve basic fact problems prohibits a student from being able to successfully perform more complex operations. Problems at this level tend to persist for diverse learners even in the higher grades (Dixon, 1990).

Kirby and Becker (1988) indicated that lack of automaticity in basic operations and strategy use—either the use of an inefficient strategy or the use of the right strategy at the wrong time—were responsible for the majority of math problems that children experience. As they stated, the results of their studies "do not suggest that children with learning problems in arithmetic have any major structural defect in their information processing systems or that they are qualitatively different from normally achieving children in any enduring sense. Instead, the results are consistent with the interpretation that such children may not be carrying out even simple arithmetic in the correct manner, and that they require extensive practice in the correct strategies" (p. 15).

Similarly in reading, apparent differences in effective strategy use between diverse learners and average achievers may be partly attributable to problems with more fundamental learning strategies. For example, the finding that diverse learners use passage context less efficiently than average achievers to learn the meaning of new vocabulary words may be the result of strategy difficulties in reading comprehension. Both Spear and Sternberg (1986), who examined the literature on the reading problems of diverse learners, and Weisberg (1988), who reviewed the research on reading comprehension, arrived at a similar conclusion: diverse learners do not use reading comprehension strategies effectively. Weisberg noted that diverse learners have difficulty using strategies to integrate their background knowledge with text material to better increase comprehension. Spear and Sternberg indicated there was strong evidence that diverse learners are less efficient at scanning text, more passive in their approach to reading, and less flexible in adjusting their reading strategies to suit varying purposes.

Spear and Sternberg (1986) made a critical point, however, in noting that even the apparent reading comprehension strategy deficiencies of diverse learners may be mediated by a more fundamental problem: generalized low word-reading skills. Part of what is interpreted as inherent strategy problems may be the result of reading failure itself. As Spear and Sternberg suggested, "because of their prolonged difficulty learning to read, these youngsters do not profit sufficiently from the experiences with text through which normal children seem to induce and practice strategies" (p. 9). Thus, in coming full circle, it may be that apparent strategy deficiencies on the part of some diverse learners have root causes in basic skill deficiencies. In reading, lack of strategy use in determining vocabulary meaning from context may stem from deficient reading comprehension strategies. Deficient reading comprehension strategies, in turn, may stem from more fundamental problems with basic word reading skills and the consequences of prolonged reading failure.

It is important to emphasize that differences between diverse learners and average achievers in their use of learning strategies do not stem from organic, "inside-the-head" problems. There seem to be understandable reasons why diverse learners sometimes use different learning strategies than average achievers. They may be focusing on more fundamental aspects of a particular learning task than other students, and thus using different strategies to solve the task. In some cases they may be more reluctant than average achievers to give up strategies they have learned for strategies with which they are unfamiliar but which are necessary to solve complex problems efficiently.

Vocabulary Knowledge

The problems diverse learners have with retaining information and using strategies to learn efficiently and meaningfully have learning consequences beyond the boundaries of each characteristic. For example, poor retention has implications for the efficient use of strategies to summarize a text. More profoundly, the learner characteristics discussed thus far have implications for skills not easily addressed by specific instructional design principles, nor easily implemented during specific instructional sessions. Rather, some skills require an instructional focus that extends across all curricular activities, in nearly all contexts. Vocabulary knowledge is perhaps the best example. Vocabulary development must occur in multiple curricular areas and in the context of multiple instructional techniques if the vocabulary gap between diverse learners and average achievers is to be substantially reduced.

Important learning and instructional considerations regarding diverse learners' knowledge and use of vocabulary are presented in Table 2–3.

The number of words students learn per year is extremely large. Early estimates of new words learned per year varied from 1,000 (Clifford, 1978) to 7,000 (Miller, 1985). More recently, Baumann, Kame'enui, and Ash (2003) reviewed the literature and suggested that 3,000 new words is probably the most accurate estimate of yearly vocabulary growth (Baumann, Kame'enui, & Ash, 2003; Beck & McKeown, 1991). Researchers have found consistently that, in addition to important differences in vocabulary size between diverse learners and average achievers, diverse learners also

TABLE 2–3
Learning and Instructional Considerations in Addressing Diverse Learners'
Vocabulary Knowledge and Use

Important Considerations for Diverse Learners	Instructional Implications for Diverse Learners
• Vocabulary difficulties are apparent early and increase over time, both in the number of words known and depth of knowledge • Word learning is partly attributable to exposure quantity; diverse learners are exposed to unknown words less frequently than average achievers • Reading is an important vehicle for vocabulary growth; diverse learners read much less than average achievers, primarily because reading is a frustrating and failure-prone experience	• Address vocabulary problems early and comprehensively • Match vocabulary goals with instruction • Combine direct instruction in word meanings with techniques to help students become independent word learners • Set goals for students to learn many words at basic levels of meaning and fewer, critical words at deeper levels • Have students tie new vocabulary to their own experiences • Ensure that strong beginning reading program is primary vehicle for helping students become independent word learners

acquire significantly fewer new words per year than average achievers (Hart & Risley, 1995; White, Graves, & Slater, 1990).

As Nagy and Anderson (1984) pointed out, the number of words diverse learners need to learn to catch up to their average-achieving peers is too great to expect direct instruction alone to make a serious impact. These researchers suggested that "any approach to vocabulary instruction must include some methods or activities that will increase children's ability to learn words on their own" (p. 325), and that "for enhancement of children's vocabulary growth and development, there can be no substitute for voluminous experience with rich, natural language" (Anderson & Nagy, 1991, p. 722). Anderson and Nagy recommend that the primary way for diverse learners to be exposed to "rich, natural language" is through structured reading opportunities.

Unfortunately, but not surprisingly, diverse learners do much less reading than average achievers. Nagy and Anderson (1984) estimated that students in grades 3 through 9 read between 500,000 and 1,000,000 words of text a year and that "the least motivated children in the middle grades might read 100,000 words a year while the average children at this level might read 1,000,000. The figure for the voracious middle-grade reader might be 10,000,000 or even as high as 50,000,000. If these guesses are anywhere near the mark, there are staggering individual differences in the volume of language experience, and therefore, opportunity to learn new words" (p. 328).

The reasons why diverse learners read less than average achievers are not surprising, but the consequences may be far more debilitating than even educators who recognize the importance of reading might assume (Beck & McKeown, 1991; Stanovich, 1986). Because diverse learners do not read as well, they are exposed to fewer words in print than average achievers, and given an equal amount of reading time, they naturally do not cover as much text. In addition, because diverse learners frequently find reading a frustrating experience, they typically engage in just about any activity other than reading if given the option (Stanovich, 1986). When Juel (1988) talked to beginning readers about activities they would rather do than read, 40 percent of diverse readers said they would rather clean their room than read, compared to 5 percent of average achievers. As one child put it, "I'd rather clean the mold around the bathtub than read" (p. 442).

Language Coding

The final characteristic is an important aspect of the language-based memory problems of diverse learners that has particularly strong implications for the development of reading proficiency. These language-based problems may be attributable, in part, to the way diverse learners store verbal information for use. For example, someone who hears an individual say, "the balance of power is an important concept in our democracy," is able to store and retrieve that phrase beyond the instance in which it was spoken. Research has shown that retrieving information stored in both long-term memory (Liberman & Liberman, 1990; Liberman & Shankweiler, 1985; Mann & Brady, 1988; Snowling, 1991; Torgesen, 1985; Torgesen et al., 1990; Wagner, 1988) and working memory (Liberman & Shankweiler, 1985; Mann & Brady, 1988; Stanovich, 1985; Wagner, 1988; Wagner & Torgesen, 1987) depends, in part, on how the information is stored. Important learning and instructional considerations related to the way language is coded by diverse learners are presented in Table 2–4.

TABLE 2–4
Learning and Instructional Considerations in Addressing Language Coding of Diverse Learners

Important Considerations for Diverse Learners	Instructional Implications for Diverse Learners
• Language coding has critical implications for reading development • Diverse learners rely primarily on semantic features to code language; average achievers rely primarily on phonological features • The way language is coded is strongly influenced by early literacy experiences involving the "nature" of words	• Provide rich and varied experiences involving the meaning and sounds of words • Provide abundant explicit experiences in connection between sounds in words and alphabetic counterparts

For example, in beginning reading, it is likely that the problem diverse learners have retrieving verbal information stored in memory emanates from weakly established phonological codes. Phonological codes represent the sounds constituted in words and aid in efficiently storing verbal information (Liberman & Liberman, 1990). Average achievers store information primarily in terms of its phonological codes— that is, on the basis of the *sounds* in words. Diverse learners, on the other hand, store information primarily in terms of its semantic features—that is, on the basis of the *meaning* of words (Liberman & Shankweiler, 1985; Snowling, 1991; Torgesen, 1985; Torgesen et al., 1990; Wagner, 1988).

Studies investigating the verbal errors committed by different groups of students provide evidence that linguistic information is stored differently by diverse learners and average achievers. Torgesen (1985) reported that when diverse learners and average achievers were given word-recognition tasks, diverse learners committed more errors when the distracter words were similar in meaning to the target words (e.g., dog, puppy), whereas average readers made more errors when the distracter words were similar phonologically to the target words (e.g., dog, log). Numerous studies using both auditory and visual presentations of letters, words, and sentences found large differences in recall between diverse learners and average achievers when the items are phonologically distinct (e.g., *a, f, r, z; hat, dog, fun, time*), because average achievers do not encounter phonological interference when storing the different-sounding items. Recall differences between diverse learners and average achievers decrease when the items are less distinct (e.g., *b, c, e, z; hat, fat, sat, rat*), because average achievers encounter more confusion when storing the similar-sounding items (Torgesen, 1985). Other studies have established that when diverse learners and average achievers store verbal information similarly, differences in accessing information in working memory are greatly reduced (Wagner & Torgesen, 1987).

The way children temporarily or permanently store language in memory is a difficult characteristic to address directly through instructional design because the process of storing language is not easily observed, inferred, or described. In essence, learners exert little control over whether information is stored on the basis of its semantic or phonological features. Thus, it is difficult for teachers to determine the extent of storage problems, receive feedback on how students store information, and evaluate the effectiveness of approaches to enhance learners' phonological coding.

One hypothesis as to why average achievers tend to store information on the basis of its phonological codes more naturally than diverse learners is that, prior to beginning school, the average achievers have been exposed to environments that foster knowledge about the composition of words, including awareness that words can be mapped onto symbols (i.e., print), and that words are composed of discrete sounds (Adams, 1990). Phonological coding, therefore, becomes a natural and effective storage tool. On the other hand, many diverse learners do not naturally acquire facility with the phonological code and thus rely more heavily on semantic strategies, with which they are more familiar, to store information.

SUMMARY

Diverse learners and average achievers can be differentiated on many other learning characteristics besides those presented in this chapter. However, it is necessary to distinguish between characteristics that are merely consequences of other, more primary characteristics and characteristics that play a causal role in contributing to academic learning problems. For example, Stanovich (1986) has shown that characteristics such as eye movements during reading and the use of context in word recognition distinguish diverse learners from average achievers. Differences between diverse learners and average achievers on these characteristics resulted in numerous misguided intervention efforts. In fact, eye movement and context use have been shown to *result from* individual differences in reading skill, not cause them.

The learning characteristics that have the strongest causal connection to academic failure are rooted in the area of language. The connectedness among four of these characteristics was stressed in this chapter. In isolation, each characteristic would present a significant challenge for students to overcome in acquiring academic proficiency. In combination, they represent too great a challenge for students with diverse learning needs to overcome given the instructional strategies currently in use. Important points to remember about the learning characteristics of diverse learners in relation to language processing, retaining information, learning strategies, and vocabulary include the following.

- Diverse learners and average achievers seem to store verbal language in memory differently. Average achievers rely much more on the phonological codes of language than diverse learners. Diverse learners focus more on the semantic features of language, perhaps to compensate for their poor phonological coding skills.
- Diverse learners do not use verbal information in working memory as efficiently as average achievers. Differences in memory performance between diverse learners and average achievers are not readily apparent with nonverbal information, such as abstract shapes and figures.
- Diverse learners do not access information in long-term memory as well as average achievers. They extract information more slowly, less accurately, and in less detail. Moreover, diverse learners may have less information in long-term memory available for access.
- Diverse learners do not use learning strategies as effectively as average achievers. Diverse learners are not devoid of strategies. In fact, they tend to use similar strategies as average achievers, but they use them less efficiently.
- Poor strategy use by diverse learners when solving complex problems may stem from difficulties they have with more fundamental aspects of the problems, which may require different strategies to solve.

- Diverse learners have vocabularies that are considerably smaller than the vocabularies of average achievers. Diverse learners have more difficulty than average achievers processing word meanings to deeper levels of understanding.
- Deficits in the vocabulary knowledge of diverse learners exist very early and grow increasingly larger each year. The consequences of vocabulary deficits are extreme. Vocabulary knowledge plays a causal role in successful reading throughout an individual's lifetime, and greatly impacts performance in many academic subject areas.

Differences between diverse learners and average achievers in these and other learning characteristics result in deficiencies in performing basic skills and more complex, higher-level problems. Basic skill deficiencies are apparent as early as the first grade (obvious language differences are apparent before students are in kindergarten) and the gap increases steadily over time (Juel, 1988; Stanovich, 1986). It is not at all surprising that when the focus shifts to content area material, diverse learners soon demonstrate significant difficulties. As the content becomes more unfamiliar and learners are expected to assume greater control over their own learning and draw more heavily on their previous learning, the academic gap between diverse learners and average achievers grows increasingly wider.

These factors are alarming considering that we have moved beyond the year 2000 when all American students were to be competent in all subject areas, highly literate, and world leaders in science and mathematics. Current trends in education and the changing demographic landscape of American society provide numerous reasons to appreciate the ambitiousness of Goals 2000 and No Child Left Behind, and the resolve necessary to meet the goals as we progress in the 21st century. However, the data—declining test scores, breakdowns in the family structure, greater numbers of children living in poverty, increases in violence, crime, drug addiction, school dropouts, and so forth—are vivid reminders of the enormity of the challenges educators face.

Educators can assert little control over most of these factors. They can, however, assert a great deal of control over what occurs in the classroom (Carroll, 1963). One of a teacher's primary responsibilities is to teach students how to transform massive amounts of information into knowledge that can be used to solve increasingly complex academic problems. One of the most likely ways to ensure high-quality instruction is to provide teachers with effective strategies to assist their students. Instructional strategies should provide means for teachers to structure opportunities for students to turn information into knowledge, just as blueprints provide builders with the plans for transforming raw materials into buildings. Just as a builder is responsible for integrating the blueprint plans with the raw materials to construct the building, teachers are responsible for integrating strategies with information to help students assemble meaningful knowledge. The chances of success are greatly enhanced if builders begin construction with high-quality blueprints. Likewise, teachers must begin instruction with high-quality strategies.

REFERENCES

ADAMS, M. J. (1990). *Beginning to read: Thinking and learning about print*, Cambridge, MA: MIT Press.

ANDERSON, R. C., & NAGY, W. E. (1991). Word meanings. In R. Barr, M. L. Kamil, P. B. Mosenthal, & P. D. Pearson (Eds.), *Handbook of reading research* (pp. 690–724). New York: Longman.

BAUMANN, J. F., KAME'ENUI, E. J., & ASH, G. E. (2003). Research on vocabulary instruction: Voltaire redux. In J. Flood, J. Jensen, D. Lapp, & J. R. Squire (Eds.), *Handbook of research on teaching the English language arts* (pp. 752–785). New York: MacMillan.

BECK, I., & MCKEOWN, M. (1991). Conditions of vocabulary acquisition. In R. Barr, M. Kamil, P. Mosenthal, & P. D. Pearson (Eds.), *Handbook of reading research* (Vol. 2, pp. 789–814). New York: Longman.

BLOOM, B. (1982). *Human characteristics and school learning*. New York: McGraw-Hill.

BROWN, A. L. (1978). Knowing when, where, and how to remember: A problem of metacognition. In R. Glaser (Ed.), *Advances in instructional psychology* (Vol. 1, pp 77–165). Hillsdale, NJ: Edbaum.

CALIFORNIA DEPARTMENT OF EDUCATION. (1999). *Reading/language arts framework for California Public Schools: Kindergarten through grade twelve*. Sacramento, CA: California Department of Education.

CALIFORNIA DEPARTMENT OF EDUCATION. (2000a). *Eastin releases additional star 2000 test results*. Retrieved from http://star.cde.ca.gov

CALIFORNIA DEPARTMENT OF EDUCATION. (2000b). *Star 2000 reports*. Retrieved November 1, 2001 from http://star.cde.ca.gov

CARNINE, D. W., & KAME'ENUI, E. J. (Eds.). (1992). *Higher order thinking: Designing curriculum for mainstreamed students*. Austin, TX: Pro-Ed.

CARROLL, J. B. (1963). A model of school learning. *Teachers College Record, 64,* 723–733.

CLIFFORD, G. J. (1978). Words for schools: The applications in education of the vocabulary researchers of Edward L. Thorndike. In P. Suppes (Ed.), *Impact of research on education: Some case studies* (pp. 107–198). Washington, DC: National Academy of Education.

COLEMAN, J. S., CAMPBELL, E. Q., HOBSON, C. J., MCPARTLAND, J., MOOD, A. M., WEINFELD, F. D., ET AL. (1966). *Equality of educational opportunity*. Washington, DC: U.S. Government Printing Office.

DANEMAN, M. (1991). Individual differences in reading skills. In R. Barr, M. L. Kamil, P. B. Mosenthal, & P. D. Pearson (Eds.), *Handbook of reading research* (Vol. 2, pp. 512–538). New York: Longman.

DIXON, B. (1990). *Research review of mathematics instruction*. Eugene, OR: Technical Report for the National Center to Improve the Tools of Educators.

DUBOW, E. F., & IPPOLITO, M. F. (1994). Effects of poverty and quality of the home environment on changes in the academic and behavioral adjustment of elementary school-age children. *Journal of Clinical Child Psychology, 23* (4), 401–412.

GERSTEN, R., & BAKER, S. (2000, July). *Research in diverse populations*. Presentation at Annual Research Project Director's Conference, Washington, DC.

GERSTEN, R., BAKER, S. K., & PUGACH, M. (2001). Contemporary research on special education teaching. In V. Richardson (Ed.), *Handbook of research on teaching* (4th ed., pp. 695–722). Washington, DC: American Educational Research Association.

GRISWOLD, P. C., GELZHEISER, L. M., & SHEPHERD, M. J. (1987). Does a production deficiency hypothesis account for vocabulary learning among adolescents with learning disabilities? *Journal of Learning Disabilities, 20* (10), 620–626.

HART, B., & RISLEY, R. T. (1995). *Meaningful differences in the everyday experience of young American children.* Baltimore: Paul H. Brookes.

HODGKINSON, H. L. (1992). *A demographic look at tomorrow.* Institute for Educational Leadership, Center for Demographic Policy.

HODGKINSON, H. (1993). American education: The good, the bad, and the task. *Phi Delta Kappan, 74* (8), 619–623.

HOFF, D. J. (2000). Gap widens between Black and White students on NAEP. *Education Week, 20,* 6–7.

JOHNSTON, P. H., & WINOGRAD, P. N. (1985). Passive failure in reading. *Journal of Reading Behavior, 17* (4), 279–301.

JUEL, C. (1988). Learning to read and write: A longitudinal study of fifty-four children from first through fourth grade. *Journal of Educational Psychology, 80* (4), 437–447.

KIRBY, J. R., & BECKER, L. D. (1988). Cognitive components of learning problems in arithmetic. *Journal of Learning Disabilities, Remedial and Special Education, 9* (5), 7–16.

KOLLIGIAN, J., & STERNBERG, R. J. (1987). Intelligence, information processing, and specific learning disabilities: A triarchic synthesis. *Journal of Learning Disabilities, 20,* 8–17.

LIBERMAN, I. Y., & LIBERMAN, A. M. (1990). Whole language vs. code emphasis: Underlying assumptions and their implications for reading instruction. *Annals of Dyslexia, 40,* 51–76.

LIBERMAN, I. Y., & SHANKWEILER, D. (1985). Phonology and the problems of learning to read and write. *Remedial and Special Education, 6* (6), 8–17.

MANN, V. A., & BRADY, S. (1988). Reading disability: The role of language deficiencies. *Journal of Consulting and Clinical Psychology, 56* (6), 811–816.

MATHES, P. G., & TORGESEN, J. K. (2000). A call for equity in reading instruction for all students: A response to Allington and Woodside-Jiron. *Educational Researcher, 29,* 4–14.

MESSICK, S. (1989). Validity. In R. L. Linn (Ed.), *Educational measurement* (3rd ed., pp. 13–103). New York: Macmillan.

MILLER, P. H. (1985). Metacognition and attention. In D. L. Forrest-Pressely, G. E. MacKinnon, & T. G. Waller (Eds.), *Metacognition, cognition and human performance* (pp. 181–218). New York: Academic Press.

NAGY, W., & ANDERSON, R. C. (1984). How many words are there in printed school English? *Reading Research Quarterly, 19,* 304–330.

NATIONAL CENTER FOR EDUCATIONAL STATISTICS. (1996). *Are limited English proficient students being taught by teachers with LEP training?* Washington, DC: Office of Educational Research and Improvement, U.S. Department of Education.

NATIONAL CENTER ON EDUCATIONAL OUTCOMES. (1999). *1999 state special education outcomes: A report on state activities at the end of the century.* Retrieved August 10, 1998 from http://education.umn.edu/nceo/OnlinePubs/99StateReport.htm

NATIONAL RESEARCH COUNCIL. (1998). *Preventing reading difficulties in young children.* Washington, DC: National Academy Press.

PALINCSAR, A. S., DAVID, Y. M., WINN, J. A., & STEVENS, D. D. (1991). Examining the context of strategy instruction. *Remedial and Special Education, 12* (3), 43–53.

PALINCSAR, A. S., & KLENK, L. (1992). Fostering literacy learning in supportive contexts. *Journal of Learning Disabilities, 25* (4), 211–225, 229.

PRAWAT, R. S. (1989). Promoting access to knowledge, strategy and disposition in students: A research synthesis. *Review of Educational Research, 59* (1), 1–41.

SAMUELS, S. J. (1995). Home factors and success in school: A response to Allington [Letter to the editor]. *The Reading Teacher, 48,* 647–648.

SILBERT, J., CARNINE, D., & STEIN, M. (1990). *Direct instruction mathematics* (2nd ed.). Upper Saddle River, NJ: Merrill/Prentice Hall.

SNOWLING, M. J. (1991). Developmental reading disorders. *Journal of Child Psychology Psychiatry, 32* (1), 49–77.

SPEAR, L. D., & STERNBERG, R. J. (1986). An information processing framework for understanding reading disability. In S. Ceci (Ed.), *Handbook of cognitive, social, and neuropsychological aspects of learning disabilities* (Vol. 1, pp. 3–31). Hillsdale, NJ: Erlbaum.

STANOVICH, K. E. (1985). Explaining the variance in reading ability in terms of psychological processes: What have we learned? *Annals of Dyslexia, 35,* 67–96.

STANOVICH, K. E. (1986). Matthew effects in reading: Some consequences of individual differences in the acquisition of literacy. *Reading Research Quarterly, 21* (4), 360–407.

STAPLES, B. (2000, June 23). The 'Mississippification' of California Schools. *The New York Times.*

STEINBERG, J. (2000, August 20). English immersion successful. *The New York Times,* reprinted in *The Register Guard,* pp. A1, A13.

SWANSON, H. L. (1987). Information-processing theory and learning disabilities: An overview. *Journal of Learning Disabilities, 20,* 3–7.

SWANSON, H. L., & COONEY, J. B. (1991). Learning disabilities and memory. In B. Y. L. Wong (Ed.), *Learning about learning disabilities* (pp. 104–127). San Diego, CA: Academic Press.

THURLOW, M. (2000, JULY). *Research in diverse populations.* Paper presented at the Annual Research Project Director's Conference, Washington, DC.

TINDAL, G., HEATH, B., HOLLENBECK, K., ALMOND, P., & HARNISS, M. (1998). Accommodating students with disabilities on large-scale tests: An experimental study. *Exceptional Children, 64,* 439–450.

TORGESEN, J. K. (1977). The role of nonspecific factors in the task performance of learning disabled children: A theoretical assessment. *Journal of Learning Disabilities, 10,* 33–39.

TORGESEN, J. K. (1985). Memory processes in reading disabled children. *Journal of Learning Disabilities, 18* (6), 350–357.

TORGESEN, J. K., & HOUCK, G. (1980). Processing deficiencies in learning disabled children who perform poorly on the digit span task. *Journal of Educational Psychology, 72,* 141–160.

TORGESEN, J. K., WAGNER, R. K., SIMMONS, K., & LAUGHON, P. (1990). Identifying phonological coding problems in disabled readers: Naming, counting, or span measures. *Learning Disability Quarterly, 13,* 236–243.

U.S. CENSUS BUREAU. (2004a). Population and housing narrative profile: 2004. Retrieved October 21, 2005 from http://factfinder.census.gov.

U.S. CENSUS BUREAU. (2004b). Selected economic characteristics: 2004. Retrieved October 21, 2005 from http://factfinder.census.gov.

U.S. DEPARTMENT OF EDUCATION. (1991). *America 2000: An education strategy,* Washington, DC: Author.

WAGNER, R. K. (1988). Causal relations between the development of phonological processing abilities and the acquisition of reading skills: A meta-analysis. *Merrill-Palmer Quarterly, 34* (2), 261–279.

WAGNER, R., & TORGESEN, J. (1987). The nature of phonological processing and its causal role in the acquisition of reading skills. *Psychological Bulletin, 101,* 192–212.

WEISBERG, R. (1988). 1980s: A change in focus of reading comprehension research: A review of reading/learning disabilities research based on an interactive model of reading. *Learning Disability Quarterly, 11* (2), 149–159.

WHITE, T. G., GRAVES, M. F., & SLATER, W. H. (1990). Growth of reading vocabulary in diverse elementary schools: Decoding and word meaning. *Journal of Educational Psychology, 82* (2), 281–290.

WONG, B. Y. (1991). The relevance of metacognition to learning disabilities. In B. Y. Wong (Ed.), *Learning about learning disabilities* (pp. 232–258). San Diego, CA: Academic Press.

YSSELDYKE, J. E., THURLOW, M. L., LANGENFELD, K. L., NELSON, J. R., TEELUCKSINGH, E., & SEYFARTH, A. (1998). *Educational results for student with disabilities: What do the data tell us?* Retrieved August 10, 1998 from http://education.umn.edu/nceo/OnlinePubs/TechnicalReport23/ TechnicalReport23.html

CHAPTER 3

Effective Strategies for Teaching Beginning Reading

Deborah C. Simmons
Texas A&M University

Edward J. Kame'enui
University of Oregon

Michael D. Coyne
University of Connecticut

David J. Chard
University of Oregon

THE PURPOSE OF this chapter is to apply the findings of current research on beginning reading to the design of effective instructional strategies for children with diverse learning needs. The chapter is organized in three sections: (a) a discussion of current issues in beginning reading, (b) an analysis of beginning reading instruction using the six-principle framework detailed in Chapter 1, and (c) guidelines for applying the six principles for developing, selecting, and modifying instructional programs.

CURRENT ISSUES IN BEGINNING READING

"Reading is essential to success in our society" (National Research Council, 1998, p. 1). Reading opens up the world for children and is the doorway to learning. Unlike any other ability, the capacity to read allows children access to the collective knowledge, history, and experiences of our shared symbolic humanity.

The benefits of learning to read in the early grades are significant. Research suggests consistently that the establishment of strong beginning reading skills is fundamental to cognitive development and later school success (Cunningham & Stanovich, 1998; Foorman, Francis, Shaywitz, Shaywitz, & Fletcher, 1997; Stanovich, 1986). Children who become confident, independent readers are not only well-prepared for the academic tasks they will encounter, but also well-positioned with the essential skills necessary to enter into a technological society with ever-increasing literacy requirements (National Research Council, 1998). At no other time in our history has the ability to read been so important to *all* members of society.

As the need for early established reading increases, there exists a significant portion of our children who do not gain entry to the world of reading. According to the National Assessment of Educational Progress, approximately 40 percent of U.S. fourth-grade students read below a "basic level" and have "little or no mastery of the knowledge or skills necessary to perform work at each grade level" (National Center for Educational Statistics, 2005). Almost 20 percent of the nation's children encounter severe reading problems before third grade, which translates into more than 10 million children in America who are struggling, unsuccessfully, to read (National Reading Panel, 2000). The magnitude of this reading problem in the United States results in increasing numbers of students that become eligible for special education services under the category of specific learning disabilities. A full 80–85 percent of students with learning disabilities have reading as their primary area of difficulty. Moreover, there is consistent evidence that children with low reading achievement in the early grades have greater likelihood of school dropout, pregnancy, and unemployment (McGill-Franzen & Allington, 1991; Slavin, 1989), and consequently face great risks of negative academic, social, and economic outcomes.

Currently, the convergence of two factors has the potential to impact significantly the pervasiveness and seriousness of reading failure among children in the United States (Coyne, Kame'enui, & Simmons, 2001). The first factor is a growing coalition of support for research-based efforts directed at improving reading outcomes for all students, and especially students at risk of reading disability and reading failure (e.g., Learning First Alliance, 1998; U.S. Department of Education, 2002).

This broad coalition spans multiple segments of society and includes parents, educators, policy makers, and leaders in business and technology. The growing support for reading reform can be seen in increased calls for school accountability and is reflected in the proliferation of ambitious reading standards and reading assessments at the local, state, and national level (e.g., California Department of Education, 1999; Texas Department of Education, 1997).

The second factor is the consolidation of a substantial knowledge base built on the sizable body of converging, multidisciplinary research evidence accumulated over the past 40 years (e.g., McCardle & Chhabra, 2004; National Reading Panel, 2000; National Research Council, 1998). This scientific knowledge base reflects a significant advancement in our understanding of both the nature of reading difficulties and the ways in which educators can work to ensure that all children become successful readers. In this chapter, we highlight the extensive convergence of research on beginning reading and summarize one of its most significant conclusions, the importance of learning to read in the early grades.

Research on Beginning Reading

In 1998, the National Academy of Sciences concluded that the weight of empirical research evidence in beginning reading was sufficient to reach broad consensus within the field. Reflecting on the National Research Council's (1998) final report, *Preventing Reading Difficulties in Young Children,* Kame'enui (1999) wrote that the "fact that the National Academy of Sciences agreed to establish a committee to address the prevention of reading problems represents a clear, serious, and momentous signal to the field that a 'scientific' basis does indeed exist that requires our full attention and consideration" (p. 6). Extending the work of the committee, the National Research Panel (2000) applied an objective quantitative review methodology to "undertake comprehensive, formal, evidence-based analyses of the experimental and quasi-experimental research literature relevant to a set of selected topics judged to be of central importance in teaching children to read" (p. 1).

The work of the National Research Council and the National Reading Panel has the potential to allow researchers and educators to move past the divisive and rancorous "reading wars" that plagued the field for more than 100 years (McPike, 1998; Kame'enui, 1993). We can now reject unsubstantiated rhetoric and point to scientific evidence to guide reading instruction that will promote a solid and successful start in reading and literacy for every child in America (see also What Works Clearinghouse, 2004).

One of the most salient conclusions from the research on beginning reading is the importance of learning to read in the early grades. As early as kindergarten, "meaningful differences" exist between students' literacy experiences (Hart & Risley, 1995). While some children enter school with thousands of hours of exposure to books and a wealth of rich oral language experiences, other children begin school with very limited and impoverished knowledge of print and language. These diverse learners (i.e., those students at risk of reading disability and reading failure) already face the "tyranny of time," the enormous task of constantly trying to catch up (Kame'enui, 1993).

Students disadvantaged in reading skills have an extremely difficult time catching up to their peers (Juel, 1988; Felton & Pepper, 1995). These initial differences in skills between students only grow larger over time. Stanovich (1986, 1999) described this phenomenon in reading as "Matthew effects," referring to the biblical adage in the Book of Matthew declaring that the "rich get richer while the poor get poorer." The consequences of establishing, or failing to establish, early reading skills are striking. Without strategic intervention, Juel's (1988) longitudinal research found that good readers in first grade had a .88 chance of staying good readers in fourth grade while poor readers in first grade had a .87 probability of remaining poor readers.

After third grade, when the requirements of reading shift from *learning to read* to *reading to learn,* students' trajectories of reading progress become even more stubbornly resistant to change (Good, Simmons, & Smith, 1998). From third grade onward, students who are in the *bottom* trajectory almost never become good readers in the *top* trajectory (Felton & Pepper, 1995; Juel, 1988). Children who are not competent and fluent readers by the end of grade 3 are at serious risk, not only for reading problems, but also for dropping out of school (Slavin, 1994).

Children with diverse learning needs face overwhelming odds from the outset of schooling. To close the reading gap between these students and their peers, and to help all children ultimately become successful readers, we are compelled to draw a clear and unwavering "line in the sand." Children must be readers by the end of grade 3. This is a formidable goal that requires schools to commit to beginning reading as a top instructional priority in the primary grades beginning in kindergarten (Coyne, Kame'enui, & Simmons, 2004; National Research Council, 1998).

Moreover, to optimize the precious instructional period between kindergarten and third grade, beginning reading instruction must provide diverse learners with effective strategies based on validated principles of instructional design. These principles are central to designing reading instruction that responds to the acute instructional needs of diverse learners, those students who are vulnerable and need intensive and systematic methods to achieve the complex rules and strategies required of reading (Simmons & Kame'enui, 1998). In the next sections we outline how the six-principle framework introduced in Chapter 1 (i.e., big ideas, mediated scaffolding, conspicuous strategies, strategic integration, primed background knowledge, and judicious review) can be used to maximize the effectiveness of instruction in beginning reading to ensure that all students become accurate and fluent readers by the end of third grade.

PRINCIPLES FOR IMPROVING INSTRUCTIONAL STRATEGIES

Beginning Reading: Designing Instruction Around Big Ideas

In content areas such as science (see Chapter 7), efficient and effective teaching is gained by designing instruction around a limited number of important concepts, principles, facts, laws, and theories called "big ideas." By understanding a few big ideas, such as convection and scientific inquiry (e.g., identifying variables to control and test), students are equipped with a governing principle, concept, or pattern for organizing, unifying, and understanding other ideas, principles, concepts, and patterns. For example, understanding the workings of a convection cell in the context of a pot of boiling water should help naïve learners understand the same circular patterns of movement in the atmosphere and the earth's mantle (see Chapter 6 of this text). Moreover, in "big idea"-based instruction, the convection cell is intentionally designed and used to represent the same processes that occur in very different contexts.

In beginning reading instruction, big ideas don't come in the form of a unifying concept such as the convection cell. In this chapter, we use big ideas in beginning reading to refer to *a set of unifying curriculum activities* necessary for successful beginning reading. Such curricular activities are instructional anchors that, when accomplished and routinized, provide learners enormous capacity to identify printed words and translate alphabetic codes into meaningful language. In their synthesis of research on beginning reading, Simmons and Kame'enui (1998) identified three foundational concepts or big ideas that were common to all theoretical models of early reading acquisition and consistent across the architecture of effective beginning reading interventions. The following three big ideas, *phonological awareness, alphabetic understanding,* and *automaticity with the code,* should serve as a "minimum" framework for beginning reading instruction (see also National Reading Panel, 2000). We present these big ideas with phonological awareness a prerequisite to alphabetic understanding and alphabetic understanding fundamental to automaticity with the code. In addition, we provide a set of "curriculum maps" (Simmons & Kame'enui, 1999) in Appendix B to illustrate one way the skills and strategies associated with these three big ideas can be sequenced over the course of the primary grades.

Phonological Awareness. The first priority, or big idea, in beginning reading is phonological awareness (National Research Council, 1998). One of the most compelling and well-established findings in beginning reading research is the important relation between phonological awareness and reading acquisition (National Reading Panel, 2000). While it would be overly simplistic to point to a single cause of reading failure, the research reviewed suggests that poor readers have difficulty using the sounds of the language in processing written and oral information (Al Otaiba & Fuchs, 2002; Wagner et al., 1997; Wolf & Bowers, 1999).

Phonological awareness refers to the conscious understanding and knowledge that language is made up of sounds. Most important is phonemic awareness, the insight that words consist of separate sounds or phonemes and the subsequent ability to manipulate these individual sound units (Adams, 1990; Spector, 1995). Stated differently, "before children can make sense of the alphabetic principle, they must understand that the sounds that are paired with letters are one and the same as the sounds of speech" (Adams, Foorman, Lundberg, & Beeler, 1998, p. 19). In addition, beginning readers must also come to know that individual sounds combine to make up a word. Moreover, they must recognize that the same sounds are found in many different words (e.g., the /sssss/ in *sit* has the same sound as the /sssss/ in *miss*).

In phonological awareness instruction, students *do not* see any written words or letters, but rather listen and respond to what they hear. Phonological awareness involves activities like the following:

1. Orally blending sounds to make a word (e.g., "What word do you have if you put these sounds together: /c/, /aaaa/, /t/?"—*cat*)
2. Isolating beginning, middle, and ending sounds (e.g., "What is the first sound in *rose?*"—/*rrrrr*/)
3. Segmenting a word into sounds (e.g., "Say the sounds in the word *sat.*"—/*ssss*/–/*aaaa*/–/*t*/)
4. Manipulating sounds within a word (e.g., "What word do you have if you change the /ssss/ in *sat* to /mmmm/?"—*mat*)

Path analyses by Torgesen, Wagner, and Rashotte (1994) indicated that phonological awareness is a construct comprised of multiple dimensions (e.g., rhyming, blending, segmenting) that relate differentially to reading acquisition. More specifically, the difficulty of phonological awareness components and their relation to reading acquisition exist on a continuum. Components such as rhyming are easier and less directly related to reading, while those requiring synthesis (e.g., blending) and analysis (e.g., segmenting) at the individual sound (i.e., phoneme) level are more difficult and more directly associated with reading achievement (National Reading Panel, 2000; O'Connor, Jenkins, & Slocum, 1995). These advances in phonological awareness research carry significant instructional implications. Therefore, to suggest that students need phonological awareness training is useful but overly simplistic. Instruction should, at a minimum, focus on the two fundamental skills of orally blending and segmenting words at the phoneme level and allocate less time to other phonological activities (e.g., rhyming, syllable clapping, etc.).

Many children seem to develop phonological awareness intuitively. Considerable evidence suggests that children who enter kindergarten with a facility for hearing sounds in words are the same children who come from language-rich environments in which oral language, word play, reading, and print experiences are commonplace. For some learners, this immersion in the sounds and meaning of language forms the rudiments for early reading acquisition. For other learners, this incidental and indirect approach is simply insufficient to address the phonological deficits they bring to the literacy environment (Stanovich, 1986). For pedagogical purposes, the evidence appears convincingly clear: Students who enter school with little phonological awareness experience less success in reading than students with the ability to analyze and synthesize the sound structure of words (Juel, 1988; Smith, Simmons, & Kame'enui, 1998).

Ideally, children have phonological awareness before they begin formal schooling, but because many children do not, phonological awareness instruction must begin as early as possible. This instruction is obligatory, not optional (Adams, 1990; Smith, Simmons, & Kame'enui, 1998). Adams (1990) made the strongest case for teaching phonemic awareness when she stated, "This is not hard to do, and it is just too risky not to" (p. 71). The research also shows that phonological awareness skills *can* and *should* be taught to children with diverse learning needs. Intervention studies that included instruction in phonological awareness have consistently reported positive effects on both measures of phonologic skills and word reading skills. These results are consistent across studies that included samples of normally achieving students (Ball & Blachman, 1991; Byrne & Fielding-Barnsley, 1995; Lundberg, Frost, & Petersen, 1988) as well as studies that focused specifically on students at risk of reading failure and reading disability (Foorman, Francis, Fletcher, Schatschneider, & Mehta, 1998; Hatcher, Hulme, & Ellis, 1994; Lovett, Borden, Lacerenza, Benson, & Brackstone, 1994; O'Connor, Notari-Syverson, & Vadasy, 1996; Torgesen et al., 1999).

Alphabetic Understanding.   The second big idea in beginning reading is alphabetic understanding, which is a necessary requirement for operating in an alphabetic writing system (Perfetti & Zhang, 1996; National Research Council, 1998). According to Perfetti (1985), "acquisition of the alphabetic code is a critical component—indeed, the definitive component—of reading in an alphabetic language" (p. 501). Alphabetic understanding refers to a child's understanding that words are composed of individual letters, and is concerned with the "mapping of print to speech," or the establishment of a clear link between a letter and a sound. A beginning reader must come to know each letter as a "discrete, self-contained" visual pattern that can be printed or pointed to "one by one" (Adams, 1990, p. 247). As Adams (1990) stated, "Very early in the course of instruction, one wants the students to understand that all twenty-six of those strange little symbols that comprise the alphabet are worth learning and discriminating one from the other because each stands for one of the sounds that occur in spoken words" (p. 245).

The importance of developing an awareness and facility with mapping sounds to letters is furthered by the apparent limitation of whole-word identification strategies (Liberman & Liberman, 1990). In learning to identify printed words represented by an alphabet, facility in whole-word naming will rapidly reach its limit unless accompanied by a facility in applying the alphabetic code to decipher or "sound out" unknown words. Such facilities are not easily or simply acquired. A code-emphasis approach to beginning reading "makes intellectual demands of the child" (Liberman & Liberman, 1990). Juel (1991) noted that "learning the rules that underlie alphabetic writing systems is deemed neither easy nor natural" (p. 775). In fact, Torgesen (2000) pointed out the fundamental difficulty that students struggling with reading have using alphabetic understanding to read individual words, "Perhaps the most important single conclusion arising from the last 20 years of research on children who have specific difficulties learning to read is that these children experience a major bottleneck to reading growth in the area of skilled word identification" (p. 56).

To read words, a reader must see a word and access its meaning in memory. But to get from the word to its meaning, beginning readers must first apply alphabetic understanding. The reader must:

1. Sequentially translate the letters in the word into their phonological counterparts (the letters in the word *sat* are translated into their individual sounds or phonemes, /ssss/, /aaaa/, and /t/)
2. Remember the correct sequence of sounds
3. Blend the sounds together (/ssssaaaat/ – /sat/)
4. Search her memory for a real word that matches the string of sounds (/sat/)

More advanced readers must also use the alphabetic principle to recognize complex letter combinations and patterns (e.g., ea, -igh, silent-e patterns, r-controlled vowels, etc.). Skillful readers do this so automatically and rapidly that it looks like the natural reading of whole words and not the sequential translation of letters and letter combinations into sounds and sounds into words.

Converging research accentuates three realities that would be reckless to ignore:

1. A primary difference between good and poor readers is the ability to use letter–sound correspondences to identify words (Lyon & Moats, 1997; Torgesen, 2000).
2. Students who acquire and apply alphabetic understanding early in their reading careers reap long-term benefits (Stanovich, 1986).
3. Teaching students to listen to, remember, and process the sounds and letters in words is a difficult, demanding, yet achievable goal with long-lasting effects (Moats, 1999; Liberman & Liberman, 1990).

It is important to emphasize that the ultimate goal of reading is to construct meaning from print. Because the rewards of reading and understanding are so great, however, it is easy to overlook the skills that facilitate reading comprehension. One of the more compelling and reliable conclusions from research is that reading comprehension and other higher-order reading activities—that is, cognitive access to meaning—depend on strong word recognition skills (Chard, Simmons & Kame'enui, 1998; Lyon & Moats, 1997). The National Reading Panel (2000) highlighted this conclusion when they noted the "strong evidence substantiating the impact of systematic phonics instruction on learning to read" (p. 2-92). Interventions that included instruction in alphabetic understanding and a code-emphasis approach to reading words showed strong effects on the reading ability of students with diverse learning needs (Foorman et al., 1998; Hatcher, Hulme, & Ellis, 1994; Lovett et al., 1994; Torgesen et al., 1999; Torgesen et al., 2001; Vellutino et al., 1996).

Not all "phonics" instruction, however, is equally effective (National Reading Panel, 2000). The *quality* of code-based reading instruction (i.e., attention to instructional design principles) is critical. Given the converging evidence of the importance of understanding the alphabet (National Research Council, 1998), the role of instructional strategies should be to reduce the intellectual demands of this complex activity. Strategies can promote alphabetic understanding by identifying requisite components and carefully designing instruction to communicate their effective and efficient acquisition.

Automaticity with the Code.   The third big idea in beginning reading instruction is automaticity with the phonological/alphabetic code, or the ability to translate letters to sounds and sounds to words fluently. LaBerge and Samuels (1974) described the fluent reader as one whose decoding processes are automatic. Automatic processes are fast, effortless, autonomous, and require little conscious attention (Logan, 1997). There is considerable and converging evidence that many students experiencing reading difficulties lack the ability to read words automatically. This lack of decoding fluency places increasing demands on a reader's ability to remember and process information. Unless readers become automatic with the alphabetic code, the time and attention required to identify a word limits the cognitive resources available to process the meaning of the sentence in which the word appeared.

Directly stated, if a reader has to spend too much time and energy figuring out what the words *are,* she will be unable to concentrate on what the words *mean.* Stanovich (1994) explained this relation by indicating that comprehension fails "not because of overreliance on decoding, but because decoding skill is not developed enough" (p. 283). For the nonfluent reader, "reading becomes a slow, labor-intensive process that only fitfully results in understanding" (National Reading Panel, p. 3-8). The close relationship between reading fluency (i.e., decoding words accurately and quickly) and reading comprehension (i.e., deriving meaning from print) has strong empirical and theoretical support (Fuchs, Fuchs, Hosp, & Jenkins, 2001; RAND Study Group, 2002; Shinn, Good, Knutson, Tilly, & Collins, 1992). Thus, the third big idea underscores the importance of readers moving beyond the ability to just translate letters to sounds to the ability to use alphabetic understanding to decode words automatically with little or no conscious effort. It is only when students reach this degree of fluency that they are able to truly grasp the full meaning of what they read.

According to Ehri and McCormick (1998), children in the initial stage of reading focus largely on individual letters and sounds. Once students gain competence at this level of processing, they are able to develop an awareness of patterns in which letters frequently appear (e.g., spelling patterns). Readers can then begin to process these familiar sequences of letters as units and use such sequences to speed up word reading. Ehri and McCormick (1998) noted that because skillful readers are more likely to identify words by recognizing the samenesses in them, there is value in teaching students to read unfamiliar words by detecting known words and familiar word parts. Cunningham and Stanovich (1998) determined that the ability to use patterns of letters was highly related to word identification skills and that individual differences in this ability were largely explained by differences in exposure to print. Additionally, Felton (1993) asserted that "the child must be exposed to words (decodable words) enough times that the words become automatically accessible. . . . For some children . . . developing automaticity requires tremendous amounts of practice" (p. 588).

It is important to note that exposing children to familiar words does not suggest that words always be decontextualized and presented in isolated lists. Rather, students should also practice reading connected text such as engaging in repeated readings of familiar passages with peer or teacher feedback. Guided repeated oral reading strategies are well-researched and effective approaches for increasing text-reading fluency (McCardle & Chhabra, 2004; National Reading Panel, 2000). Repeated readings can include fixed-time activities in which students reread as much of a passage as they can in a set time or fixed-length activities in which they reread a set number of words and record their reading time (Texas Center for Reading and Language Arts, 1998; Mastropieri, Leinart, & Scruggs, 1999).

At this early stage of reading, children must read materials that facilitate successful identification and understanding of words, instead of text in which the words are too difficult or unfamiliar. Children should read stories, passages, texts, or materials with a high percentage of decodable words (i.e., words for which the student knows each letter–sound correspondence and can apply the appropriate blending or decoding skills) (Carnine, Silbert, Kame'enui, & Tarver, 2003). Reading decodable texts communicates to the beginning reader the importance of accessing meaning through accurate word identification. For fluency building, children should read text in which they can accurately identify at least 95 percent of the words (Texas Center for Reading and Language Arts, 1998).

At the risk of oversimplifying this important stage of reading, automaticity of the code appears to result from prerequisite ability with phonemic awareness and alphabetic understanding combined with repeated opportunities to practice and apply these capacities in connected text to the point of overlearning (Adams, 1990; Felton, 1993). Clearly, automaticity of word reading is not the end goal of reading instruction. However, fluent reading marks the critical transition to more advanced stages of literacy learning.

Designing Conspicuous Strategies.   The first instructional design principle organizes beginning reading instruction around the big ideas of phonological awareness, alphabetic understanding, and automaticity with the code. Big ideas in beginning reading set the stage for teaching effective strategies. Students who are at risk of experiencing reading difficulties need to be taught conspicuously a set of strategies to be able to use the skills associated with these three big ideas.

Strategies are a series of steps that can be purposefully employed to achieve a particular outcome. Although some students are able to infer intuitively the strategies necessary for successful beginning reading, many students, especially those with diverse learning needs, are not able to induce effective or efficient strategies (National Research Council, 1998). Strategies that beginning readers need to be successful are both simple (e.g., knowing to say the sound that corresponds with a letter) and complex (e.g., sequentially decoding a difficult word). Because phonological awareness and alphabetic understanding are learned concepts (Perfetti & Zhang, 1996; Liberman & Liberman, 1990), instruction must make *all* strategies conspicuous by explicitly teaching them in a manner that is systematic and sequential. Such instruction involves multiple steps, systematic teacher actions, and a careful sequence of teaching events. For example, according to Felton (1993), teaching children with phonological problems should be clear and unambiguous: "Children who do not have age-appropriate phonological awareness skills must be taught such skills directly. . . . Instruction should be explicit with no aspects of the process (including blending) left to intuition" (p. 587).

Phonological Awareness.   Many children have a difficult time developing strategies and skills associated with phonological awareness. This is not surprising. The understanding that language is made up of discrete sounds is an unnatural insight because words are pronounced as whole units in conversational language (Moats, 1999). As Ball and Blachman (1991) pointed out, the individual sounds in words are "coarticulated"—that is, merged and not pronounced as separate, discrete parts—and require more "abstraction than discrimination" (p. 52). They stated: "Although we may teach children to 'hear' three sounds in *cat,* the three sounds are not separated in the acoustic stimulus itself" (p. 51). In other words, we are not programmed to be consciously aware of the individual sounds within words (Liberman, 1999). Facilitating phonological awareness, therefore, requires directly teaching children strategies to "attend to that which we have learned not to attend to" (Adams, 1990, p. 66). Because many learners do not naturally recognize the importance or purpose of the discrete sounds of language, instruction must make this purpose and process conspicuous.

There are a number of characteristics that are common to effective instruction designed to teach conspicuously the critical phonological strategies of oral blending and segmenting (Smith, Simmons, & Kame'enui, 1998). First, teachers regularly model skills for students by overtly drawing attention to the sounds within words and clearly demonstrating strategies. Second, after teacher modeling, students are given multiple opportunities to demonstrate their skills orally. Third, students' mental manipulations of sounds are made overt with concrete representations.

Figures 3–1 and 3–2 illustrate conspicuous instruction of phonological awareness strategies for oral blending and segmenting taken from the *Optimize* beginning reading program developed by researchers from the Institute for Development of Educational Achievement (IDEA) at the University of Oregon (Project Optimize, 1999). In this first oral blending activity, the teacher has "Diz," a dinosaur puppet, say the sounds in words "stretched out." The teacher first models blending the stretched out sounds into words and then gives the students opportunities to practice this strategy.

In this next oral segmenting activity, students say the sounds in words slowly while touching a square for each sound. The teacher models the strategy and then

"I'll show you how to figure out what Diz the Dinosaur is saying."
"If Diz says 'mmmmmooooop', he means '<u>mop</u>'."
(The teacher points to the picture of <u>mop</u>.)

"Now it's your turn to figure out what Diz is saying."
"If Diz says 'lllleeeaffff', what does he mean?"
(The students respond "<u>leaf</u>", and point to the correct picture.)

FIGURE 3–1

Conspicuous Instruction of an Oral Blending Strategy

Note. From *Project Optimize* kindergarten intervention program, 1999, Eugene, OR: University of Oregon, Institute for the Development of Educational Achievement. Reprinted with permission.

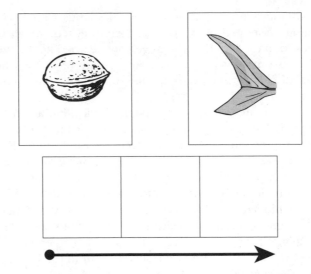

"**The first picture is <u>nut</u>.**"
"**I'll say the sounds in <u>nut</u> slowly, and touch a square for each sound.**
/nnnn/ – /uuuu/ – /t/."
(The teacher points to a square while saying each sound.)

"**This next picture is <u>fin</u>.**"
"**Now it's your turn to say the sounds in <u>fin</u> slowly, and touch a square for each sound.**"
(The students respond "/ffff/ – /iiii/ – /nnnn/", and point to a square while saying each sound.)

FIGURE 3–2
Conspicuous Instruction of an Oral Segmenting Strategy
Note. From *Project Optimize* kindergarten intervention program, 1999, Eugene, OR: University of Oregon, Institute for the Development of Educational Achievement. Reprinted with permission.

gives students practice segmenting words. The three-square strip acts as a concrete representation of the sound segments in the words and also makes students' application of the steps of the strategy overt.

We reiterate the importance of differentiating instruction according to learner needs. All children do not enter school with phonological awareness deficits. Some children already have mastered the phonologic basis of language and do not need additional intensive instruction in this area. However, teachers have become increasingly aware of the number of diverse learners whose experiential, physiological, linguistic, or socioeconomic histories have hampered phonological awareness development. For these children, conspicuous instruction of phonological awareness skills and strategies is essential.

Alphabetic Understanding.   Instruction that conspicuously teaches alphabetic understanding provides students with strategies for producing letter–sound correspondences and decoding words (Chard, Simmons, & Kame'enui, 1998). What may appear to be a simple process of translating letters into sounds has been found particularly troublesome for students with diverse learning needs (Adams, 1990; Felton, 1993). More importantly, analyses of prominent beginning reading programs have revealed the absence of systematic procedures to teach students to translate letters to sounds and blend them into words (Stein, 1993). Therefore, it is not surprising that students fail to make the connections between learning the alphabetic code and reading.

First, instruction must teach individual letter–sound correspondences, such as /rrrr/, /ssss/, or /aaaa/. In teaching letter–sound correspondences, it is important to teach letters that occur frequently in common words (e.g., *ran, sat*) and also to limit the number of letters introduced per lesson. Conspicuous teaching of a strategy for identifying letter–sound correspondences could consist of the teacher first displaying a single letter symbol and modeling the corresponding sound (e.g., the teacher points to the letter *m* on the board and says, "This letter makes the sound /mmmm/."), and then testing students to verify acquisition (e.g., the teacher points to the letter *m* again and asks, "What sound does this letter make?"). This instruction is simple and unambiguous. Each letter–sound pair is presented in isolation without the distractions of other letters. The connection between the letter and its sound is made clear to the learner.

Once students have mastered two to three letters, the next step is for students to blend the sounds of isolated letters into meaningful words. Because students have practiced the process of oral blending at the phonological awareness stage, they are prepared to blend the sounds that correspond to printed letters to read words. Figure 3–3 demonstrates the word-reading strategy from the *Optimize* beginning reading program. The teacher makes the steps for reading words conspicuous by clearly modeling the strategy before students have opportunities to practice.

Automaticity with the Code.   In his review of automaticity in reading, Logan (1997) concluded that experience with words and consistent practice are necessary to develop automatic word reading skills. Therefore, the more readers are exposed to and experience words that they can accurately decode, the more likely they are to develop automaticity and fluency with the patterns (Share & Stanovich, 1995). Building on the word-reading strategy described above, students would be given frequent opportunities to use the strategy to read words containing letter–sound correspondences and patterns that have been systematically taught, both in isolation and in meaningful connected text. Giving students the opportunity to read the same words in books that they have practiced reading in isolation makes conspicuous the linkage between accurately decoding words and accessing the meaning of what they read.

As Adams (1990) noted, the purpose of strategy instruction is to make explicit those processes to which we do not typically attend. The conspicuous instruction described in the sections above provides students with simple, effective and reliable beginning reading strategies through presentations that are direct and unambiguous, in effect, making explicit the implicit techniques that good readers regularly use to recognize sounds in words, relate sounds to letters, and blend sounds into words.

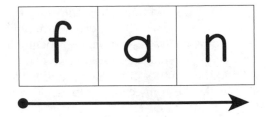

"My turn to read a word. First I'll say the sounds in the word slowly and
then I'll say them fast."
"Watch my finger. Each time I touch a letter, I'll say its sound. I won't stop
between the sounds. /ffffaaaannnn/."
(The teacher moves his finger underneath each letter and says each sound for
1–2 seconds.)
"Now I'll say it fast. Fan. The word is fan."
(The teacher moves his finger quickly across the arrow as he says the word fast.)

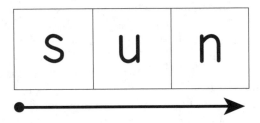

"Now it's your turn to read a word. First you'll say the sounds in the word
slowly and then you'll say them fast."
"When I touch a letter, say its sound. Keep saying the sound until I touch
under the next letter. Watch my finger!"
(The teacher moves his finger underneath each letter while the students say the
sounds. /ssssuuuunnnn/.)
"Now say it fast."
(The teacher moves his finger quickly across the arrow as the students say the
word fast. Sun.)

FIGURE 3–3
Conspicuous Instruction of a Word-Reading Strategy

Note. From *Project Optimize* kindergarten intervention program, by Project Optimize, 1999, Eugene,
OR: University of Oregon, Institute for the Development of Educational Achievement. Reprinted with
permission.

In the following section we describe design procedures used to ensure that such
strategies are achieved by students with diverse learning needs.

Designing Mediated Scaffolding

The third design principle, mediated scaffolding, is particularly important for students
who may not profit fully from traditionally sequenced and structured curricula. Scaf-

folds provide the learner with personal guidance or support during the initial phases of learning new and difficult information. Students with diverse learning needs require substantial supports to gain cognitive access to the complexities of our alphabetic writing system.

When scaffolding instruction, an important guideline is to align the amount of structure and support with the needs of the learner. Another recommendation is to scaffold instruction through prompts and supports that can be easily and authentically embedded in instructional materials. Finally, it is important to withdraw scaffolds gradually once learners demonstrate mastery of a skill or strategy, so that they do not become overly dependent on a prop.

In beginning reading, scaffolds may be provided in two ways: through assistance by teachers or peers, and through the sequence and selection of tasks. During initial learning, teachers scaffold instruction by modeling the precise process students will need to perform. Gradually, responsibility is transferred to students until they have internalized strategies and are able to perform tasks independently. For example, Carnine, Silbert, Kame'enui and Tarver (2003) designed a carefully scaffolded sequence of lessons for teaching students to decode words that progressively moves from a high degree of teacher support to students decoding words independently. The following sequence would progress gradually over the course of multiple lessons each of which would contain modeled examples, guided examples, and learner practice.

Scaffold 1—Model.   The teacher says the sounds in a word while touching under each letter: "My turn to sound out this word. When I touch a letter, I'll say its sound. I'll keep saying the sound until I touch the next letter."

Scaffold 2—Overt Sound Out.   The teacher touches under each letter while *students* say each sound: "Your turn to sound out this word. When I touch a letter, you say its sound. Keep saying the sound until I touch the next letter."

Scaffold 3—Internal Sound Out.   The teacher touches under each letter while students say each sound *in their head*: "You are going to read this word without saying the sounds out loud. As I point to the letters, sound out this word to yourself."

Scaffold 4—Whole-Word Reading.   The teacher points to the word and students sound it out independently: "You are going to read this word the fast way. When I point to a word, sound it out to yourself. When I signal, say the word the fast way."

Task scaffolds are embedded in the tasks themselves and designed to allow students to focus on reading processes and strategies by initially reducing the information they must generate independently. Instruction should begin with easy tasks and systematically progress to more difficult ones. For example, phonological awareness tasks that deal with larger linguistic units are easier for learners to process than smaller units. Instruction in segmenting, therefore, could begin with students breaking sentences into words, progress to breaking words into syllables, and conclude with the ultimate goal of breaking words into individual phonemes. Even at the phoneme level, it is easier for students to isolate the first sound than to completely segment the word. In both phonological and reading tasks, certain types of sounds/letters and words are more demanding than others. Continuous sounds that can be held out (e.g., /mmmm/) are less difficult than stop sounds, which can only be said for an instant (e.g., /t/). Consonant–vowel–consonant words (e.g., fun) are easier to decode than words with consonant blends (e.g., *stop, hand*) which, in turn, are easier than words with more complicated letter patterns (e.g., *lake, train*). Reading instruction should be designed or scaffolded to mirror this progression of difficulty.

Other task scaffolds include introducing a manageable amount of information in a lesson and the purposeful separation of highly similar and potentially confusing concepts (e.g., separating the introduction of *b* and *d* by a number of lessons, or initially teaching only the most common sound for the *ea*. letter combination). Careful consideration of the information communicated in a lesson focuses attention on the specific skill or concept being taught and decreases the likelihood that students will form a misrule or become confused. Types of student responses can also be scaffolded. Tasks can be sequenced so that learners are required to first recognize the correct response (e.g., choose the correct letter from a set of letters) and then produce a response (e.g., write the letter from memory).

Designing Strategic Integration

The fourth design principle, strategic integration, involves the logical and purposeful connections between skills and strategies. The purpose of strategic integration is to connect prerequisite skills to develop more sophisticated applications in higher order skills. For example, identifying words in connected text requires that a reader integrate phonological awareness, alphabetic understanding, and automaticity with the code. Students with diverse learning needs often fail to induce the connections between these big ideas; thus, it is imperative that instructional strategies are designed to communicate these relations. Beginning reading strategies are not discrete but are integrally related. Students must not only understand these strategies as separate entities, but also learn the relations among strategies that lead to a complete and integrated strategy for reading words.

One of the most consistent conclusions of research on beginning reading and strategic points of integration concerns combining phonological awareness with letter–sound and word-reading instruction (National Research Panel, 2000). Repeatedly, experimental investigations have documented the insufficiency of either phonological awareness or letter–sound correspondence training, unless combined with direct instruction in reading (Spector, 1995). Relatedly, Ball and Blachman (1991) found that letter–name and letter–sound training without phonological awareness training is not enough to improve early reading skills. The combination of instruction in phonological awareness and letter–sound correspondences appears to be most favorable for successful early reading (O'Connor, Jenkins, & Slocum, 1995; National Research Panel, 2000).

An example of integrating a phonological awareness activity (i.e., first sound isolation) with an alphabetic activity (i.e., knowledge of letter sounds) is illustrated

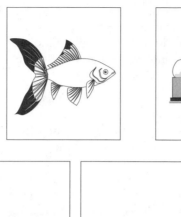

"The first picture is <u>fish</u>. The first sound in <u>fish</u> is /ffff/."
"I'm going to point to the letter that matches this picture's first sound."
(The teacher points to the letter <u>f</u>.)
"The letter <u>f</u> says /ffff/ like the /ffff/ in <u>fish</u>."

"The next picture is <u>pie</u>. What is the first sound in <u>pie</u>?"
(The students respond /p/.)
"Now you're going to point to the letter that matches this picture's first sound."
(The students point to the letter <u>p</u>.)
"That's right, the letter <u>p</u> says /p/ like the /p/ in <u>pie</u>."

FIGURE 3–4
Strategic Integration of a Phonological Awareness Activity (i.e., first sound isolation) with an Alphabetic Activity (i.e., knowledge of letter sounds)

Note. From *Project Optimize* kindergarten intervention program, 1999, Eugene, OR: University of Oregon, Institute for the Development of Educational Achievement. Reprinted with permission.

in Figure 3–4. In this activity from the *Optimize* beginning reading program, students identify the first sound of a picture (phonological awareness) and then choose a letter that goes with the sound (alphabetic understanding). Students could also write the letter that matches the picture's first sound.

Although phonological awareness, alphabetic understanding, and automaticity with the code increase in complexity with one set of skills being a prerequisite to the next, instruction shouldn't proceed in only a linear fashion. Skills need to be integrated strategically and teaching should progress simultaneously (Simmons & Kame'enui, 1998). Students who know some letter–sound correspondences and are able to orally blend and segment words should begin word reading. Similarly, students who are able to read simple words should move into reading connected, decodable texts to develop automaticity and fluency.

The following steps should be considered in the strategic integration of phonological awareness, letter–sound correspondence, word-reading, and text-reading instruction:

1. Design phonological awareness tasks emphasizing sounds that correspond to the letters that students are learning.
2. Initially teach letter–sound correspondences that have the greatest generality and use in reading words. (This is similar to the "Wheel of Fortune" strategy, in which contestants select consonants that appear frequently in many words (e.g., s, r, t, l, m) to assist them in identifying the word puzzle.)
3. For word reading, select examples for which students know all the letter–sound correspondences, and in which the most common sounds are represented (e.g., /nnnnn/ in *man* and *nut*).
4. Have students read stories that contain a high percentage of words and word types already taught and practiced in phonological awareness and word-reading instruction.
5. Make explicit the connection between the strategies through instruction (e.g., "Do you remember how we heard the sounds in words and blended those sounds together to make words? Today, we will sound out letters to read words").

A frequent criticism of code-emphasis approaches to beginning reading instruction is the lack of integration of code-based activities with other activities, such as story reading, spelling, and writing even though including such activities has been shown to be an effective method for strategically integrating phonologic and alphabetic skills (Ehri, 1997; Santoro, Coyne, & Simmons, in press). It has been argued that children too often receive a phonics lesson that has limited application to the other activities in language arts. As Juel reported, "It is unfortunate that many basal series treat phonics lessons as if they had no relation to story reading (Beck, 1981, cited in Juel, 1991). This "propped-on" phonics method fails to communicate the utility of learning component letter sounds. Beginning reading instruction that includes the strategic integration of skills results in students achieving a more meaningful and complex level of knowledge and understanding.

Designing Primed Background Knowledge

The fifth design principle is primed background knowledge. Perhaps in no other facet of literacy does background knowledge exact such consequences as in beginning reading. Successful reading acquisition depends largely on (a) the knowledge the learner brings to the reading task, (b) the accuracy of that information, and (c) the degree to which the learner accesses and uses that information. For diverse learners, priming background knowledge is critical for success because these students often have memory or strategy deficits. In effect, priming is a brief reminder that alerts the learner to the requirements of a task and prompts the learner to retrieve known information.

In beginning reading, there are multiple concepts, skills, and strategies that learners must bring to bear to any given task (Adams, 1990). To spell a word, for instance, a student must be able to orally segment the word into individual phonemes (a phonological awareness skill), map each sound to its corresponding letter (alphabetic understanding and knowledge of letter–sound correspondences), write the letters in the correct order, and read back the word to see if it is correctly spelled (a decoding strategy). If a student is unable to access prerequisite knowledge quickly or accurately, he or she will be unsuccessful at spelling the word. However, diverse learners may not access information in memory as efficiently and effectively, or may not consistently rely on effective strategies. In such cases, the task of priming background knowledge is paramount to subsequent reading success. The following discussion identifies three facets to guide the design of primed background knowledge.

First, identify essential preskills or background knowledge most proximal (i.e., relevant) to the new task. This step may seem obvious; however, for beginning reading, a thorough understanding of the components of phonological awareness, alphabetic understanding, and automaticity, and of the relations among them, is pivotal to efficient and effective instruction and learning. Because diverse learners are often playing catch-up with their peers, priming the knowledge most proximal to the task will increase instructional efficiency. For instance, there are multiple dimensions to phonological awareness that are related differentially to reading acquisition. Specifically, while rhyming is a common phonological awareness task, other tasks, such as blending and segmenting, are more highly related and therefore proximal to beginning word identification. Effective priming of background knowledge requires a careful analysis of the intricate components of beginning reading and the selection of information most relevant to the instructional objective.

Second, once proximal tasks are identified, one must determine whether the background knowledge needs to be primed or taught. Priming is a brief reminder or exercise that requires the learner to retrieve known information. For example, practicing a few examples of isolating initial sounds in words before teaching how to segment whole words primes or readies the learner for the more complex task. On some occasions, teachers may assume that learners have background knowledge such as knowledge of letter–sound correspondences or how to match words with the same beginning sounds. If learners never mastered the letter–sound correspondences, then a brief reminder that the letter *r* makes the /rrrr/ sound will not suffice. Therefore, a second step is to determine whether priming will allow the learner to retrieve and use the information accurately and reliably. If so, then priming is the appropriate instructional strategy; if not, then a more thorough instructional sequence must be designed to teach the information.

Third, priming is a prompt that elicits the correct information or readies the learner by focusing attention on a difficult task or component of a task. For example, prior to reading a short passage to improve automaticity, learners may be prompted to pay attention to words that have not been recently reviewed or words that may have been problematic in word lists. This may involve modeling how to segment a word or merely pointing to a previously problematic letter and reminding students to pay careful attention when they come to that letter.

The functions of priming background knowledge are to increase the likelihood that students will be successful on tasks by making explicit the critical features of tasks, and to motivate learners to access information they already know. Therefore, in most cases the level of priming should be brief and strategic. Prolonged priming that fosters dependence on teacher-provided information should be discouraged.

Designing Judicious Review

Effective beginning reading instruction depends on the sixth design principle, judicious review, to reinforce the essential building blocks of phonological awareness, alphabetic understanding, and automaticity with the code. The critical dimensions of judicious review were presented in Chapter 1 (i.e., sufficient, distributed, cumulative, and varied). So how do teachers select information for review, schedule review to ensure retention, and design activities to extend beginning readers' understanding of the skills, concepts, and strategies specific to beginning reading? These issues are discussed in the sections that follow.

Determining What To Review.   Judicious review requires that teachers select information to review that is useful and essential for further reading success. For example, Carnine, Silbert, Kame'enui, and Tarver (2003) suggested that review include high-utility, frequently occurring letter sounds, spelling patterns, and exercises. The specific content of review, however, should vary from learner to learner. To ensure that review is judicious for diverse learners, students' progress must be monitored carefully to ensure that the information reviewed is the information in need of review. Informal methods of documenting learner performance (e.g., collecting data on difficult words during oral reading practice) can provide information about what should be included in review.

Scheduling Review.   Review is more effective when it is distributed over time and presented in shorter time increments (Dempster, 1991). Such distributed activities lend themselves particularly well to the range of skills and strategies in beginning reading. For example, when developing automaticity with the code, words could be clustered into sets and reviewed over time. The amount of spacing between review sets must be determined by the facility of the reader. Initially, frequent review sessions would be scheduled, and as fluency develops, greater amounts of time would be interjected between review sessions.

It is important to avoid the common but fatal practice of removing items (e.g., words, letter sounds, phonological activities) from review sets completely once a learner attains a high level of initial learning. Judicious review involves continually reexamining important information to enhance retention. This suggests that teachers must retain a cumulative list of essential and high-utility information, and must continue to present this information in spaced reviews and in different activities. Fortunately, in beginning reading, spaced review will take care of itself if students read often and extensively.

Designing Review Activities.   A common misconception is that review is synonymous with rote rehearsal. The purpose of a judicious review is to provide learners with more opportunities to demonstrate what they know. The means and methods for having students demonstrate this knowledge can be as flexible and creative as teachers desire. Decisions as to what to review, how often, and when depend to a large extent on exactly what has been taught, how often, and when, and on the particular outcome the teacher desires. For example, auditory blending tasks to develop phonological awareness will require a different kind and schedule of review than letter–sound correspondence tasks to develop alphabetic understanding. Because auditory skills require no visual materials, they can be reviewed more spontaneously and for brief periods of time. For example teachers can call students to line up by the first sounds in their names (e.g., "Everybody whose name begins with the sound /b/, please line up".). Letter–sound correspondence review requires systematic analysis of visual and auditory information that may predispose students to failure, and therefore requires more deliberate planning (e.g., the careful separation of letters, like *b* and *d,* which are easily confused). Of course, review activities will also depend on the learner's performance; that is, which phonological awareness or alphabetic understanding activities were unsuccessful and why.

In general, developing successful reading skills requires careful scheduling of review activities (Carnine, Silbert, Kame'enui, & Tarver, 2003). The following guidelines should be considered in designing review activities for developing phonological awareness, alphabetic understanding, and automaticity with the code:

1. Examine the types of errors (e.g., omission errors, substitution errors, no responses, slow responses) students made during reading activities to recognize patterns.
2. Create "review sets" for particular beginning reading activities. For example, when teaching letter–sound correspondences, include in the review set letters most recently introduced, letters that were particularly difficult (i.e., letters missed consistently and frequently) for learners, as well as a judicious sample of letters *not* reviewed recently.
3. Schedule review activities for brief periods on multiple occasions within a lesson. For example, it requires approximately 15 seconds to orally blend one word. This phonological awareness skill could be reviewed periodically (three to four times) throughout a 10–15-minute word-reading lesson.
4. Schedule review activities for brief periods (30 seconds to 1–2 minutes) on multiple occasions throughout a school day; that is, space the activities across the full range of teaching lessons in a day.
5. Devote more review time to new reading tasks than to familiar tasks.

THE APPLICATION OF INSTRUCTIONAL DESIGN PRINCIPLES

In the preceding sections we discussed the six design principles, specifically in relation to beginning reading instruction. These principles can be applied, however, in a number of ways for different purposes. Three possible applications include using the six principles to *develop, select,* or *modify* instructional tools in beginning reading. For example, curriculum developers could use the six principles to guide the design or creation of a new beginning reading program, district curriculum committees could use the principles to evaluate a number of possible reading programs under consideration for adoption, and classroom teachers could use the principles to modify or strengthen an existing program. In the next sections, we provide guidance on applying instructional design principles for each of these purposes in beginning reading.

Developing Instructional Tools

Moats (1999) declared that teaching reading *is* rocket science. This assertion underscores the complexities inherent in teaching children to read in an alphabetic writing system and the difficulties associated with developing a comprehensive beginning reading program. Curriculum designers, developers, and publishers need to attend carefully to each of the six principles described in this chapter to ensure that reading programs are designed to meet the needs of diverse learners.

When designing a beginning reading program, developers should allocate considerable time and attention to teaching the big ideas of phonological awareness and alphabetic understanding and to the development of automaticity with the code. This is in contrast to distributing equal time and resources to a multitude of topics, in essence going an inch deep and a mile wide.

Programs should include explicit instruction of strategies for applying big ideas. Strategies should not be too narrow because they would likely result in rote learning and the need to learn too many strategies. Neither should they be too broad, like some of the common "strategies" for reading words (e.g., What words do you know that begin with _____? or What word would make sense in this sentence?). Students need to be taught more specific strategies with broad potential for transfer of knowledge across letters, sounds, and words (e.g., sequentially sounding out the letters in words and then blending the sounds together). Strategies for reading words, such as this one, are straightforward, yet accurate and reliable.

Scaffolded tasks should be built into programs, particularly around the selection of letters and words to include when introducing skills associated with phonological awareness, alphabetic understanding, and automaticity with the code. The introduction of letters and word types should be carefully sequenced and controlled to maximize student success and reduce misunderstanding, especially with letters and words that are visually and auditorially similar and that predictably cause confusion for many students (e.g., b/d, p/q: was/saw). Tasks should also progress from teacher directed to student directed. For example, tasks can be designed so that the teacher (a) models the skill for students, (b) performs the skill with students, and (c) gives students opportunities to perform the skill independently. Programs should also include tasks and activities that specifically integrate phonological awareness, alphabetic understanding, and automaticity with the code.

Developers should (1) create assessment tools that determine whether students possess background knowledge for learning the strategies in a program, and (2) provide instruction on essential background knowledge for those with gaps. For diverse learners, it is risky to assume that material taught "last year" will be fully retained as background knowledge for strategies being taught this year. Developers also do a great service to teachers when they provide plentiful review in beginning reading programs, because it is infinitely easier for teachers to skip review activities than to create additional ones. Programs with well-distributed and varied review are far more efficient than those without it, and programs with built-in cumulative review promote strategic integration, as described above.

Selecting Instructional Tools

Schools and districts face an important, difficult, and highly consequential task when selecting a beginning reading program for adoption. Whether or not a program has incorporated quality design features in its basic architecture can make the critical difference in the success or failure of students with diverse learning needs. The six instructional design principles can serve as a guide for evaluating different beginning reading programs.

Begin by examining beginning reading programs to determine the extent to which the majority of time/attention is allocated to the big ideas of phonological awareness, alphabetic understanding, and automaticity with the code. Examine the program to see whether conspicuous strategies exist at all, and if so, whether they generally appear to be "intermediate in generality." Try to imagine yourself as a diverse learner just learning to read an alphabetic language based solely on the strategies taught in the program you are evaluating. Does the program provide students with simple, effective, and reliable beginning reading strategies through presentations that are direct and unambiguous? Does the instruction make explicit the implicit techniques that good readers regularly use to recognize sounds in words, relate sounds to letters, and blend sounds into words?

Examine both *model* or demonstration tasks associated with reading strategies and the tasks students will eventually do independently. Ask yourself, "Are there in-between tasks that will help students gradually achieve independence and understanding? Is there enough support built into tasks to accommodate diverse learners? Do tasks gradually progress from teacher directed to student directed?"

Examine the scope and sequence of instructional tools, look specifically to see whether some chapters (or units or lessons) are designated as "summary or review" or "integration" or "consolidation." In a well-integrated tool, in-program assessments will include tasks representing all topics taught previously, not just those taught immediately preceding assessment.

A strategy for teaching an important big idea in beginning reading (e.g., phoneme segmentation, word decoding) should be dissected into its component parts. Then, examine how those component parts are introduced or developed in lessons *preceding* the introduction of the strategy. Ideally, components are taught or reviewed a few lessons before the introduction of the new strategy. Also tools should be checked to determine the extent to which assessment tools identify potential problems with background knowledge.

To evaluate review activities, locate a particularly difficult skill in beginning reading, such as reading words that end in *ing* or *ed,* then trace the review throughout the remainder of the program to determine whether review is plentiful, distributed, cumulative, and appropriately varied.

Modifying Instructional Tools

Many beginning reading programs have not been developed with sufficient attention to instructional design principles. Therefore, teachers may find that they need to modify existing programs to accommodate the needs of diverse learners. This is a very difficult and time-consuming endeavor, especially if the program is not organized around big ideas and does not include explicit instruction of conspicuous strategies. However, teachers can use the six principles to significantly improve and strengthen flawed programs.

First, examine the program and identify the most important beginning reading concepts and principles associated with the big ideas of phonological awareness, alphabetic understanding, and automaticity with the code and reallocate instructional time so that you may teach those concepts and principles thoroughly. Note that valid and useful assessment should also focus on these three big ideas.

When students struggle with concepts and principles that are not directly taught in the program, teachers must develop explicit instruction to teach those concepts and principles. This explicit instruction should be focused on providing students with effective and reliable beginning reading strategies. When strategies are included in the program, but are too narrow or broad, teachers should explain the underlying principles that make strategies work and introduce more effective strategies.

If the program doesn't include sufficient support for difficult tasks, teachers can provide scaffolding by first modeling skills and then performing skills with students before requiring students to demonstrate skills independently. Without consuming too much time, teachers can also convert independent tasks into scaffolded tasks by providing hints, cues, or prompts for some of the more difficult steps in the strategies associated with those tasks.

Teachers can improve the effectiveness of program notably by identifying common confusions (e.g., b/d, p/q; was/saw), introducing and practicing components first in isolation, and later providing students with additional integrated practice around them. To some extent, teachers can analyze important strategies in advance of their introduction and provide essential background knowledge based on that analysis. For example, teachers can review new or difficult letters before students read them in words, and practice reading difficult words in isolation before reading the same words in a passage or book.

Teachers can modify programs to improve the judiciousness of review by (1) taking an extensive set of review tasks and distributing them over a period of days, (2) making review cumulative by reintegrating previously learned skills into currently reviewed material, and (3) developing thoughtful, creative, and varied review activities that help students transfer skills to new situations.

SUMMARY

A primary purpose of educational research is to identify the things that matter and result in reliable, trustworthy reading improvements for all learners. More than three decades of research validate that we know a great deal about what matters in beginning reading instruction. However, it is perplexing that this converging body of knowledge on prerequisites and requisites of beginning reading acquisition does not consistently find its way into the instructional strategies of classrooms and schools. Although we are encouraged by new reading programs we have had the opportunity to review and their reliance on empirically-based principles (e.g., American Federation of Teachers, 1999), there is still a need for more research-validated beginning reading instruction. Our synthesis of the research literature leads us to conclude that beginning readers must develop an awareness of the phonological properties of language, and insight, utility, and, ultimately, automaticity with the alphabetic code. To accomplish this, instruction for beginning reading should be designed and selected according to the following criteria:

1. Beginning reading instruction should be organized around the three *big ideas* of phonological awareness, alphabetic understanding, and automaticity with the code.

2. Effective instruction provides explicit teaching of *conspicuous strategies* for beginning reading. Such instruction should teach phonological awareness strategies for oral segmenting and blending, and teach alphabetic understanding strategies for identifying letter–sound correspondences, recognizing common word parts or spelling patterns, and decoding words. Moreover, instruction must ultimately result in students becoming proficient enough with skills and strategies to decode words automatically and read text fluently with little or no conscious effort.

3. Beginning reading instruction should include *mediated scaffolding*. Students with diverse learning needs require substantial support during the initial stages of learning to read in our complex alphabetic writing system. The level of support needs to align with the needs of the learner and should be gradually withdrawn to promote reading independence. Instruction should include extensive teacher modeling of skills and strategies. Task supports should be built into instructional programs and include a carefully designed sequence for introducing and practicing letters, words, and texts that promotes success and reduces confusion.

4. Effective instruction provides *strategic integration* of beginning reading skills and strategies. Phonological awareness instruction should be complemented by instruction in letter–sound correspondences and word-reading strategies. Students who are able to read simple words should move into reading connected, decodable texts to develop automaticity and fluency.

5. Beginning reading instruction is more effective when students have *primed background knowledge*. This requires that instructional programs (a) identify the essential preskills that students need to successfully apply beginning reading strategies, (b) assess whether or not students possess those preskills, and (c) include instruction that either prompts or reteaches essential preskills.

6. Effective beginning reading instruction includes *judicious review.* Review is judicious when it is structured to ensure mastery, automaticity, and retention of beginning reading skills and strategies, and results in broad transfer across multiple reading tasks and situations.

As expectations for students increase, accountability for achievement grows. As classrooms become more complex environments and the needs of learners become more diverse, teachers must rely on beginning reading instruction that incorporates effective principles of instructional design that result in more effective and efficient student learning. Educational research and our substantial knowledge base in beginning reading has brought us closer to identifying the factors that determine effective reading instruction. Now, our task is to ensure that this information is translated into strategies that we can use successfully with all students in classrooms around the nation, allowing *every* child to enter in the world of reading.

REFLECTION AND APPLICATION

Case Study

Terri Washington is a special educator at East School, an elementary school that serves students in kindergarten through grade 6. Terri primarily supports students with learning disabilities in fourth through sixth grade. Terri likes to say that she gets to do a little bit of everything. For example, on any given day she may co-teach a social studies unit with a fifth-grade teacher, help sixth-grade students develop a plan for organizing their homework in the resource center, develop an instructional plan for a paraprofessional to implement one-on-one with a student struggling with math, and teach a systematic reading program to a small group of fourth graders. Terri likes the variety of her job and knows that she is good at what she does.

Terri feels strongly about supporting students who are experiencing reading difficulties because, as she often says, "Reading is the gateway skill. If a child can't read, he won't be successful in any other area." Over the years, Terri has adopted and implemented an explicit, systematic, and intensive reading program with the students on her caseload with IEP goals in reading. Because of the success of her students in reading, she has been recognized by the principal and upper-grade teachers as the resident "expert" and is often consulted about how to better teach reading in the general education classrooms.

Another component of Terri's job is to conduct eligibility evaluations for students who are referred for special education. Both Terri and the administration have noticed that referrals at East School have been gradually increasing over the past few years, especially in fourth grade. This fall, for example, the fourth-grade teachers submitted five new referrals, all for students experiencing significant reading difficulties. To discuss the increase in referrals, the principal set up a meeting with the two fourth-grade teachers and Terri. After discussing different options, the principal decided that the only way to reduce the number of referrals was to strengthen reading instruction in the early grades. As the school's reading expert, Terri was given the job of consulting with the primary teachers. Terri felt somewhat wary about this new role, as she was already overscheduled with trying to support the students on her caseload. On the other hand, she understood that a preventive approach could result in fewer students identified with learning disabilities down the road. She agreed to give it a shot.

Terri's first undertaking was to meet with the first-grade teachers. Both teachers were concerned about the increase in referrals and were happy to talk with Terri about their approach to teaching beginning reading. They said that their first priority in the fall was to ensure that all students had established phonemic awareness skills and were firm in their knowledge of letters and sounds. "We each post alphabet cards around our rooms and make sure children know that when they see a letter, they say its most common sound." The teachers also said they teach a strategy for reading words. "All our children know that when they see a word that they don't know, they should look at the picture, think about what makes sense, and look at the first letter." After hearing about the first-grade teachers' approach to reading instruction, Terri knew that she could offer some targeted advice.

- Why might the first-grade teachers' strategy for reading words be problematic for students at risk of reading difficulties? What advice could Terri give regarding teaching word reading?

The conclusion of the case study can be found later in this chapter.

Content Questions

1. What are two factors that could potentially help to decrease the pervasiveness of reading difficulties in the United States?

2. What was the conclusion of the National Academy of Sciences in the 1998 report of the National Research Council?

3. Name one important conclusion from the research on beginning reading.

4. What are the three big ideas in beginning reading instruction?

5. Why do many children have difficulty developing phonological awareness?

6. What are the alphabetic understanding strategies that should be taught conspicuously?

7. Describe a sequence for scaffolding decoding instruction.

8. Name four task scaffolds in beginning reading instruction.

9. How should phonological awareness, alphabetic understanding, and automaticity with code be integrated strategically?

Reflection and Discussion

1. The chapter states that after third grade, the requirements of reading shift from *learning to read* to *reading to learn*. What do the authors mean by this statement? What are the implications of this statement for designing beginning reading instruction? What are the instructional implications of this statement for older students who have not yet mastered beginning reading skills?

2. How would you respond to this statement? "Teachers don't need to provide explicit instruction in beginning reading skills, most kids pick it up on their own. Even the kids that don't will figure it out sooner or later." In your response, refer to both the research on beginning reading as well as principles of effective instruction.

Application

1. The Florida Center for Reading Research provides reviews of reading programs on their website (http://www.fcrr.org/FCRRReports/reportslist.htm). Read a review of a program that you are familiar with or that seems relevant to your interests. Do you think that this review provides useful information about whether programs are designed around principles of effective instruction? Would these reviews be helpful to educators trying to evaluate and select reading programs?

2. Figure 3–3 shows an example of word-reading instruction that was designed around principles of effective instruction. Evaluate the instruction according to the following questions. What big idea does the instruction focus on? How is the instruction conspicuous? How is the instruction scaffolded? What background knowledge do students need to successfully complete the instruction? How could the instruction be extended to provide judicious review?

Case Study (Conclusion)

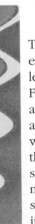

Terri knew from reading the research as well as from personal experience that a strategy such as "look at the picture, think about what makes sense, and look at the first letter" would not be a reliable or effective word-reading strategy for many students. First, she knew that good readers rely primarily on phonics and decoding to read and spell words. Although using context can help students confirm the accuracy of a word they have already read, it is not a reliable strategy for initially identifying the word. Terri knew that a word students think "makes sense" is very often not the word that is correct. Second, she knew that many of the students with learning disabilities she worked with in the upper grades relied almost entirely on context to read words, mostly because they lacked an effective phonics or decoding strategy. Terri wished she had a dime for every time she worked with a student whose approach to reading words was to look at the first letter and guess.

Terri introduced the first-grade teachers to a more effective strategy for reading words. She shared with them the approach for introducing a decoding strategy from the systematic intervention program that she used with her students with individualized education programs (IEPs). (This strategy was similar to the example in Figure 3–3.) She also talked with them about how to present or "teach" the strategy in a way that would support successful learning for all students. The first-grade teachers appreciated Terri's clear and conspicuous procedures for explaining and modeling the strategy as well as the carefully selected and scaffolded examples she provided for initial student practice. Both first-grade teachers agreed to try teaching this new strategy and Terri agreed to meet with the teachers again the following week.

Although Terri was pleased with how open the first-grade teachers were to working with her and modifying their practices, she wondered if she had taken on more than she could handle. She felt confident that she could offer advice and help design or modify individual lessons, but certainly the first-grade teachers needed something more systematic and comprehensive. And she hadn't even met yet with the kindergarten, second-or third-grade teachers. Nevertheless, she was committed to improving the overall reading instruction at East School and would do everything she could to make that happen.

1. Do you believe it is appropriate for special educators like Terri to support general education teachers, even if those teachers have no students with identified disabilities? What are some pros and cons of a special educator taking on a role like Terri's?
2. Terri is hoping that improved reading instruction in the primary grades will lessen the number of students who are later identified with learning disabilities. Do you think early intervention can "prevent" learning disabilities?
3. The first-grade teachers in Terri's school were open to changing their instructional practice. How might you engage teachers who are resistant to adopting research-validated practices that support diverse learners?

The reflection and application section of this chapter was written by Maureen F. Ruby, Richard P. Zipoli, Jr., and Michael D. Coyne, all of the University of Connecticut.

REFERENCES

ADAMS, M. J. (1990). *Beginning to read: Thinking and learning about print.* Cambridge, MA: MIT Press.

ADAMS, M. J., FOORMAN, B. R., LUNDBERG, I., & BEELER, T. D. (1998). The elusive phoneme: Why phonemic awareness is so important and how to help children develop it. *American Educator, 22* (1–2), 18–29.

AL OTAIBA, S., & FUCHS, D. (2002). Characteristics of children who are unresponsive to early literacy intervention. *Remedial and Special Education, 23* (5), 300–316.

AMERICAN FEDERATION OF TEACHERS (1999). *Building on the best, learning from what works: Seven promising reading and English language arts programs.* Washington, DC.

BALL, E. W., & BLACHMAN, B. A. (1991). Does phoneme awareness training in kindergarten make a difference in early word recognition and developmental spelling? *Reading Research Quarterly, 24,* 49–66.

BECK, I. L. (1981). Reading problems and instructional practices. In G. E. MacKinnon & T. G. Waller (Eds.), *Reading research: Advances in theory and practice* (Vol. 2, pp. 53–95). New York: Academic Press.

BYRNE, B., & FIELDING-BARNSLEY, R. (1995). Evaluation of a program to teach phonemic awareness to young children: A 2- and 3-year follow-up and a new preschool trial. *Journal of Educational Psychology, 87,* 488–503.

CALIFORNIA DEPARTMENT OF EDUCATION. (1999). *Reading/language arts framework for California Public Schools: Kindergarten through grade twelve.* Sacramento, CA: California Department of Education.

CARNINE, D. W., SILBERT, J., KAME'ENUI, E. J., & TARVER, S. (2003). *Direct instruction reading.* (4th ed.). Upper Saddle River, NJ: Prentice Hall.

CHARD, D. J., SIMMONS, D. C., & KAME'ENUI, E. J. (1998). Word recognition: Research bases. In D. C. Simmons & E. J. Kame'enui (Eds.), *What reading research tells us about children with diverse learning needs.* Mahwah, NJ: Erlbaum.

COYNE, M. D., KAME'ENUI, E. J., & SIMMONS, D. C. (2001). Prevention and intervention in beginning reading: Two complex systems. *Learning Disabilities Research & Practice, 16,* 62–72.

COYNE, M. D., KAME'ENUI, E. J., & SIMMONS, D. C. (2004). Improving beginning reading instruction and intervention for students with learning disabilities: Reconciling "all" with "each". *Journal of Learning Disabilities, 37,* 231–239.

CUNNINGHAM, A. E., & STANOVICH, K. E. (1998). What reading does for the mind. *American Educator, 22*(1–2), 8–15.

DEMPSTER, F. N. (1991). Synthesis of research on reviews and tests. *Educational Leadership, 48,* 71–76.

EDITOR. (1998). Every child reading: An action plan of the Learning First Alliance. *American Educator, Spring/Summer,* 52–63.

EHRI, L. C. (1997). Learning to read and learning to spell are one and the same, almost. In C. A. Perfetti, L. Rieben, & M. Fayol (Eds.), *Learning to spell: Research, theory, and practice across languages.* Mahwah, NJ: Erlbaum.

EHRI, L. C., & MCCORMICK, S. (1998). Phases of word learning: Implications for instruction with delayed and disabled readers. *Reading and Writing Quarterly, 14,* 135–163.

FELTON, R. H. (1993). Effects of instruction on the decoding skills of children with phonological-processing problems. *Journal of Learning Disabilities, 26,* 583–589.

FELTON, R. H., & PEPPER, P. P. (1995). Early identification and intervention of phonological deficits in kindergarten and early elementary children at risk for reading disability. *School Psychology Review, 24,* 405–414.

FOORMAN, B. R., FRANCIS, D. J., FLETCHER, J. M., SCHATSCHNEIDER, C., & MEHTA P. (1998). The role of instruction in learning to read: Preventing reading failure in at-risk children. *Journal of Educational Psychology, 90,* 37–55.

FOORMAN, B. R., FRANCIS, D. J., SHAYWITZ, S. E., SHAYWITZ, B., & FLETCHER, J. M. (1997). The case for early reading intervention. In B. Blachman (Ed.), *Foundations of reading acquisition: Implications for intervention and dyslexia* (pp. 103–115). Hillsdale: NJ: Erlbaum.

FUCHS, L. S., FUCHS, D., HOSP, M. K., & JENKINS, J. R. (2001). Oral reading fluency as an indicator of reading competence: A theoretical, empirical, and historical analysis. *Scientific Studies of Reading, 5,* 239–256.

GOOD, R., III, SIMMONS, D. C., & SMITH, S. (1998). Effective academic interventions in the United States: Evaluating and enhancing the acquisition of early reading skills. *School Psychology Review, 27,* 740–753.

HART, B., & RISLEY, R. T. (1995). *Meaningful differences in the everyday experience of young American children.* Baltimore: Paul H. Brookes.

HATCHER, P., HULME, C., & ELLIS, A. W. (1994). Ameliorating early reading failure by integrating the teaching of reading and phonological skills: The phonological linkage hypothesis. *Child Development, 65,* 41–57.

JUEL, C. (1988). Learning to read and write: A longitudinal study of 54 children from first through fourth grades. *Journal of Educational Psychology, 80,* 437–447.

JUEL, C. (1991). Beginning reading. In R. Barr, M. L. Kamil, P. B. Mosenthal, & P. D. Pearson (Eds.), *Handbook of reading research* (pp. 759–788). New York: Longman.

KAME'ENUI, E. J. (1993). Diverse learners and the tyranny of time: Don't fix blame; fix the leaky roof. *The Reading Teacher, 46,* 376–383.

KAME'ENUI, E. J. (1999). The National Research Council's report on preventing reading difficulties in young children and the process of dubitation. *Journal of Behavioral Education, 9* (1), 5–22.

LABERGE, D., & SAMUELS, S. J. (1974). Toward a theory of automatic information processing in reading. *Cognitive Psychology, 6,* 293–323.

LEARNING FIRST ALLIANCE. (1998). Every child reading: An action plan of the Learning First Alliance. *American Educator, Spring/Summer,* 52–63.

LIBERMAN, A. M. (1999). The reading researcher and the reading teacher need the right theory of speech. *Scientific Studies of Reading, 3*(2), 95–111.

LIBERMAN, I. Y., & LIBERMAN, A. M. (1990). Whole language vs. code emphasis: Underlying assumptions and their implications for reading instruction. *Annals of Dyslexia, 40,* 51–76.

LOGAN, G. D. (1997). Automaticity and reading: Perspectives from the instance theory of automatization. *Reading and Writing Quarterly, 13,* 123–146.

LOVETT, M. W., BORDEN, S. L., LACERENZA, L., BENSON, N. J., & BRACKSTONE, D. (1994). Treating the core deficits of developmental dyslexia: Evidence of transfer of learning after phonologically- and strategy-based reading training programs. *Journal of Educational Psychology, 30,* 805–822.

LUNDBERG, I., FROST, J., & PETERSEN, O. -P. (1988). Effects of an extensive program for stimulating phonological awareness in preschool children. *Reading Research Quarterly, 23* (3), 263–284.

LYON, G. R. & MOATS, L. C. (1997). Critical conceptual and methodological considerations in reading intervention research. *Journal of Learning Disabilities, 30,* 578–588.

MASTROPIERI, M. A., LEINART, A., & SCRUGGS, T. E. (1999). Strategies to increase reading fluency. *Intervention in School and Clinic, 34,* 278–283.

MCCARDLE, P. & CHHABRA, V. (2004). *The voice of evidence in reading research.* Baltimore: Paul H. Brookes.

MCGILL-FRANZEN, A., & ALLINGTON, R. L. (1991). Every child's right: Literacy. *The Reading Teacher, 45,* 86–90.

MCPIKE, E. (1998). The unique power of reading and how to unleash it. *American Educator, 22* (1–2), 4–5.

MOATS, L. C. (1999). *Teaching reading is rocket science: What expert teachers of reading should know and be able to do.* Washington, DC: American Federation of Teachers.

NATIONAL CENTER FOR EDUCATION STATISTICS. (2005). *The nation's report card: Reading 2005.* Washington, DC: U.S. Department of Education.

NATIONAL READING PANEL. (2000). *Teaching children to read: An evidence-based assessment of the scientific research literature on reading and its implications for reading instruction.* Washington, DC: National Institute of Child Health and Human Development/National Institutes of Health.

NATIONAL RESEARCH COUNCIL. (1998). *Preventing reading difficulties in young children.* Washington, DC: National Academy Press.

O'CONNOR, R. E., JENKINS, J. R., & SLOCUM, T. A. (1995). Transfer among phonological tasks in kindergarten: Essential instructional context. *Journal of Educational Psychology, 87,* 202–217.

O'CONNOR, R. E., NOTARI-SYVERSON, A., & VADASY, P. A. (1996). Ladders to literacy: The effects of teacher-led phonological activities for kindergarten children with and without disabilities. *Exceptional Children, 63,* 117–130.

PERFETTI, C. A. (1985). *Reading ability.* New York: Oxford University Press.

PERFETTI, C. A. & ZHANG, S. (1996). What it means to learn to read. In M. F. Graves, P. Van den Broek, & B. M. Taylor (Eds.), *The first R: Every child's right to read* (pp. 37–61). New York: Teachers College Press.

PROJECT OPTIMIZE. (1999). *Project Optimize kindergarten intervention program.* Eugene, OR: University of Oregon, Institute for the Development of Educational Achievement.

RAND READING STUDY GROUP. (2002). *Reading for understanding.* Washington, DC: RAND.

SANTORO, L. L., COYNE, M. D., & SIMMONS, D. C. (in press). The reading–spelling connection: Developing and evaluating a beginning spelling intervention for children at risk of reading disability. *Learning Disabilities Research & Practice.*

SHARE, D. L. & STANOVICH, K. E. (1995). Cognitive processes in early reading development: Accommodating individual differences into a model of acquisition. *Issues in Education, 1,* 97–100.

SHINN, M. R., GOOD, R. H., KNUTSON, N., TILLY, W. D., & COLLINS, V. (1992). Curriculum-based reading fluency: A confirmatory analysis of its relation to reading. *School Psychology Review, 21,* 458–478.

SIMMONS, D. C., & KAME'ENUI, E. J. (1998). *What reading research tells us about children with diverse learning needs: Bases and basics.* Mahwah, NJ: Erlbaum.

SIMMONS, D. C., & KAME'ENUI, E. J. (1999). *Curriculum maps: Mapping instruction to achieve instructional priorities in beginning reading, kindergarten-grade 3:* Unpublished manuscript.

SLAVIN, R. E. (1989). PET and the pendulum: Faddism in education and how to stop it. *Phi Delta Kappan, June,* 752–758.

SLAVIN, R. E. (1994). School and classroom organization in beginning reading. In R. E. Slavin, N. L. Karweit, & B. A. Wasik (Eds.), *Preventing early school failure: Research, policy, and practice* (pp. 122–142). Boston: Allyn & Bacon.

SMITH, S., SIMMONS, D. C., & KAME'ENUI, E. J. (1998). Phonological awareness: Research bases. In D. C. Simmons & E. J. Kame'enui (Eds.), *What reading research tells us about children with diverse learning needs: Bases and basics.* Mahwah, NJ: Erlbaum.

SPECTOR, J. E. (1995). Phonemic awareness training: Application of principles of direct instruction. *Reading and Writing Quarterly, 11,* 37–51.

STANOVICH, K. E. (1986). Matthew effects in reading: Some consequences of individual differences in the acquisition of literacy. *Reading Research Quarterly, 21,* 360–406.

STANOVICH, K. E. (1994). Constructivism in reading education. *The Journal of Special Education, 28,* 259–274.

STANOVICH, K. E. (1999). The sociopsychometrics of learning disabilities. *Journal of Learning Disabilities, 32*(4), 350–361.

STEIN, M. L. (1993). *The beginning reading instruction study.* Washington, DC: Office of Educational Research and Improvement, U.S. Department of Education.

Texas Center for Reading and Language Arts. (1998). *Professional development guide: Reading fluency: Principles for instruction and progress monitoring.* Austin, TX: Author, University of Texas at Austin.

Texas Department of Education. (1997). *English language arts and reading: Texas essential knowledge and skills.* Austin, TX: Texas Education Agency.

Torgesen, J. K. (2000). Individual differences in response to early interventions in reading: The lingering problem of treatment resisters. *Learning Disabilities Research & Practice, 15,* 55–64.

Torgesen, J. K., Alexander, A. W., Wagner, R. K., Rashotte, C. A., Voeller, K. K. S., & Conway, T. (2001). Intensive remedial instruction for children with severe reading disabilities: Immediate and long-term outcomes from two instructional approaches. *Journal of Learning Disabilities, 34,* 33–58, 78.

Torgesen, J. K., Wagner, R. K., & Rashotte, C. A. (1994). Longitudinal studies of phonological processing and reading. *Journal of Learning Disabilities, 27,* 276–286.

Torgesen, J. K., Wagner, R. K., Rashotte, C. A., Rose, E., Lindamood, P., Conway, T., & Garvan, C. (1999). Preventing reading failure in young children with phonological processing disabilities: Group and individual responses to instruction. *Journal of Educational Psychology, 91,* 1–15.

U.S. Department of Education. (2002). *Reading First.* Retrieved November 1, 2005 from http://www.ed.gov/programs/readingfirst/index.html

Vellutino, F. R., Scanlon, D. M., Sipay, E. R., Small, S. G., Pratt, A., & Chen, R. (1996). Cognitive profiles of difficult-to-remediate and readily remediated poor reader: Early intervention as a vehicle for distinguishing between cognitive and experiential deficits as basic causes of specific reading disability. *Journal of Educational Psychology, 88,* 601–638.

Wagner, R. K., Torgesen, J. K., Rashotte, C. A., Hecht, S. A., Barker, T. A., & Burgess, S. R. (1997). Changing relations between phonological processing abilities and word-level reading as children develop from beginning to skilled readers: A 5-year longitudinal study. *Developmental Psychology, 33,* 468–479.

What Works Clearinghouse. (2004). U.S. Department of Education. Retrieved November 1, 2005 from http://www.whatworks.ed.gov/

Wolf, M., & Bowers, P. G. (1999). The double-deficit hypothesis for the developmental dyslexias. *Journal of Educational Psychology, 91* (3), 415–438.

CHAPTER 4

Effective Strategies for Teaching Reading Comprehension

Michael D. Coyne
University of Connecticut

David J. Chard
University of Oregon

Richard P. Zipoli, Jr.
University of Connecticut

Maureen F. Ruby
University of Connecticut

FROM THE CONVERGENCE of more than 30 years of scientific research, we have a solid understanding of essential components in early literacy development and instruction (Adams, 1990; National Research Council, 1998; National Reading Panel, 2000). Whitehurst and Lonigan (1998) have categorized these essential components in literacy development into two domains, inside-out components and outside-in components. Both inside-out and outside-in components are related to later reading development and are important aspects of children's early literacy experiences (Storch & Whitehurst, 2002).

Inside-out components include phonological awareness, alphabetic understanding, and automaticity with the code. These three components, discussed in Chapter 3, relate to students' ability to understand and use our complex alphabetic code to read words and connected text. These code-based components require students to grapple with sounds, letters, and words; in a sense, working from the inside out. Outside-in components relate to comprehending text. These components are associated with students' ability to draw on their understanding of language, word meanings, prior knowledge, and strategies for extracting and constructing meaning. These meaning-based components require students to bring larger concepts and constructs to bear as they read text, in a sense, working from the outside in. The purpose of this chapter is to apply the six-principle framework to the design of effective reading comprehension instruction for students with diverse learning needs.

CURRENT ISSUES IN READING COMPREHENSION

Over the past decade, there has been an increased focus nationally on the development of literacy for all students. This increased focus has spawned several important documents to assist teachers in providing effective reading instruction to prevent reading difficulties (National Research Council, 1998) and to improve overall reading performance (National Reading Panel [NRP], 2000). Each of these documents identified reading comprehension as an essential literacy outcome for students and the ultimate goal of reading instruction. However, these national panels also acknowledged a need for more research on reading comprehension. In comparison to existing research on the code-based components of reading (i.e., phonemic awareness, alphabetic understanding, automaticity with the code), research on reading comprehension, including vocabulary development, is less extensive, rigorous, and current. This conclusion was echoed by the RAND Reading Study Group (2002) which determined that "evidence-based improvements in the teaching practices of reading comprehension are sorely needed" (p. xxiii). As a result, a number of important research initiatives, sponsored by the U.S. Department of Education's Institute of Education Sciences, are currently underway that could significantly add to our understanding of ways to support reading comprehension for all students.

Perfetti, Marron, and Folz (1996) divided the factors that contribute to reading comprehension into two general areas: processes and knowledge. Processes involve decoding, working memory, inference-making, and comprehension monitoring. In contrast, knowledge factors include word meanings and domain knowledge related to the content of what is being read. These factors provide a framework for thinking about current trends in reading comprehension instructional research. Much of the research over the past several years has focused on the teaching of specific comprehension strategies that reflect those used by good readers (Pressley, 2000) and this continues to be an important focus for researchers. However, there is renewed interest in other aspects of reading comprehension. For example, an area of interest in contemporary reading comprehension research relates to the importance of individual word knowledge and decoding and its contribution to text comprehension. Another current issue is how strategic processing interacts with specific domain knowledge in content area reading. We briefly discuss each of these areas in the next sections.

The Role of Decoding in Comprehension Development

Before children learn to read, they are dependent on oral language and pictures to make sense of the world around them (Carlisle & Rice, 2003). Once children begin to grasp the alphabetic principle, they are increasingly able to use their understanding of orthography and phonology to read words, strings of abstract symbols that represent concepts in their world. This shift from the concrete to the abstract is not abrupt. Rather it is a gradual process that occurs as students gradually acquire proficiency with the symbolic system. However, for many students, especially those who experience difficulties learning to read, the development of word recognition skills acts much like a traffic bottleneck on a highway. Regardless of students' level of listening comprehension, they have to learn the process of word recognition, much like every car on the highway, regardless of its power or speed, must slow down and pass through the bottleneck. Once through this bottleneck, the speed and power of a car again become paramount. Similarly, once children learn how to read words, their proficiency with language comprehension once again becomes an important contributor to their understanding of texts.

Because text comprehension, in part, relies on proficient decoding, the relation between children's listening and reading comprehension grows stronger as they grow older and more fluent. According to Carlisle and Rice (2003), reading and listening comprehension grow more similar by about fifth grade compared to earlier grades for both good and poor readers. Good word readers are able to read a lot. The consequences of reading well include maximal exposure to new words and phrases, opportunities to read different types of texts, and practice monitoring one's understanding (Stanovich, 1986; Cunningham & Stanovich 1998). In contrast, however, poor word readers remain at the mercy of their word reading difficulties. As a result of not reading, they fail to learn many new words, do not develop proficiency in understanding texts, and often learn to dislike reading (Baker & Wigfield, 1999).

Strategy Instruction versus Content Knowledge

In the 1980s, research on comprehension focused on how proficient readers understand what they read. The combined results of these studies suggest that good readers are strategic, orchestrating multiple strategies before, during, and after reading to help make sense of what they read. More recently, some researchers have questioned whether our almost singular focus on strategy instruction has distracted us from trying to understand instructional approaches that result in enhanced content knowledge or content engagement.

In a recent international study of fourth-grade reading achievement, researchers reported that U.S. fourth graders outperformed many other countries on measures of narrative comprehension, but did relatively poorly on measures of expository text comprehension (Mullis, Martin, Gonzalez, & Kennedy, 2003). While this study did not establish the cause of this poor performance, we might infer that it is a result of insufficient content knowledge. Recent research efforts have turned to examine the relative effects of strategy instruction versus content engagement or the combined effect of strategy instruction and content engagement.

It seems reasonable that effective comprehension instruction involves both strategy instruction (NRP, 2000) and content engagement (Beck, McKeown, Sandora, Kucan, & Worthy, 1996). What we still need to understand is how best to integrate these two key instructional areas. Despite several unanswered questions about comprehension instruction, the knowledge base regarding the development of comprehension is robust. In the next section, we discuss the big ideas in reading comprehension development.

BIG IDEAS IN READING COMPREHENSION

Comprehension, or a reader's interaction with text to construct meaning, is an immensely complex process. There are a number of important components, or big ideas, that contribute to understanding text. Each big idea plays a role in determining whether comprehension is successful. Some big ideas are related to the knowledge, skills, and strategies that readers bring to the task. For example, a reader must understand the meanings of the individual words that appear in the text. They must also have a repertoire of strategies to regulate and use flexibly to help them understand what they read and to monitor their success. There are also big ideas that affect comprehension that are related to the text itself. For example, a text may have a narrative or informational structure. A reader needs to think differently in either case, because each type of text is organized differently, possesses different features, and is of a different level of difficulty. Finally, if a student can't read a text fluently, comprehension suffers or is nonexistent.

In the next sections, we describe four big ideas related to comprehension: fluency, vocabulary knowledge, strategic processing, and text features. Each of these big ideas is critical in comprehending text. Most importantly, each of these big ideas can be addressed instructionally in ways that can increase students' ability to comprehend what they are reading.

Fluency

Reading fluency is the rapid, efficient, and accurate application of word recognition skills that permits a reader to comprehend (Pikulski & Chard, 2005). Fluent reading also includes expressive oral reading and the rapid, efficient, and accurate application of word-recognition skills used during silent reading (Chard, Vaughn, & Tyler, 2002; Dowhower, 1991). Similar to learning to ride a bike, some children's reading is so wobbly and slow that they either forget what they are reading or lose their place, effectively falling off the bike. Children who are not fluent focus so carefully on decoding that they are unable to think about the meaning of what they are reading.

In many ways, fluent reading serves as a bridge between accurate decoding and understanding the text (Pikulski & Chard, 2005; Rasinski & Hoffman, 2003). A significant positive relationship between reading fluency and reading comprehension has been clearly established (Pinnell et al., 1995). In order for reading to be efficient and effective, the reader cannot focus attention on decoding and comprehending simultaneously. Though the nonfluent reader can alternate attention between the two processes, thorough understanding of texts requires uninterrupted attention. When attention is required for decoding words, little is left for constructing and responding to the meaning of a text. Therefore, fluency, or automaticity with the code, is essential for comprehension and high levels of reading achievement.

A second reason that fluency is important is that fluent readers are more likely to spend time reading than their peers who are not fluent. Nonfluent readers can find reading punishing. They may be so unmotivated to read that they don't choose to read and, therefore, do not enjoy the benefits of reading such as increased vocabulary and fluency. This is a vicious cycle that can result in a trajectory of poor achievement that is difficult to reverse (Stanovich, 1986).

Vocabulary Knowledge

For the purposes of this chapter, we will refer to vocabulary knowledge as knowing the meanings of individual words, for example knowing that the word *enormous* means "very big." Note that this conceptualization of vocabulary knowledge, sometimes referred to as meaning vocabulary, applies equally across both reading and listening tasks. In other words, if a student knows the meaning of the word *enormous*, she will understand what an *enormous crocodile* means regardless of whether she reads the words "enormous crocodile" or hears them.

Teachers and researchers have long recognized the important and prominent role that understanding words, or vocabulary knowledge, plays in comprehension (Becker, 1977; National Research Council, 1998; RAND Reading Study Group, 2002; Storch & Whitehurst, 2002). Understanding the relationship between vocabulary knowledge and comprehension is relatively straightforward. If students don't know the meanings of individual words, it interferes with their ability to understand the overall meaning of a sentence or paragraph (Stahl, 1991). If meanings of many of the words in a passage are unknown or a single unknown word is particularly important to the overall meaning of a sentence, comprehension may not occur at all. For example, consider the sentence "We were completely surprised to see a pluff emerge from the box!" If a reader or listener didn't know the meaning of *pluff*, it would be difficult to make sense of the entire sentence. If, however, a reader knows that *pluff* means "kitten," the sentence becomes comprehensible.

There are a number of dimensions of vocabulary knowledge that have implications for both reading and listening comprehension. First is breadth of knowledge. This refers to the total number of word meanings that students possess. Students have a greater chance of comprehending at a high level if they know the meanings of more of the words they are reading or listening too. Another dimension is depth of knowledge. Individual words can be known at different levels from totally unknown, to partial known, to fully known (Nagy & Scott, 2000; Schwanenflugel, Stahl, & McFalls, 1997). For example, a reader could know that *miserly* has a negative connotation, but know nothing else about the meaning of the word. On the other hand, a reader may not only know that *devour* means "eat," but also understand what it would mean to "devour a book" (Beck, McKeown, & Kucan, 2002). Depth of word knowledge plays an important role in how well students comprehend text. Greater depth of knowledge leads to higher levels of comprehension.

There are important individual differences in vocabulary knowledge among students with diverse learning needs (see also Chapters 2 and 9). For example, children with disabilities, children from low SES backgrounds, and English language learners often have access to fewer learning opportunities and early literacy experiences than their peers, contributing to less developed vocabulary knowledge (Hart & Risley, 1995; Van Kleeck, Stahl, & Bauer, 2003). As a result, even as early as kindergarten "meaningful differences" exist between students' vocabulary knowledge (Hart & Risley, 1995). This vocabulary gap only grows larger in the early grades as children with limited vocabulary knowledge grow much more discrepant over time from their peers who have rich vocabulary knowledge. Biemiller and Slonim (2001) found that much of the vocabulary differences between children occur before grade 3, at which point children with high vocabularies know thousands of more word meanings than children who are experiencing delays in vocabulary development. Compounding this, children who have difficulty learning word-identification skills are also less able to develop their vocabulary knowledge through independent reading (Cunningham & Stanovich, 1998). In sum, deficits in vocabulary knowledge play a large role in the comprehension difficulties of diverse learners. Over time, as the vocabulary gap widens and texts becomes more complex, vocabulary knowledge becomes even more of a critical determinant of successful comprehension (Storch & Whitehurst, 2002).

Strategic Processing

Cognitive Strategies. Comprehension doesn't occur automatically. Readers must intentionally and purposefully work to extract and construct meaning from text by actively applying a variety of cognitive strategies. A convergence of evidence has identified a number of strategies that can be taught that reliably improve comprehension (NRP, 2000). Some of these include summarizing, finding the main idea, generating and answering questions, developing concept maps, and self-monitoring. When readers use appropriate strategies, they are better able to retain, organize, and evaluate the information they read (Pressley 2000; RAND Study Group, 2002). See Table 4–1 for a list of lay comprehension strategies.

TABLE 4–1
Key Comprehension Strategies

Strategy	Definition	Comments
Identifying Important Information	Reading a text and identifying the most important elements. In narrative texts, these are the elements of a story map (setting, characters, problem, key events, and outcome). In expository text these are the main ideas.	This strategy is essential to knowing what the author is saying explicitly. Readers often use several strategies in combination to fully understand a text.
Inferring/Predicting	Judging, concluding, or reasoning from some given information. This can include anticipating what is going to happen or come next. This is the process of predicting.	This strategy helps students read between the lines and determine information that is not directly stated. It also helps students have a purpose for reading.
Monitoring/Clarifying	Knowing whether what you are reading is making sense and having a plan to clear up your understanding if it does not make sense.	This strategy enables students do things such as reread, look at diagrams and illustrations, think about how to figure out an unknown word, etc.
Generating and Answering Questions	Posing questions before reading or during reading, which requires students to integrate information and think as they read. In addition to answering questions of their own, students also profit from answering questions from the teacher and/or other students.	This strategy helps students set a purpose for their reading. When students ask questions of each other, the one asking the question must always know the answer.
Visualizing	Forming mental pictures in your head as you read.	This strategy is somewhat like inferential thinking where the reader forms visuals in his/her mind as reading takes place.
Summarizing	Pulling together the essential elements in a longer piece of text. This is like retelling in your own words.	For narrative text this strategy is focused on story elements, and for expository text it is focused on main ideas.
Synthesizing	Pulling together the key ideas from several sources of information.	This strategy requires the same basic process as summarizing except it is applied across several sources. This strategy is important as students study content areas such as science or social studies.
Evaluating	Making judgments about what has been read.	This includes making judgments about the text, the way characters responded to certain situations, and judging the validity and accuracy of the content. This is the process of critical reading.

An example of a basic strategy that students use to better understand what they are reading involves finding the main idea of a group of informational sentences. Because students can't remember everything they read, they must strategically focus on the most important ideas and concepts in a passage. Although it may seem like we do this automatically, "finding the main idea" is in fact a highly active process. Good comprehenders are continually evaluating what they are reading and selectively identifying what is most important. Therefore, teaching an explicit strategy for "finding the main idea" helps students learn how to actively read text in a way that focuses on what is most important and, therefore, improves comprehension. It is the same with other comprehension strategies. Students that possess a repertoire of cognitive strategies are better prepared with the tools to engage in the type of active reading that results in higher levels of comprehension. Instruction plays a critical role in providing students with effective strategies at the initial stages of learning that mirror the kind of processing that expert readers engage in to understand what they read (Gersten, Fuchs, Williams, & Baker, 2001; NRP, 2000).

Metacognition.   Possessing a set of cognitive strategies does not ensure comprehension. Students also need to know how, when, and where to apply these strategies. Again, because constructing meaning from text is not automatic, readers need to make ongoing decisions about which strategies are most likely to be successful in different situations. Moreover, students must be able to apply strategies flexibly, sometimes in combination, and evaluate whether they are successful. Monitoring one's strategy use requires metacognition, which is the ability to manage and control cognitive activities in a reflective manner or to "think about one's thinking" (Gersten et al., 2001). Readers who possess metacognitive ability are able to ask themselves questions such as: How do I know when I'm not understanding what I'm reading? When should I use different comprehension strategies? Did my strategy work? If not, what do I try next?

There is evidence to suggest that some of the most important differences between good and poor comprehenders are related to strategic processing and metacognition (Baker, Simmons, & Kame'enui, 1998). Students with diverse learning needs who are experiencing difficulties with comprehension seem to have particular difficulty regulating and monitoring their strategy use, as well as evaluating the success of their strategies. Even when students possess an effective strategy, they might not realize when they should apply it, or whether or not it was successful.

Metacognition influences comprehension before, during, and after reading. For example, consider the following two readers, Ben and Yuan. Before reading, Ben thinks about the task, sets a purpose for reading, and activates prior knowledge. During reading, he actively applies a variety of strategies, knows when comprehension is occurring, and more importantly, knows when he is becoming confused. When comprehension breaks down, he goes back, rereads, and adjusts his strategy use. After reading, he reflects on what was read and evaluates whether he was successful in meeting his goals for reading. In contrast, Yuan begins reading without setting a purpose and without considering the task ahead. During reading, she does not regulate her strategy use, does not realize when comprehension isn't occurring, and doesn't know what to do when she doesn't understand. After reading, she moves on to the next task without reflecting on what she just read. It is clear that Ben is able to approach the entire comprehension process in a reflective and thoughtful manner, an approach that greatly increases the likelihood of his strategy use resulting in successful comprehension. On the other hand, because Yuan is unable to approach the reading task strategically and reflectively, her comprehension is likely to suffer.

Text Features

Comprehension requires more than the extraction of meaning from an author's message, it is generally understood that a reader must read and interpret text. This interpretation depends on many factors of the text being read, including the density of new concepts introduced, the sophistication of syntax, sentence length, and number of pronouns. Many of these text features facilitate or detract from a student's understanding depending on how the author uses them and on the ability and experience of the reader. One way to help students understand what they read is to help them see the underlying structure of the text they are reading. This is referred to as *text structure*.

Text structures are abstract text features that serve as a frame or pattern to help readers identify important information and connections between ideas (Dickson, Simmons, & Kame'enui, 1998; Englert & Thomas, 1987; Goldman & Rakestraw, 2000; Pearson & Fielding, 1991). Strong evidence links readers' awareness of text structure to successful reading comprehension.

There are many different types of text structures. The most common structure introduced in the elementary grades is narrative, sometimes referred to as story structure. Narrative structure is used to relate stories, fiction or nonfiction. In contrast, there are many different text structures used to convey information. Many scientific texts present ideas hierarchically by first describing a key concept followed by categorizing subordinate concepts. For example, a biology text might describe the class of animals referred to as insects and then identify several subclasses or genera such as lepidoptera and hemiptera. Another type of informational text structure is persuasive text. Persuasive text is often used in editorials or essays in which the author is trying to influence the readers' opinions on a particular issue. Letters to the editor in local newspapers arguing for naming a new school in honor of a specific influential public figure is an example of persuasive texts.

In general, teaching children to be aware of text structure enhances their abilities to retell stories and comprehend text (Baker, Gersten, & Grossen, 2002; Weaver & Dickinson, 1982; Williams, 2005). One reason that students' understanding of text structure may support reading comprehension is that these structures are common across texts. Consequently, being aware of these "samenesses" across texts allows children to consider authors' messages in a broader context of literature and the world (Carnine & Kinder, 1985).

Narrative is the earliest text structure that children acquire but there is a great deal of variability among students in terms of what they know about narrative structures when they enter school (Adams, 1990). Whereas many early picture books are episodic and focused on several experiences that a character has, narratives normally involve (a) animate beings as characters with goals and motives; (b) a time and setting usually presented at the beginning of the story; (c) a problem or goal faced by the main character; (d) plots or a series of episodes that eventually resolve the problem; (e) the impacts upon the reader's emotions and arousal levels; and (f) points, morals, or themes. The predictability of narrative texts makes the primary grades an ideal time to help children develop a conventional understanding of narrative elements prior to and along with independent reading.

Traditionally, young children received less exposure in reading informational texts (Caswell & Duke, 1998; Duke, 1999). However, as reading development progresses, children are eventually expected to read expository or information books. Reading informational text requires a different set of skills and is generally not taught until fourth grade, if at all. Informational texts follow text organizational patterns (e.g., compare and contrast, cause and effect) or a combination of patterns that are more difficult to understand than narrative texts for nearly all students (Williams, 2000). Reading informational texts often involves reading to locate particular information (Dreher, 1993, Guthrie & Kirsch, 1987). A number of recent studies suggest that even young children, including students with diverse learning needs, can benefit from exposure to informational text (Smolkin & Donovan, 2003; Duke & Kays, 1998).

CONSPICUOUS STRATEGIES

To successfully comprehend text, readers must possess sufficient vocabulary knowledge, be able to read fluently, be familiar with the features of text, apply comprehension strategies flexibly, and monitor and regulate their use. However, many students with diverse learning needs will not gain access to these big ideas in reading comprehension without explicit instruction. For example, a consistent finding in the learning disabilities research literature is that most students experiencing difficulties with reading comprehension fail to "discover" strategies that are presented in an implicit fashion (Gersten et al., 2001). This is because the skills and strategies that experts rely upon to understand texts are effectively hidden from students experiencing learning difficulties. The role of instruction, therefore, is to let these students "in on the secret" of reading success by making essential reading comprehension strategies conspicuous.

Recently, the RAND Study Group (2002) concluded that converging evidence suggests that "the explicitness with which teachers teach comprehension strategies makes a difference in learner outcomes, especially for low-achieving students" (p. 33). Conspicuous comprehension instruction is direct and explicit. Concepts, skills, and strategies are broken down and taught systematically in a series of carefully sequenced steps. Teachers use language that is clear and consistent to reduce confusion and prevent misunderstanding. The goal of conspicuous instruction is to present and communicate new information in a manner that is easy to understand and unambiguous. In this way, learners struggle less with acquiring comprehension strategies and instead can focus their energies on applying them in more authentic reading and learning situations.

A primary characteristic of conspicuous instruction is extensive teacher modeling. At every stage in the learning process, teachers explain and demonstrate strategies multiple times before asking students to apply them independently. Models of proficient performance provide students with visible and overt illustrations of how comprehension strategies are used successfully. Moreover, teachers can draw attention to the step-by-step process applying strategies by verbalizing their actions. These types of "think-aloud" procedures make the cognitive processes used by proficient readers that are typically internalized and invisible more conspicuous and obvious to students at the beginning stages of strategy acquisition.

An example of instruction that reflects the principle of conspicuous strategies is presented in Figure 4–1. This lesson, adapted from Honig, Diamond, and Gutlohn (2000), was designed to introduce the big idea of finding the main idea to elementary school students. Finding the main idea in informational text is a big idea in reading comprehension because it is a cognitive strategy that can help students actively and strategically focus on what is most important as they read.

The activity includes instruction that is conspicuous. The instruction presents the strategy explicitly and directly through a series of steps using language that is clear and unambiguous (i.e., "There are two steps in thinking of a main-idea sentence. First, we name the person in the paragraph. Second, we will tell the main thing that the person did in all the sentences.") It also includes opportunities for teachers to model or demonstrate the application of the strategy multiple times before asking students to find the main idea independently. Additionally, the instruction also includes a "think-aloud" component in which the teacher verbalizes his thinking as he works his way through the steps of the strategy.

Effective comprehension instruction provides explicit modeling of comprehension strategies. However, because expert readers use strategies in a way that is flexible and personalized, instruction must also explicitly teach students why, when, and how to apply comprehension strategies. Students with diverse learning needs often have difficulty developing metacognition, or the ability to regulate and monitor their strategy use. Therefore, a critical component of conspicuous comprehension instruction includes explaining, modeling, and demonstrating how strategies can be generalized and applied successfully across a range of reading materials for a variety of tasks.

MEDIATED SCAFFOLDING

Instructional scaffolding is the support provided to learners by teachers, peers, and materials during beginning comprehension instruction. In a building project, scaffolds provide considerable external support at the outset of construction, and then are removed in stages as internal structures become stronger and better able to function

Tell students that it is impossible to remember everything that they read—especially when they are reading expository text. Explain that learning how to identify the most important, or main, idea of a passage will make it easier for them to remember what they read. Point out that a main idea can be summed up in one sentence.

Say: *"We are going to figure out the main idea of a group of sentences. There are two steps in thinking of a main-idea sentence. First, we name the person in the paragraph. Second, we will tell the main thing that the person did in all the sentences."*

Albert Einstein enjoyed sailing. He liked to play the violin. He had fun putting together jigsaw puzzles. He liked riding his bicycle everywhere.

Say: *"I'll come up with a sentence that tells the main idea. First, I have to name the person the sentences are about. That's easy. The sentences are about Albert Einstein. Then, I have to figure out how all the things that Albert Einstein did are related to each other. Hmmm, I think he enjoyed all of them. That's it, that's the main idea: Albert Einstein enjoyed doing many different things."*

(The teacher then models applying the strategy and thinking aloud to two other passages.)

When Benjamin Banneker was twenty-one, he took apart a pocket watch to see how it worked. He built a clock entirely out of wood, carving all the gears by hand. He also built the first American-made striking clock.

Teacher: *"Now you are going to practice telling the main idea.* (Reads the paragraph aloud as students follow along.) *What is the first step?"*

Student: *"First, I name the person in the sentences."*

Teacher: *"Yes, that's right. Who is the person?"*

Student: *"The person is Benjamin Banneker."*

Teacher: *"Great job naming the person. Now, what is the second step?"*

Student: *"The next step is to tell what the person did in the first sentence."*

Teacher: *"The next step is to tell what the person did in* <u>all</u> *the sentences. What is the second step?"*

Student: *"Oh yeah, the next step is to tell what the person did in all the sentences. Let's see, all the sentences seem to be about clocks or making clocks. I think the main idea sentence would be Benjamin Banneker built clocks."*

Teacher: *"Very good! Excellent job telling the main idea!"*

(The teacher then gives students opportunities to practice in other different passages.)

FIGURE 4–1
Curriculum Example: Identifying the Main Idea

independently. The same process applies to instruction. Many students require substantial supports during the initial stages of learning comprehension strategies. As they progress in their understanding and internalize their learning, supports are gradually withdrawn so that students can begin to apply strategies independently and in a personalized fashion. For students with diverse learning needs, instruction that is carefully scaffolded is essential to successful learning.

Researchers have identified the control of task difficulty as a critical component of instructional scaffolding (Swanson & Hoskyn, 1998; Vaughn, Gersten, & Chard, 2000). One way in which task difficulty can be scaffolded in comprehension instruction is by carefully selecting and sequencing reading passages for initial strategy instruction. For example, the instruction in Figure 4–1 includes examples in which it is very easy to find the main idea using the newly taught strategy. Both the Albert Einstein and Benjamin Banneker paragraphs include one character and a series of simple sentences that have a clear relationship to each other. These scaffolded examples increase the likelihood that students will be successful when learning to apply the main idea strategy. Over time, as students gain expertise with the strategy in carefully controlled paragraphs, example selection should expand to illustrate the complete range of applications for which the strategy is relevant. In this way students are gradually exposed to all example types they will encounter during independent reading.

The instructional example in Figure 4–1 is also scaffolded so that student practice is carefully supported. Once the teacher models applying the main idea strategy, he gives a student an opportunity to practice using the strategy. However, instead of simply asking the student to read a paragraph and find the main idea, he asks a series of questions that prompts the student to articulate each step of the process. In this way, the teacher is able to provide immediate corrective feedback. For example, when the student misstates the second part of the strategy ("The next step is to tell what the person did in the first sentence"), the teacher is able to immediately correct the error by modeling the correct response and giving the student another opportunity to tell the strategy ("The next step is to tell what the person did in *all* the sentences. What is the second step?"). When errors are corrected when they are first made during initial strategy learning, they are less likely to become internalized and repeated as misrules. This type of ongoing, guided practice provides learners the support and feedback needed to become fluent with comprehension strategies. Again, over time, this high level of teacher prompting and feedback should be progressively and systematically faded so that students are able to use strategies independently and successfully.

Material scaffolds also support comprehension instruction. For example, graphic organizers can help students learn text structures by making the underlying organization of stories and informational text explicit and overt. The graphic organizer presented in Figure 4–2 shows a "story map" for a narrative text. Teachers can use this type of material scaffold to help teach story structure conspicuously and then students can use the story map to identify elements of story structure in texts they are reading. Material scaffolds can also be modified over time to reflect students' increasing level

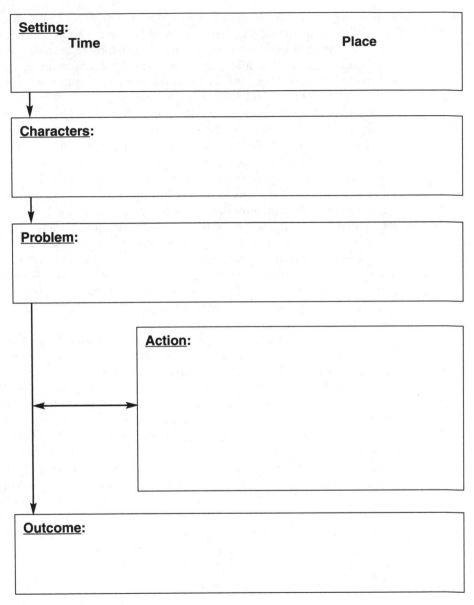

FIGURE 4–2
Story Map

of expertise and sophistication with text features. For example, a story map for
kindergarten students might only include boxes for "beginning," "middle," and "end."
In contrast, a story map for students in the upper grades might include more complex
ideas, concepts, and information, such as theme and increasingly in-depth information
about character attributes, motivation, and feelings.

STRATEGIC INTEGRATION

Strategic integration is the careful and systematic planning of instruction in ways that help students to combine important information, strategies, and skills. This instructional principle allows learners to develop new or more complex knowledge, deeper understanding, and higher-level thinking skills. Strategic integration also promotes more versatile application of learning strategies and skills. There are several ways in which strategic integration might support reading comprehension among students with diverse learning needs.

Successful readers use multiple cognitive strategies in a flexible and personalized manner to comprehend text. These readers also utilize metacognitive processes to regulate their use of strategies, monitor for comprehension breakdown, and apply alternate strategies to improve their understanding. Therefore, an important way to promote strategic integration and allow students to more effectively transfer strategy use to novel situations is to teach students to apply multiple comprehension strategies flexibly and in combination. A recent review of reading comprehension instruction for students with learning disabilities indicated that these students benefited from instruction that supported the simultaneous application of comprehension strategies (Gersten et al., 2001). Importantly, the simultaneous use of multiple comprehension strategies appeared to enhance transfer of skills to other texts.

Students with diverse learning needs might benefit from an initial emphasis on teaching specific comprehension strategies one at a time. As students gain mastery with individual strategies, instruction and practice can systematically focus on the application of multiple strategies. An example of a procedure that involves the integration of multiple strategies to increase students' understanding of expository text is reciprocal teaching (Palincsar & Brown, 1984; Honig, Diamond, & Gutlohn, 2000). In reciprocal teaching, students are initially provided with explanations and models of four successive strategies: predict, question, summarize, and clarify. Students gradually take on the "teacher" role, with increasing responsibility for combining and applying these strategies as their proficiency increases.

Figure 4–3 illustrates how a student might lead classmates and the teacher through the combined use of these four strategies to facilitate their understanding of information from a social studies text on world history. This lesson might occur later in the process of reciprocal teaching when students have already received explicit instruction, modeling, and practice in using each strategy individually. The lesson marks a transition toward growing autonomy and an attempt to integrate strategies in order to enhance comprehension.

Another strategy for promoting strategic integration is to systematically instruct students on varied expository text structures and to provide opportunities to practice with combined organizational patterns. Expository text is generally more difficult to comprehend than narrative text. Moreover, reading instruction in the primary grades tends to emphasize the understanding of narrative text structures, and systematic training on the features of expository text is sometimes neglected until the fourth grade and beyond. Adding to the challenge of reading comprehension, expository texts utilize varied organizational patterns to convey information, including compare/contrast,

Tell students that this lesson will start with a review of strategies that help us to understand and remember what we read.

Teacher: *"When we predict, we use what we know to tell what we think will happen. When we read about the decline of the League of Nations, we might have predicted that this would contribute to conflict in the world."*

Teacher: *"When we clarify, we try to explain something that seems unclear to us. We might have clarified which nations were fighting in World War I by inspecting a map in our book."*

Teacher: *"When we question, we ask for information. When we read about the United States entry into World War II, we might have asked, 'What factors led the country into war?'"*

Teacher: *"When we summarize, we tell important ideas using our own words. We might summarize our readings on the League of Nations by saying that it was an association of nations that attempted to protect the independence and sovereignty of its members."*

Have students silently read the first three paragraphs from a section of the text on Mohandas Gandhi's role in the independence movement in India. Then ask a student to assist in reciprocal teaching.

Teacher: *"Who would like to have a turn being the teacher?"*

Ask the "student teacher" to model the use of all four strategies in an attempt to help the other students and the teacher to better understand this material. Scaffold instruction by providing an outline with brief descriptions of each strategy during initial student teaching. Offer verbal support as needed.

Student teacher: *"The first strategy is to predict. When you predict, you say what you think will happen."*

Teacher: *"Good start. What do you use to make a prediction?"*

Student teacher: *"Things that I already know."*

Teacher: *"Good."*

Student teacher: *"Gandhi was smart and very determined. I predict that he was able to help people in India to gain their independence."*

Teacher: *"Nice example of how to predict. What's another strategy that we can use?"*

Student teacher: *"You can clarify, or find out more about something that is unclear. If you were not sure where India was located, you could use the map on that page in the book to find it."*

Teacher: *"Great job telling us how to clarify."*

Student teacher: *"Next, you can ask a question in order to get information. You might want to know if Gandhi ever became the head of the government or the leader of his country."*

Teacher: *"That would be an interesting question."*

Student teacher: *"There is another strategy. You should summarize, or tell about important information."*

Teacher: *"Good. Give an example of a summary."*

Student teacher: *"Gandhi wanted India to be independent. He used nonviolent ways to bring about changes."*

Teacher: *"Excellent summary. The strategies that you taught would really help us to understand this material!"*

FIGURE 4–3
Curriculum Example: Reciprocal Teaching

cause–effect, description, problem/solution, and time order structures (Honig et al., 2000). These different patterns are sometimes combined within the same text.

All students should receive systematic and explicit instruction in the features of expository text. Different organizational patterns should initially be taught separately in order to develop skill with particular patterns. After students have demonstrated proficiency understanding these organizational patterns, they might be provided with instruction and opportunities for guided practice using passages that combine patterns (e.g., description and compare/contrast). This allows students to better integrate their knowledge of differing organizational patterns and develop skill comprehending increasingly complex expository text structures.

A third method of developing strategic integration is to apply research validated reading comprehension strategies across multiple content domains. In a review of research evidence on reading comprehension instruction, the RAND Reading Study Group (2002) concluded that "teachers who provide comprehension strategy instruction that is deeply connected within the context of subject matter learning, such as history and science, foster comprehension development" (p. 39). This finding suggests that the cognitive strategies presented earlier in this chapter (e.g., predicting, monitoring, and summarizing) should be explicitly and systematically taught using reading materials from varied content domains. Thus it will be important for specialists (e.g., teachers in social studies, science, languagearts, and special education) working with a given student to communicate with one another, particularly at the middle school and secondary levels, to ensure that specific comprehension strategies are applied consistently and flexibly across content areas.

PRIMED BACKGROUND KNOWLEDGE

Background knowledge, or prior knowledge, is the body of information that students "bring to the table" before engaging in instruction and use to make meaningful connections to new concepts, information, or strategies. Background knowledge is derived from a cumulative set of experiences related to particular topics and is heterogeneous across any given sample of students. It is via these prior experiences that students assimilate and consolidate new knowledge. Linguistic and experiential knowledge form the foundational network upon which new knowledge is added, evaluated, and refined. Because of the importance of background knowledge in reading comprehension and the diversity of the student population in today's classrooms, teachers must be cautious not to make assumptions about students' previous experiences with language, concepts, ideas, and vocabulary.

Benson and Cummins (2000) describe background knowledge as what is already in a student's "backpack." It includes the vocabulary, ideas, and concepts accumulated from life experiences and prior instruction. For example, consider Ray as described by Cooper, Chard, and Kiger (2006):

Ray was a seventh grader who had lived his entire life on a small Midwestern farm. So when his teacher gave him an article to read on life in Mexico, he could not comprehend it because he had never been out of his county, hadn't read other things about Mexico or seen movies set there, and wasn't even sure if it was another country. In other words he had no background—or prior knowledge—related to the topic. And Ray's struggles weren't just related to Mexico—he often lacked the prior knowledge necessary to comprehend texts on many different topics. If a student has limited or inaccurate prior knowledge or concepts he or she may have problems with comprehension. (p. 35)

Successful, independent readers are active readers who set goals for reading based upon, among other things, their prior knowledge of the subject material and their personal experiences (Duke & Pearson, 2002). One important goal for teachers is to support students in developing the ability to actively set goals for reading based on what they know and what they want to know about a particular topic.

To do this effectively, teachers must assess students' prior knowledge. This entails thoughtful planning by the teacher with a text to determine what type of background information and vocabulary is pertinent to student understanding. Based on this planning, teachers can then prime prior knowledge to meet individual needs. This priming can range from activating background knowledge, to extending background knowledge, to providing information for those students who do not have previous experience with the topic. Comprehension builds understanding by connecting new ideas and concepts to those the reader already knows. Because diverse learners often lack sufficient background knowledge or are less able to activate the knowledge they possess, they may require direct instruction in strategies to develop and effectively use background knowledge before, during, and after reading.

One approach that can support students in priming and using background knowledge in reading comprehension is KWL (Ogle, 1986). This strategy utilizes a three-column graphic organizer with **K** representing "What I **K**now;" **W** representing "What I **W**ant to know;" and **L** representing "What I have **L**earned." Schmidt (1999) later added **Q** to represent "**Q**uestions I have." This strategy is one that has wide utility as it transcends the before, during, and after reading instructional periods, applies to both narrative and expository texts, and supports both listening comprehension and reading comprehension. It provides a framework that students can refer to and utilize across a variety of contexts and over time.

Table 4–2 provides an example of a KWL chart that a group of kindergarten students developed before (and following) their teacher's reading of *One Leaf Fell* by Toby Speed. After showing the students the cover of the book and reading the title to them, the teacher explains that the story follows the journey of a leaf. She tells them that the trip begins one autumn when the leaf falls from a tree. She then asks them a variety of questions to probe, extend, and clarify what the children already know. Following this, she inquires as to what new information they want to know. Responses are charted on the KWL chart.

As the teacher reads the story, her tone signals or prompts the children when she reads text that may give information that answers a "What I want to know" entry. As part of the after-reading discussion, the teacher reads through all the students' questions from the W column. If the information was found in the story, students recall or find the answers and the teacher records the responses in the L column of

TABLE 4–2
KWL Chart

What I Know: K	What I Want To Know: W	What I Learned: L
Leaves fall in autumn. Autumn comes after summer. Autumn comes before winter. Trips are fun. Leaves are crunchy when they fall on the ground. Squirrels make nests with leaves. Wind blows leaves.	Why does the rabbit on the cover look sad? Why did just one leaf fall? Why is the leaf green? Leaves are supposed to change color. Where did the leaf go? Did any animals carry the leaf?	Leaves can float and go a far way; Rivers "carry" leaves. Bugs can ride on leaves like a magic carpet. Birds can use leaves to make nests—they carry them in their beaks. Sparrows fly away after summer. The leaf just blew around and kept being with different animals. The rabbit was hiding.

the KWL chart. If there are questions in the W column that are unanswered, and students are interested in finding out from another source, a Q column can be added and used for further investigation. Older students can use the Q column for research extensions.

The initial teacher-facilitated discussion and the focus on the K framework of the KWL chart not only provides teachers with a peek into students' individual "backpacks," but also provides them with information that is helpful in planning instruction. If a majority of students bring a good deal of information to the table, the teacher can plan to extend and enrich the instruction. If the students are lacking in background knowledge, the teacher will know to provide a sufficient amount of scaffolding and direct instruction on relevant content to serve as a foundation for comprehension. Additionally, the astute use of the K column supports individualized differentiated instruction.

Older students can use the KWL or KWLQ approach in whole-group and small-group settings, or as individual graphic organizers. Teachers can support the transformation of the W column into anticipation questions, which older students can then use to navigate and outline text and further develop their metacognitive and monitoring skills. Over time, after students have had sufficient practice with teacher-mediated use of the KWL chart they are better able to independently evaluate and prime their own background knowledge and set a specific purpose for reading.

Elementary school children in the United States may not get sufficient opportunities to read and learn from interesting expository texts. The result is that their already limited background knowledge is further limited. The power of priming and extending background knowledge is that it stimulates students to read in areas of interests that they are not able to experience firsthand.

JUDICIOUS REVIEW

Judicious review provides students with repeated and sequential opportunities to apply and develop new knowledge and skills. This systematic review helps students to acquire fluency with recently acquired information and strategies, thus enhancing the effectiveness of other teaching strategies, such as conspicuous instruction and mediated scaffolding. In order to support students' attempts to construct meaning from text, judicious review should reflect big ideas in reading comprehension, including fluency, vocabulary knowledge, strategic processing, and text features.

Effective judicious review is adequate, distributed, cumulative, and varied (Carnine, Dixon, & Kame'enui, 1994). Adequate review allows students to perform tasks accurately and efficiently. The importance of adequate review was illustrated, for example, in a study by Gajria and Salvia (1992) utilizing a mastery-learning paradigm. Direct instruction in five rules for summarizing expository text was provided to students in grades 6 through 9 with learning disabilities and poor reading comprehension. These students demonstrated significantly improved performance in comprehending main ideas, concepts, inferences, and cause-and-effect relationships when compared to both students with learning disabilities and average readers who had not received instruction. Students who had received summarization instruction also outperformed learning-disabled peers when answering factual questions. Importantly, rules that had been taught in previous sessions were reviewed prior to the introduction of any new rule, and the five rules were combined only after students had demonstrated mastery of each rule in isolation. Consistent with the principle of adequate review, teaching to mastery helped to assure that students were able to apply the summarization rules accurately.

Distributed review is the frequent presentation of information and opportunities for practice. Explicit instruction and teacher modeling should be presented systematically across multiple lessons, using consistent language to describe the strategies. It is also essential to afford students with repeated opportunities for guided practice. The importance of distributed instruction and practice in reading comprehension is suggested by research indicating that students experiencing learning difficulties may need longer durations of instruction in order to maintain effective use of strategies (Gersten et al., 2001). It might not be sufficient, for example, to provide students with instruction on a comprehension strategy (e.g., generating and answering questions) in only one or two lessons. Moreover, multiple exposures also appear critical to promoting word learning during vocabulary instruction (Stahl & Fairbanks, 1986).

Cumulative review involves the integration of information or strategies into more complex tasks, while varied review allows students to apply knowledge and practice skills through diverse applications. These two aspects of the review process are closely related to the instructional principle of strategic integration. The relationship between strategic integration and review becomes apparent when considering the curriculum example presented in Figure 4–3. This lesson involved a student's first attempt at combining four different strategies (predict, clarify, question, and summarize) during reciprocal teaching. Following this initial attempt, the "student teacher" and her classmates would be likely to benefit from continued practice integrating these four strategies with progressively longer and more complex passages of expository text (cumulative review). These students might also benefit from opportunities to review the reciprocal teaching procedure using texts with different types of expository features or reading materials from different content domains (varied review).

By planning review that is adequate, distributed, cumulative, and varied, teachers may substantially improve the effectiveness of reading comprehension instruction for all students, including those with diverse learning needs.

THE APPLICATION OF INSTRUCTIONAL DESIGN PRINCIPLES

The six design principles discussed in the preceding sections of this chapter can be applied to *develop, select,* or *modify* instructional tools for use in teaching comprehension. Curriculum developers should consider the six principles to guide the design or creation of instructional materials to be used for teaching comprehension skills and strategies. Curriculum coordinators, supervisors, and textbook adoption committees may want to use the principles to evaluate the design of comprehension instruction in programs being considered for adoption or use in their district or schools. In addition, classroom teachers may find the principles useful if they need to modify or strengthen an existing program. Next, we will discuss how to use the principles for each of these purposes.

Developing Instructional Tools

Designing comprehension instruction is considerably different than designing instruction for learning to read words. Unlike word reading skills such as phonological awareness and letter–sound associations, comprehension can't be mastered. Rather, learning to comprehend text requires the development of expertise. Therefore, we don't learn to comprehend in a particular grade. As long as we continue to read widely, our ability to make sense of different types of texts and ideas conveyed through those texts will likely improve. Teaching students to understand what they read requires the teaching of comprehension skills (e.g., sequencing important events in a historical primary source document) *and* comprehension strategies (e.g., making an inference based on several pieces of information). Unlike discrete skills such as the sound associated with the letter *s,* teaching comprehension skills and strategies requires the teacher to think aloud while reading to make comprehension related activities overt to learners. Curriculum designers, developers, and publishers need to attend carefully to each of the six principles described in this chapter to ensure that diverse learners have access to sophisticated comprehension instruction.

Programs should include conspicuous instruction of comprehension skills and strategies. As noted earlier, this explicit instruction can often take the form of "think-alouds" in which the teacher models how good readers think as they strategize. For example, after reading a persuasive essay, the teacher might describe in a think-aloud format how she decides whether the author is correct or incorrect. To scaffold comprehension instruction, we recommend that even after students learn to read independently, comprehension skills and strategies be modeled initially in the context of "read-alouds." In particular, students who struggle with reading fluency benefit from the opportunity to see comprehension skills and strategies modeled without the challenge of having to read the text first. Additionally, in the primary grades, when teachers' primary objective is to help students develop their independent reading and reading fluency, curriculum designers must ensure that time is allotted to model comprehension in the contexts of read-alouds. The explicit modeling should be followed by opportunities to demonstrate and practice the new skills and strategies with corrective feedback.

Systematic and judicious review of comprehension skills and strategies is essential. Developers must ensure that key comprehension activities are revisited from year to year with more sophisticated content. In particular, as students in the intermediate grades are exposed to increasing amounts of content area text that includes multiple types of text structures, instructional materials can support the integrated review of students' comprehension strategies as well as provide opportunities for students to discuss the content of multiple related texts.

Selecting Instructional Tools

The six instructional design principles offer educators and program adoption committees valuable support in making decisions about the suitability of materials to help all students meet comprehension standards. When selecting comprehension programs, educators should examine the program to determine whether comprehension instruction plays a prominent role across the grades. In the primary grades, comprehension strategies should be introduced primarily through read-alouds. In later grades, comprehension should become more prominent with students spending significant periods of time engaged in reading both fiction and nonfiction texts in which comprehension skills and strategies are explicitly taught and practiced.

As with beginning reading skills, the adequacy of the comprehension instruction for a wide range of diverse learners should be considered. For example, educators should examine whether the instruction is scaffolded to support students who need vocabulary and background knowledge, and whether the instruction proceeds from teacher think-alouds to more independent application of skills and strategies.

When examining the program's scope and sequence, teachers should look specifically to see whether some chapters (or units or lessons) are designated as "review" or "integration." Comprehension instruction that includes opportunities to make intertextual connections assists learners to synthesize related ideas in informational texts as well as to compare characters and plot elements in narrative texts.

To evaluate the effectiveness of review activities, identify how comprehension skills and strategies are modeled within a grade and from one grade to the next. Especially for students with diverse learning needs, it is critical that instruction not assume that students be able to automatically generalize a comprehension strategy to more sophisticated texts or different text types without conspicuous instruction, ongoing support, and sufficient review.

Modifying Instructional Tools

The six instructional principles may also serve as a framework for modifying existing lessons, programs, or curricula in order to more effectively teach diverse learners to comprehend text.

Examine instructional tools to make sure that they reflect big ideas in reading comprehension: reading fluency, vocabulary knowledge, strategic processing, and text features. Reading fluency frees up cognitive resources for comprehension and may be developed through guided oral readings and repeated readings. Existing curriculum materials may be used to develop fluency, but repeated readings should be performed with text that can be read with a high degree of accuracy. Vocabulary knowledge also contributes to reading comprehension and students of all ages will benefit from learning the meanings of words that are important for understanding a given passage or topic. Comprehension strategies may be applied with storybooks, basal readers, or textbooks. Code-based instruction, for example, might be complemented with oral activities designed to promote strategic processing, such as questions, predictions, or summarization. Additionally, existing instructional materials might be used to provide explicit instruction in narrative and expository text features.

The think-aloud format may be used with existing texts to make comprehension strategies more conspicuous. This method is particularly well-suited for students with diverse learning needs, who tend to be less active and reflective in their approach to learning and benefit from explicit instruction and modeling. Scaffolding may be applied through careful consideration of task difficulty. Instruction should progress from relatively simple to more complex comprehension tasks, and models, feedback, and prompting should be systematically faded. Additionally, graphic organizers and webs are useful strategies for helping diverse learners to construct meaning from trade books or textbooks that are already available. For example, story maps may be used to enhance understanding of narrative text and graphic organizers may be used to facilitate comprehension of expository text in content areas (e.g., social studies or science).

The instructional principle of strategic integration is readily accomplished with existing materials by teaching comprehension strategies in isolation, and then supporting students in their attempts to apply strategies in combination. Students in middle and secondary school should be instructed in the use of comprehension strategies across varied content areas. Background knowledge may be primed by having students answer or generate questions based on what they already understand. However, educators must be careful to examine existing instructional tools to assure that diverse learners possess the prerequisite knowledge needed for comprehension. When important concepts are not known, these concepts should be explicitly taught to students. Finally, systematic review of comprehension strategies should be provided through repeated instruction, modeling, and practice.

SUMMARY

Comprehension is the ultimate goal of reading. Therefore, a primary purpose of reading instruction should be to help students develop the skills and strategies needed to successfully construct meaning from text. Educators and curriculum developers can optimize the effectiveness of reading comprehension instruction by attending to the six principles of instructional design. Comprehension instruction that is carefully designed and delivered is essential for successful learning, particularly for students with diverse learning needs.

Instruction in reading comprehension should be informed by the following principles.

1. Big ideas in reading comprehension include reading fluency, vocabulary knowledge, strategic processing (cognitive strategies & metacognition), and text features. Instruction should comprehensively address each of these essential big ideas.

2. Expert readers intentionally and purposefully extract and construct meaning from text by actively applying a variety of cognitive strategies. Because many diverse learners do not discover strategies independently, comprehension instruction must make strategies conspicuous through clear, intentional, and explicit teaching and modeling.

3. Instructional scaffolding supports students during initial stages of comprehension instruction. Teachers or curriculum developers can scaffold comprehension instruction by carefully controlling task difficulty, example selection, and corrective feedback. Material scaffolds such as graphic organizers and story webs can also support comprehension by making the underlying organization of stories and informational text explicit and overt. Scaffolding should be systematically faded over time so that students are able to use comprehension strategies independently.

4. Expert readers apply comprehension strategies flexibly and in combination. Therefore effective comprehension instruction systematically integrates the teaching of multiple strategies and gives students opportunities to apply strategies across different subject-area texts.

5. Comprehension occurs when a reader is able integrate new information with their own prior knowledge. Because diverse learners often lack sufficient background

knowledge or are less able to activate the knowledge they possess, instruction should help students develop, prime, and effectively use background knowledge to support comprehension.

6.   Instructional review helps diverse learners to use comprehension strategies more efficiently and consistently. Systematic review and practice with varied texts promotes fluency and flexibility in the application of strategies.

REFLECTION AND APPLICATION

Case Study

Jeff Chavez is a resource room teacher at King Academy, a large public high school in an affluent suburb. King Academy has a strong reputation as an excellent school and the teachers and community take pride in the number of seniors that are accepted by prestigious colleges each year. Despite the school's financial resources and academic successes, however, there are a significant number of students at King Academy who experience academic difficulties. Sometimes Jeff becomes frustrated with the perception that all the students at the school are academically successful. "We are just like any other school; we serve the whole range of students. My students with learning disabilities face the same challenges here that they would face in any other school, maybe even more."

Much of Jeff's time is spent supporting students with learning disabilities in ninth grade, many of whom have a period per day scheduled in the resource room. For most of these students, their time with Jeff in the resource room is the only direct special education services they receive. Like many special educators who work with secondary students, Jeff finds it challenging to address all his students' needs within the limited instructional time available. He struggles trying to balance teaching fundamental skills and strategies with helping his students stay organized and caught up with their class work.

For example, many of his students have difficulty comprehending content area texts. "These kids are overwhelmed in science and social studies. They don't know what to make of the textbooks and don't know how to even approach their reading assignments." However, instead of using his time in the resource room to teach reading comprehension strategies, he usually finds himself helping students complete homework assignments or studying for tests. "When my students come to the resource room panicked about a paper due the next day or a quiz that afternoon, I have to help them. If I don't, who will?"

Over the four years Jeff has been teaching, he's found that more and more of his time with students is taken up reacting to their immediate needs at the expense of directly teaching skills and strategies. "I feel like all I'm doing is giving out Band-Aids without addressing the root of these kids' reading problems." This year, however, Jeff has made a conscious decision to focus on teaching his students specific comprehension strategies. "The only way my kids are going to become independent learners is by developing strategies that they can rely on to read and understand their textbooks."

Jeff decided that he would focus on teaching his students strategies for recognizing the underlying structures in expository text. The ninth-grade social studies teachers require all students to develop outlines for each chapter in their textbooks. Jeff thought that by introducing his students to expository text structures, he could help them develop the expertise to complete these assignments independently. He knew that this would take resource time away from helping his students with other immediate tasks; however, he felt confident that this tradeoff would pay off in the long run by assisting his students to become strategic and independent readers.

Jeff carefully developed a four-week teaching sequence to introduce his students to expository text structures. He provided conspicuous instruction by directly explaining and modeling strategies. He intentionally scaffolded the lessons by writing his own carefully controlled text examples that clearly illustrated the text structures. He made sure that students received plentiful practice with individualized feedback applying the strategies to similarly controlled text examples. At the end of the four weeks, Jeff was very pleased with his students' understanding of text structure and mastery of the strategies. He was very much looking forward to talking with the social studies teachers and hearing about his students' performance on the most recent chapter outline.

When Jeff saw Sally Monroe, one of the social studies teachers, in the staff room the next week, he asked how his students did on the outline. Sally's response took him completely by surprise. "I don't think these kids are ever going to understand this content. This was the worst outline yet. Didn't you get a chance to help them with it in the resource room?" Jeff didn't know what to think. He had dedicated four weeks to teaching his students fundamental comprehension strategies, yet they hadn't used the strategies to improve their social studies outlines. In fact it appeared that by taking resource time away from working on the assignment itself, his students actually did worse.

- Even though Jeff's students were able to successfully use their knowledge of text structures in the resource room, they weren't able to transfer this knowledge to understanding their social studies text. Why might Jeff's students have had difficulty generalizing their comprehension strategies? What instructional principles and teaching strategies might Jeff have considered to help his students better generalize their strategy use to the social studies outline?

The conclusion of the case study can be found later in this chapter.

Content Questions

1. Describe inside-out and outside-in components of literacy development.

2. List four big ideas in reading comprehension.

3. Describe two reasons why oral reading fluency is important to reading comprehension.

4. Name and briefly describe two dimensions of vocabulary knowledge that have implications for reading and listening comprehension.

5. List eight reading comprehension strategies.

6. Describe metacognition and explain why it is important to reading comprehension.

7. Describe why experiences with informational text might benefit young children.

8. List three strategies to promote strategic integration in reading comprehension.

Reflection and Discussion

1. A fourth-grade teacher consults you for suggestions on reading comprehension strategies that might benefit one of his students. During the consultation, you note that the student's reading appears slow and effortful despite accurate decoding. Discuss how the student's lack of reading fluency might be impacting her reading comprehension. What implication would your observation have for instructional planning?

2. How might mediated scaffolding and strategic integration be used to help students more consistently apply reading comprehension strategies for different purposes across a variety of texts?

3. How might judicious review be applied in vocabulary instruction or the teaching of comprehension strategies in a manner that fosters active engagement and student interest? Conversely, how might review become rote and monotonous?

Application

1. Examine a section of expository text from relevant grade level materials. Note the particular organizational patterns (e.g., description, compare and contrast, cause and effect, problem solution, time order) or combinations of patterns that are found in the selection. Next select and examine a section of narrative text from the same grade level and draft a story map. Discuss how knowledge of these expository and narrative text structures can help students to better understand and recall what they read.

2. Choose a specific cognitive strategy for improving reading comprehension. Describe how you would use a "think-aloud" procedure to make the steps of this strategy conspicuous to students. Choose a second comprehension strategy and describe how you would apply mediated scaffolding to enhance learning. Attempt to apply control over task difficulty and material scaffolds in your example.

Case Study (Conclusion)

When Jeff asked his students why they didn't use their strategies for the social studies outline, he received blank looks. One student replied, "I didn't know the strategies would work with our social studies text. I thought it only worked with what we read in the resource room." Reflecting on this comment later, Jeff realized that he had forgotten a fundamental tenet of instruction. "I should know by now that if you don't teach kids how to generalize and strategically integrate strategies, it is unlikely that they'll figure out how to do it on their own." Moreover, although the highly scaffolded text examples that Jeff had used supported his students' initial learning, they had not demonstrated the range of texts for which the strategies would apply.

The next week, Jeff told his students that they would learn how to use their new strategies to better understand their social studies and science books. He provided conspicuous instruction on how to apply the strategies to outlining textbook chapters by modeling and thinking aloud. Instead of developing his own text examples, he used previous chapters from the students' social studies and science textbooks. Next, he gave his students extensive guided practice outlining additional chapters while providing ongoing corrective feedback. Finally, he talked with the students about times in their classes when they could use their strategies to complete assignments and better understand readings. When Jeff saw Sally next, she commented on how well his students had done on the most recent outline. This time, Jeff wasn't surprised.

- Jeff struggles trying to balance teaching fundamental skills and strategies with helping his students stay organized and caught up with class work and required content. Do you think other special and/or general educators face similar issues? How should educators allocate their time to best support students?
- Sally Monroe was unaware that Jeff was teaching his students strategies to better understand their social studies textbook. What are some challenges associated with communication and collaboration between special and general educators? How might Sally have better supported the students in her class with learning disabilities if she had been aware of Jeff's instruction in the resource room?

The Reflection and Application section of this chapter was written by Richard P. Zipoli, Jr., Maureen F. Ruby, and Michael D. Coyne, all of the University of Connecticut.

REFERENCES

ADAMS, M. J. (1990). *Beginning to read: Thinking and learning about print.* Cambridge, MA: MIT Press.

BAKER, L., & WIGFIELD, A. (1999). Dimensions of children's motivations for reading and their relations to reading activity and reading achievement. *Reading Research Quarterly, 34,* 452–477.

BAKER, S., GERSTEN, R., & GROSSEN, B. (2002). Remedial interventions for students with reading comprehension problems. In M. R. Shinn, G. Stoner, & H. M. Walker (Eds.), *Interventions for academic and behavior problems II: Preventive and remedial approaches* (pp. 731–754). Bethesda, MD: National Association of School Psychologists.

BAKER, S. K., SIMMONS, D. C., & KAME'ENUI, E. J. (1998). Vocabulary acquisition: Research bases. In D. C. Simmons & E. J. Kame'enui (Eds.), *What reading research tells us about children with diverse learning needs* (pp. 183–218). Mahwah, NJ: Erlbaum.

BECK, I. L., MCKEOWN, M. G., & KUCAN, L. (2002). *Bringing words to life: Robust vocabulary instruction.* New York: Guilford.

BECK, I. L., MCKEOWN, M. G., SANDORA, C., KUCAN, L., & WORTHY, J. (1996). Questioning the author: A yearlong classroom implementation to engage students with text. *Elementary School Journal, 96* (4), 385–414.

BECKER, W. C. (1977). Teaching reading and language to the disadvantaged: What we have learned from field research. *Harvard Educational Review, 47,* 518–543.

BENSON, V., & CUMMINS, C. (2000). *The power of retelling.* Bothell, WA: Wright Group/McGraw-Hill.

BIEMILLER, A., & SLONIM, N. (2001). Estimating root word vocabulary growth in normative and advantaged populations: Evidence for a common sequence of vocabulary acquisition. *Journal of Educational Psychology, 93,* 498–520.

CARLISLE, J. F., & RICE, M. S. (2003). *Improving reading comprehension: Research-based principles and practices.* New York: York Press.

CARNINE, D. W., DIXON, R., & KAME'ENUI, E. J. (1994). Math curriculum guidelines for diverse learners. *Curriculum/Technology Quarterly, 3*(3), 1–3.

CARNINE, D. W., & KINDER, D. (1985). Teaching low performing students to apply generative and schema strategies to narrative and expository materials. *Remedial and Special Education, 6*(1), 20–30.

CASWELL, L. J., & DUKE, N. K. (1998). Non-narrative as a catalyst for literacy development. *Language Arts, 75,* 108–117.

CHARD, D. J., VAUGHN, S., & TYLER, B. J. (2002). A synthesis of research on effective interventions for building fluency with elementary students with learning disabilities. *Journal of Learning Disabilities, 35,* 386–406.

COOPER, J. D., CHARD, D. J., & KIGER, N. (2006). *The struggling reader: Interventions that work.* New York: Scholastic.

CUNNINGHAM, A. E., & STANOVICH, K. E. (1998). What reading does for the mind. *American Educator, Spring/Summer,* 1–8.

DICKSON, S. V., SIMMONS, D. C., & KAME'ENUI, E. J. (1998). Text organization: Instructional and curricular basics and implications. In D. C. Simmons & E. J. Kame'enui (Eds.), *What reading research tells us about children with diverse learning needs: Bases and basics.* Mahwah, NJ: Erlbaum.

DOWHOWER, S. L. (1991). Effects of repeated reading on second-grade transitional readers' fluency and comprehension. *Reading Research Quarterly, 22,* 389–406.

DREHER, M. J. (1993). Reading to locate information: Societal and educational perspectives. *Contemporary Educational Psychology, 18,* 129–138.

DUKE, N. K. (1999). *The scarcity of informational texts in first grade* (Report No. 1-007). Ann Arbor, MI: University of Michigan, School of Education, Center for the Improvement of Early Reading Achievement. Retrieved August 2003 from www.ciera.org/library/reports/inquiry-1/1-007/Report%201-007.html

DUKE, N. K., & KAYS, J. (1998). 'Can I say 'once upon a time'?': Kindergarten children developing knowledge of information book language. *Early Childhood Research Quarterly, 13,* 295–318.

DUKE, N. K., & PEARSON, D. (2002). Effective practices for developing reading comprehension. In A. E. Farstrup & S. J. Samuels (Eds.), *What research has to say about reading instruction* (pp. 205–242). Newark, DE: IRA.

ENGLERT, C. S., & THOMAS, C. C. (1987). Sensitivity to text structure in reading and writing: A comparison between learning disabled and non-learning disabled students. *Learning Disability Quarterly, 10,* 93–105.

GAJRIA, M., & SALVIA, J. (1992). The effects of summarization instructions on text comprehension of students with learning disabilities. *Exceptional Children, 58*(6), 508–516.

GERSTEN, R., FUCHS, L. S., WILLIAMS, J. P., & BAKER, S. (2001). Teaching reading comprehension strategies to students with learning disabilities: A review of the research. *Review of Educational Research, 71*(2), 279–320.

GOLDMAN, S. R., & RAKESTRAW, J. A. (2000). Structural aspects of constructing meaning from text. In M. L. Kamil, P. B. Mosenthal, P. D. Pearson, & R. Barr (Eds.), *Handbook of reading research* (Vol. II, pp. 311–335). Mahwah, NJ: Erlbaum.

GUTHRIE, J. T., & KIRSCH, I. S. (1987). Distinctions between reading comprehension and locating information in text. *Journal of Educational Psychology, 79*(3), 220–227.

HART, B., & RISLEY, T. R. (1995). *Meaningful differences in the everyday experiences of young American children.* Baltimore: Paul H. Brookes.

HONIG, B., DIAMOND, L., & GUTLOHN, L. (2000). *CORE: Teaching reading sourcebook.* Novato, CA: Arena.

MULLIS, I. V. S., MARTIN, M. O., GONZALEZ, E. J., & KENNEDY, A. M. (2003). *PIRLS 2001 international report: IEA's study of reading literacy achievement in primary schools.* Chestnut Hill, MA: Boston College.

NAGY, W., & SCOTT, J. (2000). Vocabulary processes. In M. Kamil, P. Mosenthal, P. D. Pearson, & R. Barr (Eds.), *Handbook of reading research* (Vol. III, pp. 269–284). Mahwah, NJ: Erlbaum.

NATIONAL READING PANEL. (2000). *Teaching children to read: An evidence-based assessment of the scientific research literature on reading and its implications for reading instruction.* Washington, DC: National Academy Press.

NATIONAL RESEARCH COUNCIL. (1998). *Preventing reading difficulties in young children.* Washington, DC: National Academy Press.

OGLE, D. M. (1986). K–W–L: A teaching model that develops active reading of expository text. *Reading Teacher, 39,* 564–570.

PALINCSAR, A. S., & BROWN, A. L. (1984). Reciprocal teaching of comprehension-fostering and comprehension-monitoring activities. *Cognition and Instruction, 1*(2), 117–175.

PEARSON, P. D., & FIELDING, L. (1991). Comprehension instruction. In R. Barr, M. L. Kamil, P. Mosenthal, & P. D. Pearson (Eds.), *Handbook of reading research* (Vol. 2, pp. 815–860). White Plains, NY: Longman.

PERFETTI, C. A., MARRON, M. A., & FOLZ, P. W. (1996). Sources of comprehension failure: Theoretical perspectives and case studies. In C. Cornoldi & J. Oakhill (Eds.), *Reading comprehension difficulties: Processes and intervention* (pp. 137–166). Mahwah, NJ: Erlbaum.

PIKULSKI, J. J., & CHARD, D. J. (2005). Fluency: Bridge between decoding and reading comprehension. *The Reading Teacher, 58,* 510–519.

PINNELL, G. S., PIKULSKI, J. J., WIXSON, K. K., CAMPBELL, J. R., GOUGH, P. B., & BEATTY, A. S. (1995). *Listening to children read aloud.* Washington, DC: Office of Educational Research and Improvement, U.S. Department of Education.

PRESSLEY, M. (2000). What should comprehension instruction be the instruction of? In M. L. Kamil, P. B. Mosenthal, P. D. Pearson, & R. Barr (Eds.), *Handbook of reading research* (Vol. III, pp. 545–561). Mahwah, NJ: Erlbaum.

RAND READING STUDY GROUP. (2002). *Reading for understanding: Toward an R&D program in reading comprehension*. Santa Monica, CA: RAND Corp.

RASINSKI, T. V., & HOFFMAN, J. V. (2003). Oral reading in the school literacy curriculum. *Reading Research Quarterly, 38,* 510–522.

SCHWANENFLUGEL, P. J., STAHL, S. A., AND MCFALLS E. L. 1997. Partial word knowledge and vocabulary growth during reading comprehension. *Journal of Literacy Research, 29*(4), 531–553.

SCHMIDT, P. R. (1999). KWLQ: Inquiry and literacy learning in science. *The Reading Teacher, 52*(7), 789–792.

SMOLKIN, L. B. & DONOVAN, C. A. (2003). Supporting comprehension acquisition for emerging and struggling readers: The interactive information book read-aloud. *Exceptionality, 11,* 25–38.

STAHL, S. A. (1991). Beyond the instrumentalist hypothesis: Some relationships between word meanings and comprehension. In P. J. Schwanenflugel (Ed.), *The psychology of word meanings*. Hillsdale, NJ: Erlbaum

STAHL, S. A., & FAIRBANKS, M. M. (1986). The effects of vocabulary instruction: A model-based meta-analysis. *Review of Educational Research, 56*(1), 72–110.

STANOVICH, K. E. (1986). Matthew effects in reading: Some consequences of individual differences in the acquisition of literacy. *Reading Research Quarterly, 21,* 360–407.

STORCH, S., & WHITEHURST, G. (2002). Oral language and code-related precursors to reading: Evidence from a longitudinal structural model. *Developmental Psychology, 38,* 934–947.

SWANSON, H., & HOSKYN, M. (1998). Experimental intervention research on students with learning disabilities: A meta-analysis of treatment outcomes. *Review of Educational Research, 68* (3), 277–321.

VAN KLEECK, A., STAHL, S. S., & BAUER, E. B. (2003). *On reading books to children: Parents and teachers*. Mahwah, NJ: Erlbaum.

VAUGHN, S., GERSTEN, R., & CHARD, D. (2000). The underlying message in LD intervention research. *Council for Exceptional Children, 67,* 99–114.

WEAVER, P. W., & DICKINSON, D. K. (1982). Scratching below the surface structure: Exploring the usefulness of story grammars. *Discourse Processes, 5,* 225–243.

WHITEHURST, G. J., & LONIGAN, C. J. (1998). Child development and emergent literacy. *Child Development, 69,* 848–872.

WILLIAMS, J. (2005). Instruction in reading comprehension for primary-grade students: A focus on text structure. *Journal of Special Education, 39,* 6–18.

WILLIAMS, J. (2000). *Strategic processing of text: Improving reading comprehension for students with learning disabilities* (ERIC/OSEP Digest No. E599). Arlington, VA: ERIC Clearinghouse on Disabilities and Gifted Education.

Effective Strategies for Teaching Writing

Robert C. Dixon
JP Associates

Stephen Isaacson
Portland State University

Marcy Stein
University of Washington, Tacoma

WRITING IS A HIGHLY complex process that writers ultimately apply independently (Bereiter & Scardamalia, 1982). Conceivably, writing is one of the most complex human activities (Bereiter, 1980; Hillocks, 1987; Isaacson, 1989; Scardamalia, 1981.) The inherent complexity of writing suggests that acquiring writing proficiency might prove to be difficult for many students—a speculation borne out both by descriptive research and the experience of many teachers.

For example, two decades ago, Applebee, Langer, and Mullis (1986) reported that students in fourth, eighth, and twelfth grades taking the National Assessment of Educational Progress (NAEP) performed poorly on measures of nonfiction writing: approximately half wrote adequate or better narrative and informative pieces, and only about a third wrote adequate or better persuasive pieces. Eleventh-grade students performed equally as poorly on the 1990 NAEP: they did not write much, and what they did write was of poor quality (Applebee [NAEP], 1990).

Results from the 1998 NAEP were similar (Greenwald, Persky, Campbell, & Masseo [NCES], 1999). There are four levels for reporting writing on the NAEP: below basic, basic, proficient, and advanced. More than half of the students tested scored within the "basic" range. One notable conclusion from the 1998 NAEP is that low-income students score lower than those from better economic backgrounds. The NAEP data and other previous research (Applebee, Langer, Jenkins, Mullis, & Foertsch, 1990; Christenson, Thurlow, Ysseldyke, & McVicar, 1989; Flower & Hayes, 1981) suggest that students in general education experience many writing difficulties. Yet, writing is *important* for so many students (Englert et al., 1988). Writing is not just an end in itself, but a means by which students demonstrate their knowledge within various content areas (Christenson et al., 1989; Graham, 1982; Harris & Graham, 1985).

The students who experience the greatest difficulties with writing are those with learning disabilities and emotional and/or behavioral problems (Englert & Raphael, 1988; Graham, 1982; Graham, Harris, MacArthur, & Schwartz, 1991; Morocco & Neuman, 1986; Montague, Maddux, & Dereshiwsky, 1990; Nodine, Barenbaum, & Newcomer, 1985; Thomas, Englert, & Gregg, 1987). Given the increasing diversity of children in classrooms (see section on learner characteristics in Chapter 2), there is a need to identify elements of writing instruction that are likely to be most effective at helping teachers improve the writing of the broadest possible range of students. That is, given the practical limitations of the classroom, which characteristics of a *single* writing curriculum are likely to contribute to improved performance for the majority of students?

In this chapter we describe a few fundamental characteristics of writing instruction that can contribute significantly to a single writing curriculum that is effective with a broad range of students at various performance levels. First, we briefly describe some current issues in writing instruction. Then we turn to the specifics of instructional design.

CURRENT ISSUES IN WRITING INSTRUCTION

Opportunity to Learn

We stress a *single* effective writing curriculum because frequently, little or no real writing instruction takes place in regular classrooms (Applebee et al., 1990; Bridge & Hiebert, 1985; Langer & Applebee, 1986). Therefore, it seems quite impractical to advocate the implementation of two or more writing curricula in diverse classrooms as a means of accommodating the needs of diverse learners.

It goes without saying that the minimal requirement for adequate writing achievement is that effective writing instruction be made available to all students. In general, opportunity to learn has long been considered one of the major factors influencing achievement (in addition to pedagogical practice and aptitude; see Carroll, 1963). Students probably will not become better writers if they do not spend a relatively substantial part of most school days engaged in productive writing activities. Graves (1985) states, for example, that students should write for at least 30 minutes a day, at least four days a week, as opposed to a national average of writing one day in eight.

Author versus Secretary, or Author and Secretary

Allocating just any amount of time to "writing" is *not* likely to result in notable writing improvement. For example, neither "free writing" nor instruction on grammar and writing mechanics have proven, by themselves, to be effective means for improving writing performance (Hillocks, 1984). The elements of meaningful, allocated writing time are the principal subject of this chapter. (See Isaacson, 1994, for a full discussion of academic learning time and writing instruction.)

Smith (1982, cited in Isaacson, 1991) characterizes writing as a complex undertaking in which the writer works both as author and secretary throughout the processes of writing. The writer-as-author is concerned primarily with matters of content, including the origination and organization of ideas, levels of diction, and so on. Simultaneously, the writer-as-secretary is concerned with the mechanics of writing. Sometimes the secretary role is characterized as a concern related almost solely to the revision phase of writing, but for students with learning difficulties, mechanical skills such as handwriting and spelling can present severe obstacles to participation in all authoring processes (Graham, 1990).

The author-as-secretary characterization provides a framework for identifying vastly different orientations toward writing instruction. The first is the skills-dominant approach, in which instruction focuses primarily on the mechanics of writing: secretarial concerns. Based on several descriptive studies, this approach has been the predominant one in American schools for many years (Applebee, 1981; Bridge & Hiebert, 1985; Langer & Applebee, 1986; Leinhardt, Zigmond, & Cooley, 1980). Within this approach, composition activities are minimal, often limited to writing short answers or transcribing.

Even less emphasis seems to be placed on composition in skills-dominant approaches used with lower performing students. Such students receive a great deal of skills instruction (Englert et al., 1988; Graham et al., 1991; Isaacson, 1989; Roit & McKenzie, 1985), and even that instruction is poor, because it occurs in isolation and is unconnected with its presumed eventual use (Graves, 1985).

Interestingly, skills-dominant approaches are polemical ghosts, in that they have little if anything to recommend them. To our knowledge, no one advocates skills-dominant approaches in the literature. If there is a rationale for such approaches at all, we can only speculate as to what it might be. Perhaps someone believes that attention to mechanical skills will somehow result in improved composition.

Perhaps someone believes that lower performing youngsters are incapable of creating coherent text without first acquiring a full complement of mechanical skills. Or perhaps no rationale for skills-dominant approaches exists at all; for example, a teacher who is not comfortable with his or her own composition ability might inadvertently slight composition instruction in the classroom. We know for certain only that skills-dominated approaches are in widespread use, without the benefit of empirical or theoretical support.

A second, nearly opposite approach to writing may have evolved in reaction to skills-based approaches: the composition-dominant approach, concerned primarily with authoring aspects of writing. Advocates of this approach generally argue that instruction on mechanics should be restricted to those concerns students raise themselves in connection with the polishing stage of composition (DuCharme, Earl, & Poplin, 1989; Graves, 1983).

We have some general concerns with composition-dominant approaches. First, there is little research to support the hypothesis that the mechanics of writing will take care of themselves in the context of authentic writing experiences. Many of the gains reported anecdotally for students in composition-dominated programs could possibly be the result of maturation. In addition, some measures of collaborative efforts may mask individual achievement, or lack of it.

Second, there is strong evidence that mechanical difficulties can effectively preempt many students from meaningful participation in far more rewarding authoring roles (Graham, 1999; Graham, 1990; Morocco, Dalton, & Tivnan, 1990). The kinds of general difficulties experienced by many students with learning problems strongly suggest such students are not likely to acquire knowledge of any sort casually (Isaacson, 1991). In our well-justified haste to distance ourselves from skills-based approaches to writing, we should be cautious and thoughtful: mechanics are an integral part of writing.

If we envision writing as an interweaving of complexities involving both author and secretary roles, then perhaps parallel instruction is one means for resolving dominance conflicts. Within a parallel framework, instruction includes all aspects of writing from beginning to end—from conceptualization to "publication"—with a concerted focus on the integration of writing knowledge. (See Isaacson, 1989, for an in-depth discussion of this issue.)

Technology

While there have not been any startling, new pedagogical approaches to effective writing instruction in the last 15 years or so, the further proliferation of technology in recent years has had an impact on writing instruction and learning. For instance, the National Writing Project has been experimenting in recent years with professional development courses on how to teach writing, delivered by means of the Internet. Word processing remains a potentially significant tool for the improvement of writing instruction; its influence is greater than ever because more students than ever have access to it.

In recent years, some computer-based products have been developed to directly teach writing to students, integrating word processing, explicit instruction, and stimulating multimedia presentations that can serve as inspirations for writing.

Finally, assistive technology continues to grant access for many to the opportunity to write—many who would have no such access otherwise. For better or for worse, technology is, and is likely to remain for some time, an issue in writing instruction.

Writing Assessment

More than ever before, many individual states administer writing assessments at various grade levels. In some cases, high stakes are associated with such assessments. However, there are serious questions about the technical soundness of these assessments. One serious question is the extent to which the assessments are *fair* for students with disabilities, which is a dimension of *validity*. Some evidence suggests great inconsistencies in the fairness of state writing tests for students with disabilities (Isaacson, 1999).

PRINCIPLES FOR IMPROVING INSTRUCTIONAL STRATEGIES IN WRITING

The implication of time allocated to writing instruction (or the lack of time allocated to writing instruction) is clear and, it seems, unanimously advocated: more time needs to be allocated. Any controversy that exists relates to different approaches to such allocation of time.

In this chapter we apply the six design principles highlighted in Chapter 1 to both the author role and the secretary role of writers. Although we separate the roles for the sake of illustration, we wish to reemphasize that the roles co-exist and intertwine in authentic writing. Although the principles and applications we describe are research-based, we caution readers that much of the substantial research conducted on writing in recent years is descriptive, anecdotal, quasi-experimental, or otherwise questionable as the basis for making broad generalizations about effective writing instruction (Graham et al., 1991). Still, data from a few very good studies, coupled with knowledge of diverse learners and instructional design research, provide the basis for cautiously identifying some important aspects of effective writing instruction for students at diverse levels of writing proficiency.

Designing Instruction Around Big Ideas

Big Ideas and the Author Role in Writing. In general, big ideas for writing instruction are those that seem to recur across successful writing programs. However, the notion of big ideas in general is not based as much on empirical evidence as on our intuitive analysis of the alternative: teaching small, inconsequential, or marginal aspects of writing.

Writing Process. One well-known big idea in writing is usually referred to as *the writing process.* The idea that writing instruction should center on the stages through which writers most frequently work goes back more than 35 years, when Herum and Cummings (1970) wrote on the writing process for college students. Those educators may have been ahead of their time, because the widespread acceptance of their approach in public schools is usually credited to Graves (1983).

Although statements regarding the steps in the writing process vary from source to source, the following is representative of discussions on this topic:

1. *Planning.* This step often includes brainstorming, and various graphical or other ways to represent and begin to organize ideas. Sometimes, the initial brainstorming is referred to as "preplanning," while the early attempts at organization are considered mainstream planning.

2. *Drafting.* Once students have organized their ideas, they can develop their first rough draft. The goal of the draft is to focus upon the *author* role in writing, with little attention paid to the *secretary* role.

3. *Editing/Revising.* These tasks are sometimes viewed as separate operations. Regardless, revising refers primarily to rewriting portions of a draft, while editing now focuses a great deal of attention on the "secretary" role in writing.

4. *Publishing.* Many versions of the writing process include publishing as the final step in the process. Publishing (for peers or others) is thought to give students extra motivation to make their writing as good as they can, and to demonstrate how most writing "ends up" in real-world writing applications.

Presumably, professional writers and those for whom writing is a major part of their profession have always reiteratively planned, drafted, and revised their work, dating back to the classical Greek rhetoricians. Surely it is past time for school children learning to write to be let in on this fairly public "secret" of good writers.

Text Structures.   An awareness of the writing process by itself, however necessary to writing instruction, appears to be insufficient for consistent results, particularly for students with learning disabilities and with other learning difficulties (Englert et al., 1991). *Text structure* is another big authoring idea that has resulted in impressive achievement gains when combined with process writing. Each writing genre can be identified by its own set of structural characteristics. Stories, for example, always have a protagonist, a crisis, developing incidents, and a resolution. Students who are unaware of such common recurring elements might write "stories" that are more like rambling narratives or chronologies than true stories.

Several studies have shown solid promise for teaching text structures in conjunction with process writing (Graham & Harris, 1989; Hillocks, 1986; Meyer & Freedle, 1984). The work of Englert et al. (1991) is especially promising in terms of effective writing instruction for diverse learners in that it demonstrates how writing can be effectively taught simultaneously to mainstreamed learners with disabilities and their average-achieving peers.

Englert et al. (1991) also have shown a distinct advantage of focusing on big ideas: their instructional program taught *less,* but students learned *more.* That is, the program they developed taught only two text structures within a school year, but those structures (explanations and compare/contrast) were important to future schooling success, students learned them well, and the results on measures of transference were good. In contrast, our informal analysis of language arts texts reveals that between a dozen and two dozen text structures are typically "taught for exposure" within a single school year. When too much material is "taught for exposure" or merely "covered," many students appear to learn and retain little. The study by Englert et al. (1991) suggests that "less is more" when the content chosen is truly important.

Peer Interaction. Finally, peer interaction appears to be important for improved composition performance. Collaborative work has proven to be an effective instructional tool in many subject matter domains, but it has a particular benefit to writing instruction: When working in cooperative groups, each student has the opportunity to participate in authoring, editing, and revising. Although the act of writing is often a covert and solitary endeavor for mature and able writers, those *learning* to write benefit from many opportunities to talk about writing with peers.

Big Ideas and the Secretary Role in Writing. We can conceive of several potential big ideas related to writing mechanics, ideas that promote understanding and reduce the learning burden for students. Morphology may be a big idea for spelling instruction (Dixon, 1991; Henry, 1988). The idea of combining manuscript and cursive writing into a single system, as in the D'Nealian writing program (Brown, 1984), promises substantial efficiency for teaching writing. Effective keyboarding instruction also might help to reduce the burden of simply setting print to page (Brown, 1984) and promises substantial efficiency in teaching handwriting.

Hillocks's (1984) widely known research review of effective writing practices suggested that although sentence combining alone is not the most effective way to improve writing, it was more effective than other approaches examined (teaching grammar, free writing, using good models of writing). Sentence combining and manipulation, then, might be considered a significant but nondominant big idea for teaching writing mechanics. (We illustrate this possibility more fully in later sections of this chapter.)

The notion of big ideas is less an instructional design characteristic than a foundation on which to build successful instruction. We do not *design* big ideas; we *uncover* them through a careful and complete analysis of content-area literature. Big ideas do not guide us on *how* to teach; they are a major factor in determining *what* to focus on as we design instruction.

Designing Conspicuous Strategies

Conspicuous Strategies and the Author Role in Writing. Most students with learning difficulties, and many average-achieving students, do not automatically benefit from simply being exposed to big ideas, such as the steps in the writing process or text structures. A substantial body of research has accumulated that supports the teaching of conspicuous strategies for using those ideas (see Deshler & Schumaker, 1986; Pressley, Symons, Snyder, & Cariglia-Bull, 1989).

A teacher once described to the first author of this chapter the difference between the *old* and *new* ways of teaching writing for one of her students: "He used to sit, unable to get started, when trying to write about his summer vacation. Now, he sits, unable to get started, when trying to *plan* what he is going to write."

A conspicuous *planning strategy* could clarify for students some specific steps for starting and successfully completing their planning. The steps in such strategies derive from the best efforts of subject matter specialists to uncover or emulate cognitive processes that are normally employed covertly by experts. However, teaching just any set of steps to follow does not necessarily constitute a good strategy.

The best strategies appear to be those that are *intermediate in generality* (Prawat, 1989). If a strategy is too general, it is not likely to lead to reliable results. For example, "think before you write" is a general strategy and a good idea, but is too general to be of much practical value for many learners. On the other hand, a strategy that is too narrow is likely to result in the rote acquisition of some bit of knowledge with little potential for transference.

Conspicuous strategy instruction has been used with promising results to teach all phases of the writing process: planning (Harris & Graham, 1985), text structure (Englert et al., 1991; Graham & Harris, 1989), and revising (MacArthur, Graham, & Schwartz, 1991). Such strategies have appeared to meet the intermediate-in-generality criterion.

For example, Graham and Harris (1989) taught students to generate and organize story ideas by asking themselves questions related to the parts of the story: "What does the main character want to do?" (p. 98). On the one hand, the strategy was not narrow: The questions taught in the study all involved parts of stories. On the other hand, the strategy was broad enough: It directed students' attention to the elements common to all stories.

Conspicuous Strategies and the Secretary Role in Writing. Assume that a student is puzzling over the following sentence while attempting to edit and revise a draft:

All of we young people seem to like ice cream.

Is it, the student wonders, *we* or *us* young people? In terms of grammar, the answer can involve a complex array of spiraling knowledge: nominative case, objective case, objects of verbs, objects of prepositions, predicate nominatives, appositives. It is little wonder that many teachers would choose to forgo a grammatical approach in favor of nearly almost any other option, such as telling the student the answer or suggesting that the student rewrite the sentence to make the problem disappear.

Yet the problem can be attacked via conspicuous strategy instruction, with relatively little effort and complexity, and with relatively high potential for transference. The strategy is to decompose or simplify the sentence in question, then examine the results:

All young people seem to like ice cream.
All of we/us seem to like ice cream.

A native speaker of English who does not have a severe language disorder will instantly recognize *us* as the correct choice in the simpler sentence and realize that it is, therefore, the correct choice in the original sentence.

The same general strategy can be applied to far different instances of pronoun case, and to difficulties not involving pronoun case at all.

pronoun case: compounds

John gave Mary and I/me a new book.
John gave Mary a new book.
John gave me a new book.

subject/verb agreement

Original sentence: None of the boys was/were on time.
First simplification: Not one of the boys was/were on time.
Second simplification: Not one was on time.

Designing conspicuous strategies is challenging. We tend to readily recognize good strategies that others have designed, but most instructional designers agree that designing a good strategy from scratch is no simple matter. The best we can do is to suggest that anyone attempting to design conspicuous strategies begin with *something,* then evaluate the early attempts critically, using "intermediate generality" as the principal criterion for analysis. Whenever possible, promising strategies should be field-tested with students.

Designing Mediated Scaffolding

Mediated Scaffolding and the Author Role in Writing. We are using the term "scaffolding" broadly to refer to many kinds of assistance that students may receive as they move toward deeper understanding of what is being taught. Scaffolding may be provided directly by teachers, through guidance and feedback; or it may be provided by peers, through collaboration, or built into instructional materials, through devices that facilitate the successful completion of various tasks.

A primary characteristic of successful conspicuous strategy instruction, discussed above, is scaffolding and guided practice in various forms (Pressley, Harris, & Marks, 1992; Pressley et al., 1989). Two aspects of such scaffolding seem worthy of special note. First, it is provided on an *as-needed* basis and is gradually diminished over time. Second, it includes not only strategies for accomplishing writing goals but provides for self-regulation as well. That is, students are taught to regulate their own thinking about the use of composing strategies. Taken together, these features seem critical to the goal of independence for students with learning difficulties and their average-achieving peers alike.

In addition, collaborative work among students constitutes a form of scaffolding. When students work together on projects, they act as resources for one another for everything from planning a piece of writing to final revision and editing. We should caution, however, that practitioners might be careful to observe the same gradual reduction of scaffolding as advocated by Graham et al. (1991). Otherwise, there is the danger that some students will develop a dependency on collaboration. Put another way, students will fail to achieve self-regulation if scaffolding of any variety is not gradually removed—including the type of scaffolding provided through peer collaboration.

The kinds of scaffolding that are built into tasks are sometimes referred to as *procedural facilitators.* The idea of using procedural facilitation for writing originated with Bereiter and Scardamalia (1982). It is a form of help that assumes students have underlying competencies, but that they are having difficulty implementing them due to the complexity of writing. For example, if a student really *knows* the structure of a given text type, such as a story, but can't effectively plan a draft around that structure because of the complexities involved, then a procedural facilitator could help lessen the cognitive burden of the task.

Graham et al. (1991) caution that the effective use of procedural facilitators is probably dependent on integration with other forms of help whenever the cause of student difficulties is something other than inability to execute complex cognitive demands. That is, if students know how to do something complex, but have trouble using that knowledge, then a procedural facilitator alone might be enough help. But if students have not learned the complex strategy to begin with, then other types of scaffolding are probably necessary. Englert et al. (1991) used procedural facilitation, in conjunction with big ideas, strategies, and other instructional characteristics, to teach writing simultaneously to mainstreamed students with learning disabilities and their nondisabled peers.

Figure 5–1 contains a series of think sheets that illustrate how procedural facilitators for the writing process can enhance the effectiveness of other instructional considerations. All five think sheets are designed to facilitate stages in the writing process (except publication): planning, organizing, revising, and editing.

Figure 5–1A gives students guidance in planning their writing. The potential in such a procedural facilitator is probably most likely to be realized when it is used in conjunction with scaffolded strategy instruction: teacher and student models of planning, frequent discussion with teachers and peers, and frequent monitoring of student work and feedback.

Figure 5–1B specifically facilitates the drafting of one particular text structure: explanations. A different genre, such as a story, requires a different think sheet. An example of a story organization think sheet is given in Figure 5–2.

Figure 5–1C helps students understand the *inner dialogue* role of writers and helps encourage self-regulation. This self-editing think sheet gives students an opportunity to reflect on a draft and to possibly make changes before anyone else reads it.

The Editor's Feedback Worksheet illustrated in Figure 5–1D is based on the assumption that students might not only have difficulty with their own writing, but difficulty giving constructive feedback on the writing of others as well. We base that assumption less on descriptive research than on the observations of many teachers with whom we have worked.

Finally, Figure 5–1E illustrates a think sheet that could help facilitate revision. In addition to providing guided application of revision strategies, it helps put the role of editors in perspective: that of a valuable resource.

Not only can any given phase of instruction be scaffolded, but instruction on writing a given text structure from beginning to end can be scaffolded as well. Englert et al. (1991), for example, had students write their first explanation as a group project, with a great deal of interaction among students and between teachers and students. Next, students wrote individual papers, but also with substantial support from teachers and other students. Finally, students wrote a *third* explanation in which students were encouraged to write independently, but were given support as needs arose.

That sequence of events can be summarized as *four* extensive opportunities with a single text structure: a complete teacher model of all phases in the writing

Planning Think Sheet

Name of writer _____ Date _____

Topic _____

Who will the audience be? _____

What is my goal? _____

Everything I already know about this topic—anything I can think of:

_____   _____

_____   _____

Possible ways to group my ideas:

_____ _____ _____

_____ _____ _____

FIGURE 5–1A
Think Sheet for Helping Students Plan Their Writing

Organization Think Sheet
Explanation

What am I explaining? _____

What will the reader need (if anything)? Is there any special setting for this?

_____

What can I tell readers at the beginning to get them interested? _____

_____

List the steps:

1. _____

2. _____

3. _____

4. _____

5. _____

6. _____

First   Next   Then   After   Second   Third   Finally

FIGURE 5–1B
Think Sheet for Helping Students Organize an Explanation

Self-Editing Think Sheet
Explanation
My Impressions

The things I like best   The things I like least

_____   _____

_____   _____

A Good Explanation?

Everything is clear. ☐

There is a statement saying what is being explained. ☐

I've used good key words. ☐   The steps are in order. ☐

I've added something of special interest to my readers. ☐

I've included what is needed, if anything. ☐

I've finished with a good summary statement. ☐

Questions I would like to ask my editor—friends, teachers, parents—before revision:

1. _____

2. _____

Ideas for Revision

_____   _____

_____   _____

FIGURE 5–1C
Think Sheet for Helping Students Edit Their Own Drafts

Editor's Feedback Worksheet

Title of paper I am editing: _____

Author _____

1. What I like most about this paper: _____

_____

2. Parts I think are not clear: _____

_____

_____

3. Suggestions for improving:

☐ Better introduction   ☐ Better use of key words

☐ More examples   ☐ Change organization

☐ Other _____

_____

_____

_____

FIGURE 5–1D
Think Sheet for Helping Students Give Feedback to Other Students

---

Revision Think Sheet

Suggestions from my Editor

1. Read editor's feedback worksheet carefully.

2. List the suggestions you are interested in using:

_____

_____

_____

Adding Polish

1. At this point, can you think of a good way to get your readers interested right at the beginning of the paper?

_____

_____

2. Does each part of the paper make the reader want to read the next part? _____

_____

_____

3. How is your ending? Any additional ideas for summing everything up neatly?

_____

_____

Revising

Use this page, your self-edit think sheet, and your editor's feedback worksheet as the basis for beginning to revise your draft.

Consider submitting your revision to an editor for further feedback.

FIGURE 5–1E
Think Sheet for Helping Students Revise Their Drafts

FIGURE 5–2
*Think Sheet for Helping
Students Organize a Story*

Organization Think Sheet
Story

Protagonist? _____

Antagonist? _____

What is the crisis or problem the protagonist must overcome?

_____

_____

_____

Developing Incidents

_____

_____

_____

_____

_____

_____

Climax

_____

_____

Ending

_____

_____

_____

process as they apply to explanations; the complete development of a class explanation; and two individually written explanations. In the course of the study, students studied explanations extensively, and learned to write them well. This approach is in contrast to that of typical language arts texts, in which a single text structure is taught in a period of a week or less, with little evidence of effectiveness.

Mediated Scaffolding and the Secretary Role in Writing. Few students are likely to fully understand and apply sentence-manipulation strategies, such as those outlined in the last section, without support. Such support can come in a variety of forms, including teacher guidance on the use of procedural facilitators such as those illustrated in Figure 5–3.

In Level 1 tasks, strategies are modeled and heavy scaffolding is provided to ensure that students' first attempts to apply the strategy are successful. At each successive level, a piece of scaffolding is taken away, leading to self-regulated, independent application—at Level 5 in this case. This is in sharp contrast to the approach taken in many textbooks, in which students are given a model, no explicit strategy based on big ideas, and then are expected to complete several application tasks independently.

A straightforward procedure for designing scaffolded tasks is that of beginning at the end. That is, the easiest tasks to design are generally those that represent the final, independent *outcome* that we would like to see students achieve. In the example given in Figure 5–3, the Level 5 task is the outcome task. From here, the

Level 1: Interactive Model/Heavy Scaffold

Sometimes it is difficult to know when to use words such as *I* and *me* or *she* and *her.* You can usually figure out the right word to use by breaking the sentence into two simpler sentences.

Circle the correct choice in the second simpler sentence. That is the correct choice in the longer sentence.

1. Longer sentence: The doctor gave Elicia and I/me a flu shot.
   Simpler sentences:
   The doctor gave Elicia a flu shot.
   The doctor gave I/me a flu shot.

Level 2: Relatively Heavy Scaffolding

You can usually figure out what word to use by breaking a sentence into two simpler sentences.

For each sentence, one simpler sentence is given for you. First, write the other simpler sentence. Then circle the right word in the longer sentence.

1. Longer sentence: She/Her and John lived next door to us for four years.
   John lived next door to us for four years.

_____

Level 3: Minor Prompting for Scaffolding

For each sentence, write the two simpler sentences. Then circle the right word in the longer sentence.

1. Before going on our camping trip, Melinda and I/me prepared all our supplies.

_____

_____

Level 4: Only Reminder as Scaffold

Circle the correct word in each sentence. Remember, the word that's right in the simpler sentence is also right in the longer sentence.

1. After the team members left, they/them and some other friends went out for burgers.

Level 5: Independent—No Scaffolding

Circle the correct word in each sentence.

1. The movie started before Jaques and I/me arrived.

FIGURE 5–3
Levels of Scaffolding for a Sentence Manipulation Strategy

designer can work backward, modifying the outcome task slightly by making it slightly easier, then making that task slightly easier, until the designer reaches the beginning: a highly scaffolded task that ensures high success for all or nearly all students.

Designing Strategic Integration

Strategic Integration and the Author Role in Writing.   The issue of knowledge integration is crucial at several levels in language arts instruction. At the broadest level, reading and writing instruction can potentially be integrated based on the observation that writers are readers and readers, hopefully, are writers. This relationship between reading and writing has been illustrated by Raphael and Englert (1990).

Also of particular interest is the relationship between writing mechanics and composition. A genuinely holistic view of writing, we believe, must accommodate all those writing elements that in fact intertwine to produce "good writing."

Specific to composition, knowledge of basic text structure should be integrated as a means of efficiently teaching more advanced and complex structures—those used most frequently by expert writers. One major instructional contributor to such integration is cumulative review (discussed in a later section of this chapter).

The major ingredients of instruction aimed at achieving integration appear to be, first, that students acquire fluency with the knowledge to be integrated, and, second, that instruction deliberately focuses on the integration of such knowledge. All of the instructional characteristics discussed in this chapter potentially contribute to the former: a focus on big ideas, strategies, and so on. In fact, a focus on big ideas alone would tend to encourage knowledge integration because big ideas typically comprise other knowledge realms within a domain.

Strategic Integration and the Secretary Role in Writing.   In addition to integrating writing mechanics and composition, we believe that mechanics should be integrated among themselves. The Level 5 task illustrated in Figure 5–3 might be the end of isolated work on pronoun case, but it should be the beginning of integration. When students write, they must discriminately select from among their entire repertoire of writing knowledge. In authentic writing, they are not prompted to use the correct case for pronouns, for instance. Cumulative review serves as a means for making instructional tasks closely emulate the conditions of writing.

Integration is not difficult to design into instruction if the designer keeps one principle in mind: Don't force it. It might be tempting to jump on a knowledge integration bandwagon, but an instructional designer should focus on those aspects of a content area that integrate naturally. For example, if morphology is a big idea in spelling instruction, then spelling, vocabulary, etymology, and even parts of speech interrelate with one another naturally. The morphological parts of the word *alchemist*, for instance, relate to spelling (*al* + *chem* + *ist*), vocabulary (*al-* means "the" and *chem* means "to pour"), word history (the part *al-* comes from the Arabic), and parts of speech (*-ist* means "one who" and forms nouns).

Designing Primed Background Knowledge

Primed Background Knowledge and the Author Role in Writing. With respect to composition, primed background knowledge is a less critical characteristic of effective instruction relative to other content areas. Learning a given text structure, for example, is not dependent upon a large base of other foundational knowledge. The knowledge that is required to learn text structures can be characterized as the kinds of basic "knowledge of the world" that most school children, other than those with the severest disabilities, are likely to possess.

Primed Background Knowledge and the Secretary Role in Writing. Primed background knowledge is usually important with respect to the acquisition of writing mechanics skill and knowledge. Relative to grammar and usage, in particular, background knowledge can be of crucial importance, depending on the strategies employed to teach these areas. For example, the traditional approach to teaching pronoun case is through the use of grammatical rules. Those rules, in turn, depend heavily on a broad and deep range of background knowledge, including, possibly, the notion of case, and objects of verbs and of prepositions, subjects, and pronouns.

An instructional designer can determine necessary background knowledge by examining strategies closely. Are there any concepts in the strategy that students might not know fluently? One option for accommodating background knowledge is to test for it. Students who already have prerequisite background knowledge are ready to learn the material. Other students either should not be placed in the instruction, or if they are placed, the instruction should include necessary background knowledge.

Designing Judicious Review

Judicious Review and the Author Role in Writing. Review in writing instruction has received little attention in the literature. However, the general benefits of review have been shown across content areas through relatively substantial research. As discussed elsewhere in this book (see Chapter 1), Dempster (1991) summarizes that effective review is adequate, distributed, cumulative, and varied. In addition, there is reason to believe that even excellent writing instruction might be further improved through use of effective review. Graham et al. (1991) point out that we need to "continue to investigate procedures for promoting strategy maintenance and generalization" (p. 103).

The study by Englert et al. (1991) illustrates the potential benefits of *adequate* review. With a complex cognitive process such as composing, it is not surprising to find that a large amount of application opportunity is necessary for mastery.

We are unaware of direct or indirect research on distributed review as it applies to composition. However, the procedures recommended by Englert and her associates (Englert et al. 1991; Raphael & Englert, 1990) tend to strongly support cumulative review, and to a lesser degree, distributed review.

Englert and her associates initially teach distinct text structures, such as explanation and compare and contrast. They teach those structures *thoroughly:* approximately half a school year each for explanations and compare and contrast. Compared with the typical basal "one-topic-per-week" organization, this approach might be thought of as *very* massed practice. However, because scaffolding is gradually reduced as students learn, this approach has some of the attributes of distributed practice as well.

Eventually, students combine basic text structures into more complex writing, scaffolded in part by *expert* think sheets, which are more generic than those for specific text structures. Such practice, in effect, constitutes both a distribution and an accumulation of knowledge.

Finally, in order to promote transference and generalization, review should be varied. With respect to composition specifically, work on a particular text structure can be reasonably varied by simply allowing students to select different topics about which to write. There is evidence, too, of generalization from a set of basic text structures to more complex texts incorporating one or more of the basic structures. For example, in a persuasive essay it is common to find elements of nonfiction narrative, explanation, and comparison and contrast. The crucial prerequisite for such transference appears to be that the "transfer knowledge" (basic text structures) be taught thoroughly to begin with (Englert et al., 1991).

When review is not varied, the result is likely to be a rote-like acquisition of knowledge. The opposite extreme also is possible: review may be so varied that *something else* is actually being reviewed.

Judicious Review and the Secretary Role in Writing. How much review of sentence-manipulation strategies is adequate? The answer can be found only through field testing with students. However, that amount might be relatively small. First, if the strategy is meaningful, that alone enhances memory (Torgeson, 1988). Second, if the review is well distributed, less total review should be required.

Reviewing cumulatively is critical to full understanding and to realistic integration with composition. In a sense, the Level 5 task shown in Figure 5–3 is still scaffolded to some extent, simply because it applies to only one of many possible applications of sentence-manipulation strategies: first-person plural pronouns in appositives. To learn just how sentence manipulation can be applied to solve a variety of writing mechanics problems, the strategy would need to be applied to those problems cumulatively, as each type is taught (pronouns in compounds, subject-verb agreement, several punctuation applications, etc.).

Finally, the review should include widely varying examples, in order to promote transference of the strategy, but the examples should not vary to the extent that something untaught is being reviewed. We found a lesson in a language arts basal text, for example, that only addressed the pronoun case in compounds, with no instruction on appositives, but then almost immediately gave students practice on pronoun case in appositives.

THE APPLICATION OF INSTRUCTIONAL DESIGN PRINCIPLES

Developing Instructional Tools

Developers should design tools in writing that provide intensive instruction on a small number of text structures in each school year. Instruction should emphasize stages in the writing process, and provide for collaborative work as a means of clarifying the reader–writer relationship. Tools should teach mechanical skills concurrently with composition, focusing upon big ideas such as sentence manipulation to learn usage, or morphology for spelling.

Most critically, developers should provide explicit strategies. However, strategies should not only be explicit, but should be "medium" in terms of generality as well. Such strategies are not simple to develop, but they are between strategies that are too narrow or too broad. A narrow strategy might be, "Start each paragraph with a topic sentence." A broad writing strategy is "plan before writing."

After students have studied the text structure of a specific writing genre or something else new, their initial work should be supported temporarily by simplified tasks. For instance, think sheets can be provided for each genre and for many mechanics activities. Initially, such aids should lend considerable support to students by virtually *forcing* the appropriate organization of thoughts. Gradually, simplified tasks should be converted into complex, fully self-regulated tasks.

Tools should be designed to purposefully highlight knowledge that naturally integrates to promote more complex knowledge structures. Different text structures (explanations, comparisons, arguments) can and should be integrated into more complex, "expert" structures. Most importantly, in the arena of writing, composition and writing mechanics should be well integrated.

Ideally, instructional tools should include placement tools for determining the extent to which students possess relevant background knowledge. Tools should then provide for those students with gaps in background knowledge by presenting it *relatively* close to the introduction of the target knowledge for which it is prerequisite. For instance, in order for students to write good explanations, they should have some knowledge of words indicating chronology, such as *first, then, next, after, finally,* and so on. Such knowledge is likely to be a part of general background knowledge for many students, but not for some diverse learners. If these students are able to spend time using such words to sequence events prior to the introduction of an explanation text structure, then they will be in a much better position to learn that new structure on a pace with their peers.

The kind of deep understanding required for complex problem solving rarely develops within a short period of time. Review designed according to solid empirical evidence can help students acquire and maintain deep understanding, as well as the kind of fluency required to successfully complete many complex cognitive tasks (such as most writing tasks). If less material but more important material is taught thoroughly (big ideas), then there is plenty of "room" in instructional tools for review that is adequate, distributed, and cumulative. Moreover, *thorough* instruction includes many varied opportunities to apply strategies, which in turn result in better transference of knowledge. This is particularly important with respect to writing, where a given text structure can potentially be used for an nearly unlimited array of purposes.

Selecting Instructional Tools

When selecting instructional tools in writing, evaluate prospective materials to determine the extent to which they focus upon big ideas in composition and mechanics. More time should be allocated to these big ideas than to other, less critical content. Next, identify what explicit strategies, if any, are associated with important, big ideas. The following problems sometimes occur:

1. No explicit strategy can be found.
2. The strategy is explicit, but too narrow or too broad. In general, the strategies used to teach composition tend to be quite broad, and the strategies used to teach writing mechanics tend to be quite narrow.
3. The strategy is explicit and of *medium generality,* but some steps are ambiguous or confusing.

Examine the activities associated with a major topic to see whether scaffolded tasks are routinely provided. One should be able to imagine students "easing in" to full understanding and complete independence as they work from early to later tasks on a given topic. Instructional tools for writing should not, however, go to the extreme of providing scaffolding that is never disassembled. An overzealous dependence upon cooperative work, for example, can effectively prevent many students from achieving individual accountability for their work.

The evaluation of tools can focus to a great extent upon the degree to which important, big ideas are explicitly interrelated. Some tools have emerged in recent years that are excellent in that writing mechanics are not simply *exposed and dropped,* but rather, they accumulate over time to create more and more realistic writing applications. A straightforward method of evaluating materials for integration is to select an instructional unit that would normally be taught in February or March at a given grade level, and then to examine that unit to determine the extent to which earlier topics are integrated in the selected unit.

Instructional tools can be examined to determine the extent to which they accommodate prior knowledge requirements. For example, some review of basic paragraph structure a week or two before the introduction of a new text structure can help diminish differences among students. New strategies associated with big ideas, in particular, should be examined from the viewpoint of a diverse learner to determine whether the strategy assumes crucial background knowledge that some students might not possess.

A "safe" and relatively easy way to evaluate tools for review is, in general, to look for *a lot* of review. Such tools are more likely to be effective, and are the most practical for teachers to use, since eliminating review opportunities is a much simpler matter for teachers than adding them.

Modifying Instructional Tools

To modify instructional tools in writing, identify big ideas in existing materials and plan to allocate more time to them—time "borrowed" by deemphasizing or ignoring less important ideas. Select, for example, just two or three of the most useful text structures presented in materials and teach those thoroughly.

The most difficult modification for teachers or others to make with existing tools is the creation of a strategy where none exists. When strategies are provided, teachers can realistically evaluate them from the point of view of their students and modify those steps that are ambiguous or confusing.

The independent activities provided in tools can be converted to scaffolded activities in either of two major ways. First, independent writing activities can be converted to group activities, wherein students support one another, and teachers provide extensive feedback. Second, tasks can be temporarily simplified. For example, an instructional tool might provide a task in which students proofread text for errors, such as:

Rewrite these sentences to make them clearer.
Many stores make empty promises. We put ours in writing.

Cues can be added to such tasks to increase the likelihood that students will understand them:

Did the writer probably mean "our empty promises" or "our promises"?
Change the second sentence to show what the writer probably meant.
We put _____ in writing.

New activities may be created expressly to promote the integration of knowledge. For example, previously taught text structures can be combined into novel assignments as a means of promoting text structures of greater complexity. If students have mastered a compare-and-contrast text structure as a means of conveying information, and have also mastered a basic argument-and-persuasion text structure, then those two structures can be combined into a more advanced persuasive structure, in which comparing and contrasting is used as a principal means for organizing an argument.

Existing tools can't easily be modified to accommodate background knowledge because such modification implies both the development of new instruction and the "resequencing" of existing instruction. "Better late than never," however, might apply. For example, teachers can diagnose student difficulties to determine if they originate with gaps in background knowledge, and provide instruction on such knowledge as needed. If instruction on particularly crucial background knowledge isn't provided in tools, then teachers may need to identify such knowledge and teach it directly to all students.

Teachers can provide *adequate* review on big ideas by having students write a single text structure, such as an explanation, several times within the same school year. Such basic structures, when learned well to begin with, are then incorporated into more complex structures, which provides distributed review quite naturally. For writing, such a practice is principally a matter of scheduling. A teacher can readily modify a tool that covers several text structures in a year by selecting only two or three of the most important ones, then scheduling repeated assignments involving them. Developing additional review or finding appropriate review supplements is an option for tools that provide minimal review opportunities, particularly with respect to instruction on the mechanics of writing. For instance, many younger students require substantial opportunities to review handwriting in order to become fluent enough that handwriting isn't a major stumbling block to participation in the processes of writing compositions. For writing mechanics, it is most crucial that review be cumulative, in order to closely replicate authentic writing.

SUMMARY

We have looked at designing both composition instruction and instruction on writing mechanics. The research in recent years on teaching composition is heartening and promising for all students, but particularly for students with learning difficulties. Some well-designed studies have shown, for instance, that students with learning disabilities can achieve at a level equal to their average-achieving peers (Englert et al., 1991; Graham & Harris, 1989).

Big ideas in composition instruction appear to be supported strongly, if tacitly, in the work of researchers in the field. The biggest of the big ideas are process writing, text structures, and collaboration. The recommendation of making expert cognitive processes visible through explicit strategy instruction is quite directly supported by research on explicit strategy instruction, as is the scaffolding of instruction.

The effectiveness of teaching explicit strategies depends on the design of good strategies, but is likely to be influenced by students' background knowledge. There is strong research to support the characteristics of effective review, and the need for maintenance and generalization in composition instruction is clear; however, more direct research is needed on the impact of review on composition. Finally, *complete understanding* in any sense implies the full integration of important knowledge—another area that might well benefit from more direct research.

When we turn our backs on instruction in writing mechanics, we are essentially turning our backs on many diverse learners. Without doubt, there exists an endless array of examples of poor—even terrible—writing skills sheets. That does not mean, however, that thoughtful educators, informed by research on composition, cannot find effective ways to teach mechanics and to integrate them smoothly and meaningfully into composition activities. The *principal* prerequisites for this, no doubt, are that effective composition instruction take place on a regular and sustained basis, and that instruction on writing mechanics be reasoned and systematically integrated with composition.

REFLECTION AND APPLICATION

Case Study

Bo is a dually certified general education/special education teacher with a concentration in Reading and English. He's been teaching eighth-grade English for the past two years at Gateway School, which serves children in grades K–8. Through a retirement incentive program, 12 veteran teachers retired last June, five of whom were special educators. Due to budget cuts, the district personnel office tried to save teacher jobs both through the early retirement incentive program and by transferring teachers who currently teach general education, but who hold special education certification, into special education positions. Bo was assigned a position as a grade 4 special education inclusion co-teacher and resource teacher. This position primarily requires Bo to support students in reading and written language, though he may be called upon to help in other areas.

The Gateway School has an integrated approach in grades 3, 4, and 5 in which language arts, science, and social studies are interwoven within thematic units. Grade 4 students study world history within a unit entitled "In Touch With the Past" in which each student becomes a craftsman from the colonial era. The five-month investigation culminates in a reenactment of a working colonial village. As stated in the school handbook, the "integrated theme approach allows students to hone in on written language skills, find voice and develop a personal style as developing authors." The final written project is a lengthy paper representing five months of study, research, and process writing.

Bo was excited to be involved in the "In Touch With the Past" project. Writing was his passion and he particularly enjoyed history and historical fiction. Although this was his first experience in a collaborative inclusion setting, he felt comfortable working with Jenny, his assigned general education co-teacher. Unsure of exactly how the model was intended to work, he found himself doing a lot of "hanging around" in Jenny's classroom during the first few days of school.

Jenny gave the students an overview of the next five months of thematic study and told them that they must "start to do their research," "talk to their parents," and "identify" the craft they wished to focus on for their final project. Each student received a handout with a list of major writing components for the project as well as the dates that they were due. The first component was the introduction for the paper. Over the course of the week, students were directed to work through the steps of the writing process and to hand in the final version of their introductions on Friday. Bo watched Jenny in action with the students. She seemed a master manager; she had the system down.

Bo had five students from Jenny's class on his caseload, each with documented reading and written language disabilities. On Friday, when Bo looked at his students' introductions, it was clear that none of them had anything close to a final product. Moreover, although some of the other students in the class had acceptable introductions, many did not. Bo felt his enthusiasm for "In Touch With the Past" slipping away as he watched Jenny roam the room and enter checks into her green grade book as the students showed her their work folders. If this first assignment was any indication, Bo had serious concerns about whether many students would be able to successfully complete this lengthy long-term writing project without additional support. When Bo shared his concerns with Jenny, she told him that the students already knew the steps of the writing process and should be able to complete each assignment independently.

- If the students did indeed know the steps of the writing process, why might they have had difficulty producing a final version of their introductions by the due date?
- What instructional principles and teaching strategies could Bo utilize to more effectively address the learning needs of his students, as well as the other students in Jenny's class?

The conclusion of the case study can be found later in this chapter.

Content Questions

1. How does Smith (1982) characterize the writing processes?

2. What has been the predominant approach to writing instruction in American schools?

3. Explain the authors' recommendation for resolving conflicts between skills-dominant and composition-dominant approaches for writing instruction.

4. Identify and describe three big ideas of writing instruction.

5. What are "planning strategies" in writing and why should these strategies be presented conspicuously?

6. Briefly describe the conspicuous strategy that is recommended for addressing grammar problems in sentence writing.

7. Describe three conditions in which scaffolding can be provided to learners.

8. Define the term "procedural facilitators" and describe how it is used for writing instruction. What is the most effective use of procedural facilitators?

Reflection and Discussion

1. What are the potential implications of an approach to teaching writing that emphasizes composition skills at the expense of mechanical writing skills? What are the potential implications of methods that stress writing mechanics at the expense of composition skills? How can principles of effective instruction be used to develop and support a framework of writing instruction that integrates both mechanical and composition skills?

2. The authors note that limited mechanical skills, including handwriting and spelling, may substantially hinder students with learning difficulties from participation in the authoring process. What role might technology, including assistive technology, play in facilitating the development of writing skills among students with learning difficulties?

3. Given the widespread use of procedural facilitators, such as graphic organizers and think sheets, do you think that sufficient instruction and feedback is provided to support students with diverse learning needs in the effective use of these tools?

4. Do you think that the amount of time dedicated to teaching writing is generally commensurate with the inherent complexity of this skill and the emphasis placed on writing in schools and in the workplace?

Application

1. The authors note that when selecting instructional tools in writing, strategies should be *intermediate in generality*. Evaluate the following two examples of prewriting instructions and identify the appropriateness of the strategy (e.g., too broad or too narrow) for the given task.

   a. During our unit "Rocks and Minerals" we have learned many things. Write an essay describing the most important features of the types of rocks we studied in this unit. Remember our writing strategy is "Think-Plan-Write."

   b. During our unit "Rocks and Minerals" we have learned many things. Write an essay describing the most important features of the types of rocks we studied in this unit. Remember when we write an essay we always have characters, settings, problems, and an outcome.

2. Parents of fourth graders received the following information in a "Back-to-School Night" handout (see Figure 5–4). Based on your understanding of designing instruction around big ideas, comment on the appropriateness of this schedule for writing instruction. What problems might students with diverse learning needs have with this instructional sequence? What changes would you suggest to the teacher for restructuring the plan for the year?

Writing

This year students will be engaging in the writing process regularly. Research shows that writing instruction and practice must be an ongoing and continuous process to provide students with the opportunities to develop their voice as writers. Regular writing also supports our students in preparing for our state mastery tests. We will cover the following forms of writing this year:

- September: Personal Narratives—"What I Did This Summer"
- October: Creative Writing—A scary creation for the book store contest!
- November: Position Papers—"Why I'm Voting for _____."
- December: Memoir Writing—"My Favorite Holiday Memory"
- January: Poetry—"My Personal Poetry Collection"
- February: Persuasive Writing—"Why I Should Be Able To _____"
- March: Explode the Moment—Descriptive writing
- April: Writing a Thesis Statement—Science curriculum connection
- May: Writing a Research Paper—We'll use April's thesis statement.
- June: State test
- Writer's Celebration: Each student will present his/her favorite piece from a personal portfolio at our "Evening with the Authors."

As you can see, by year's end students will become proficient in various forms of writing. This will prepare them to transition to the middle school for fifth–eighth grades.

FIGURE 5–4
"Back-to-School Night" Handout

Case Study (Conclusion)

Bo knew from his training as a special educator and his role as a writing teacher that understanding the steps of the writing process was not sufficient to carry the students successfully through the project. He knew that even strong students need a highly structured, supported, and systematic approach to a long-term writing project.

For each assignment, Bo decided that he would develop procedural facilitators, such as graphic organizers and think sheets to scaffold the students' progress through the writing process. He planned to use overheads of graphic organizers at each step so the students could follow along with him. He would use "think-aloud" procedures to model his thinking while completing the graphic organizers. Following his demonstration, Bo would provide the students with a detailed schedule containing a carefully designed breakdown of necessary steps to successfully accomplish each assignment. He would provide blank copies of the graphic organizers he used in his demonstration for the students to use. Bo developed planning sheets for researching, prewriting/ planning, drafting, revision, editing, peer conferencing, and publication.

As Bo's students became familiar with the long-term planning guide and graphic organizers, all five displayed a high level of enthusiasm for the work in the "In Touch With the Past" project. Research planning sheets supported their identification of trades and informational resources. The group now included a cooper, wheelwright, saddler, milliner, and founder. Bo continued to model and think aloud, demonstrating his own use of graphic organizers, note cards, and the drafting of his writing piece. After group discussions, he conferenced with individual students to support their learning and progress in the writing process.

In Jenny's classroom, Bo's students were successfully on task. When other students saw the folders with graphic organizers and color-coded index cards that Bo's students were using, they were curious. Bo's students shared their strategies, with pride, excitement, and an impressive and sophisticated level of comprehension. Jenny invited the five "experts" to support their peers in the use of organizers and a detailed project planning sheet. The scaffolded approach that had helped Bo's students seemed to be just what the other students needed. Jenny was also convinced; she decided to incorporate the mediated scaffolding that Bo was using in the resource room systematically into her general education instruction.

- If Bo hadn't spent the time introducing and modeling the use of the detailed planner and the graphic organizers, do you think these materials would have been effective scaffolds? What else might Jenny and Bo decide to do in the future to meet the needs of all learners as they progress in the writing project?
- Many teachers use a thematic approach to instruction in which multiple content areas are integrated within a unit (e.g., writing, math, social studies). What instructional principles should teachers consider when designing such units to ensure the success of students with diverse learning needs?

The Reflection and Application section of this chapter was written by Maureen F. Ruby, and Richard P. Zipoli, Jr., of the University of Connecticut.

REFERENCES

APPLEBEE, A. (1981). *Writing in the secondary school: English and the content areas.* Urbana, IL: National Council of Teachers of English.

APPLEBEE, A. (1990). *The writing report card, 1984–88: Findings from the nation's report card.* (NAEP Report No. 19-W-01). Princeton, NJ: U.S. Department of Education, Office of Educational Research and Improvement.

APPLEBEE, A., LANGER, J., JENKINS, L., MULLIS, I., & FOERTSCH, M. (1990). *Learning to write in our nation's schools.* Princeton, NJ: Educational Testing Service.

APPLEBEE, A., LANGER, J., & MULLIS, I. (1986). *The writing report card: Writing achievement in American schools.* Princeton, NJ: Educational Testing Service.

BEREITER, C. (1980). Development in writing. In L. Gregg, & E. R. Steinberg (Eds.), *Cognitive processes in writing* (pp. 73–93). Hillsdale, NJ: Erlbaum.

BEREITER, C., & SCARDAMALIA, M. (1982) From conversation to composition: The role of instruction in a developmental process. In R. Glaser (Ed.), *Advances in instructional psychology* (Vol. 2, pp. 1–64). Hillsdale, NJ: Erlbaum.

BRIDGE, C., & HIEBERT, E. (1985). A comparison of classroom writing practices, teachers' perceptions of their writing instruction, and textbook recommendations on writing practices. *Elementary School Journal, 86,* 155–172.

BROWN, V. L. (1984). D'Nealian handwriting: What is it and how to teach it. *Remedial and Special Education, 5*(5), 48–52.

CARROLL, J. (1963). A model for school learning. *Teacher's College Record, 64,* 723–733.

CHRISTENSON, S., THURLOW, M., YSSELDYKE, J., & McVICAR, R. (1989). Writing language instruction for students with mild handicaps: Is there enough quantity to ensure quality? *Learning Disability Quarterly, 12,* 219–229.

DEMPSTER, F. N. (1991). Synthesis of research on reviews and tests. *Educational Leadership, 4,* 71–76.

DESHLER, D. D., & SCHUMAKER, J. B. (1986). Learning strategies: An instructional alternative for low-achieving adolescents. *Exceptional Children, 52*(6), 583–590.

DIXON, R. C. (1991). The application of sameness analysis to spelling. *Journal of Learning Disabilities, 24*(5), 285–310.

DUCHARME, C., EARL, J., & POPLIN, M. S. (1989). The author model: The constructivist view of the writing process. *Learning Disability Quarterly, 12,* 237–242.

ENGLERT, C. S., & RAPHAEL, T. (1988). Constructing well-formed prose: Process, structure, and metacognitive knowledge. *Exceptional Children, 54,* 513–520.

ENGLERT, C. S., RAPHAEL, T., ANDERSON, L., ANTHONY, H., FEAR, K., & GREGG, S. (1988). A case for writing intervention: Strategies for writing informational text. *Learning Disabilities Focus, 3,* 98–113.

ENGLERT, C. S., RAPHAEL, T., ANDERSON, L., ANTHONY, H., STEVENS, D., & FEAR, K. (1991). Making writing strategies and self-talk visible: Cognitive strategy instruction in writing in regular and special education classrooms. *American Educational Research Journal, 28,* 337–372.

FLOWER, L., & HAYES, J. (1981). A cognitive process theory of writing. *College Composition and Communication, 32,* 365–387.

GRAHAM, S. (1982). Composition research and practice: A unified approach. *Focus on Exceptional Children, 14*(8), 1–16.

GRAHAM, S. (1990). The role of production factors in learning disabled students' compositions. *Journal of Educational Psychology, 80,* 781–791.

GRAHAM, S. (1999). Handwriting and spelling instruction for students with learning disabilities: A review. *Learning Disability Quarterly, 22*(2), 78–98.

GRAHAM, S., & HARRIS, K. R. (1989). A components analysis of cognitive strategy instruction: Effects on learning disabled students' compositions and self-efficacy. *Journal of Educational Psychology, 81,* 356–361.

GRAHAM, S., HARRIS, K. R., MacARTHUR, C. S., & SCHWARTZ, S. (1991). Writing and writing instruction for students with learning disabilities: Review of a research program. *Learning Disability Quarterly, 14,* 89–114.

GRAVES, D. (1983). *Writing: Teachers and children at work.* Exeter, NH: Heinemann.

GRAVES, D. (1985). All children can write. *Learning Disabilities Focus, 1*(1), 36–43.

GREENWALD, E. A., PERSKY, H. R., CAMPBELL, J. R., & MASSEO, J. (1999). *NAEP 1998 writing report card for the nation and states.* (NCES 1999-462). Washington, DC: U.S. Department of Education, Office of Educational Research and Improvement.

HARRIS, K., & GRAHAM, S. (1985). Improving learning disabled students' composition skills: Self-control strategy training. *Learning Disability Quarterly, 8,* 27–36.

HENRY, M. K. (1988). Beyond phonics: Integrated decoding and spelling instruction based on word origin and structure. *Annals of Dyslexia, 38,* 258–272.

HERUM, J., & CUMMINGS, D. W. (1970). *Writing: Plans, drafts and revisions.* New York: Random House.

HILLOCKS, G. (1984, November). What works in teaching composition: A meta-analysis of experimental treatment studies. *American Journal of Education, 93,* 133–170.

HILLOCKS, G. (1986). *Research on written composition.* Urbana, IL: National Conference on Research in English.

HILLOCKS, G. (1987). Synthesis of research on teaching writing. *Educational Leadership, 44,* 71–82.

ISAACSON, S. (1989). Role of secretary vs. author: Resolving the conflict in writing instruction. *Learning Disability Quarterly, 12,* 209–217.

ISAACSON, S. (1991). Written expression and the challenges for students with learning problems. *Exceptionality Education Canada, 1*(3), 45–57.

ISAACSON, S. (1994). Process, product, and purpose: Written expression and the role of instruction. *Reading Research Quarterly 10*(1), 39–62.

ISAACSON, S. (1999). Instructionally relevant writing assessment. *Reading and Writing Quarterly, 15*(1), 29–48.

LANGER, J., & APPLEBEE, A. (1986). Reading and writing instruction: Toward a theory of teaching and learning. In E. Rothkopf (Ed.), *Review of research in education* (Vol. 13, pp. 171–194). Washington, DC: American Educational Research Association.

LEINHARDT, G., ZIGMOND, N., & COOLEY, W. (1980). *Reading instruction and its effects.* Paper presented at the American Educational Research Association Annual Meeting, San Francisco, CA.

MACARTHUR, C. A., GRAHAM, S., & SCHWARTZ, S. (1991). Knowledge of revision and revising behavior among students with learning disabilities. *Learning Disability Quarterly, 14,* 61–73.

MEYER, B. J. F., & FREEDLE, R. O. (1984). Effects of discourse type on recall. *American Education Research Journal, 21,* 121–144.

MONTAGUE, M., MADDUX, C., & DERESHIWSKY, M. I. (1990). Story grammar and comprehension and production of narrative prose by students with learning disabilities. *Journal of Learning Disabilities, 23,* 190–197.

MOROCCO, C., & NEUMAN, S. (1986). Word processors and the acquisition of writing strategies. *Journal of Learning Disabilities, 19,* 243–247.

MOROCCO, C. C., DALTON, B. M., & TIVNAN, T. (1990, April). *The impact of computer-supported writing instruction on the writing quality of 4th grade students with and without learning disabilities.* Paper presented at the Annual Meeting of the American Educational Research Association, Boston.

NATIONAL ASSESSMENT OF EDUCATIONAL PROGRESS. (1993). *What's wrong with writing and what can we do right now?* (Research Report). Washington, DC: Office of Educational Research and Improvement. (ERIC Document Reproduction Service No. ED 356 477)

NODINE, B., BARENBAUM, E., & NEWCOMER, P. (1985). Story composition by learning disabled, reading disabled, and normal children. *Learning Disability Quarterly, 8,* 167–179.

PRAWAT, R. S. (1989). Promoting access to knowledge, strategy, and disposition in students: A research synthesis. *Review of Educational Research, 59*(1), 1–41.

PRESSLEY, M., HARRIS, K. R., & MARKS, M. B. (1992). But good strategy instructors are constructivists! *Educational Psychology Review, 4*(1), 3–31.

PRESSLEY, M., SYMONS, S., SNYDER, B. B., & CARIGLIA-BULL, T. (1989). Strategy instruction research comes of age. *Learning Disability Quarterly, 12,* 16–31.

RAPHAEL, T., & ENGLERT, C. S. (1990, February). Writing and reading: Partners in construction meaning. *The Reading Teacher, 43*(6), 388–400.

ROIT, M., & McKENZIE, R. (1985). Disorders of written communication: An instructional priority for LD students. *Journal of Learning Disabilities, 18,* 258–260.

SCARDAMALIA, M. (1981). How children cope with the cognitive demands of writing. In C. H. Frederiksen (Ed.), *Writing: The nature, development, and teaching of written communication. Vol. 2, Writing: process, development, and communication* (pp. 81–103). Hillsdale, NJ: Erlbaum.

SMITH, F. (1982). *Writing and the writer.* New York: Holt, Rinehart and Winston.

THOMAS, C., ENGLERT, C. C., & GREGG, S. (1987). An analysis of errors and strategies in the expository writing of learning disabled students. *Remedial and Special Education, 8,* 21–30.

TORGESON, J. K. (1988). Studies of children with learning disabilities who perform poorly on memory span tasks. *Journal of Learning Disabilities, 21,* 605–612.

CHAPTER 6

Effective Strategies for Teaching Mathematics

Mark K. Harniss
University of Washington, Tacoma

Douglas W. Carnine
University of Oregon

Jerry Silbert
University of Oregon

Robert C. Dixon
JP Associates

THE PERFORMANCE OF students in math and science has always been a high priority in the United States, but the successful launching of the Russian satellite *Sputnik* in 1957 mobilized resources in an unprecedented way. In 1958, Congress responded to the perceived threat to American security and competitiveness by passing the National Defense Education Act to increase support for education in math, science, and languages.

Interestingly, the U.S. Department of Defense (DoD) included 10.3 million dollars in its FY 2006 budget for a new National Defense Education Act (DoD, 2005) and business and community leaders are once again making reference to *Sputnik*. Many have suggested that America needs another "*Sputnik* moment" to rally and focus resources toward improving outcomes in math and science (Leath, 2005). For example, the American Electronics Association recently released a document entitled "Losing the Competitive Advantage: The Challenge for Science and Technology in the United States" (Kazmierczach, James, & Archey, 2005). Their argument broadly addresses U.S. competitiveness in a global economy, but includes the concern that U.S. students will be unable to participate in a technological society without an increased emphasis on math and science. In a similar vein, Bill Gates, chairman of Microsoft, in a speech focused on the failure of American high schools, remarked that

> When I compare our high schools to what I see when I'm traveling abroad, I am terrified for our workforce of tomorrow. In math and science, our 4th graders are among the top students in the world. By 8th grade, they're in the middle of the pack. By 12th grade, U.S. students are scoring near the bottom of all industrialized nations. (Gates, 2005)

Gates is likely referring to the Trends in International Mathematics and Science Studies (National Center for Educational Statistics, 2003). The 1995 TIMSS showed significant performance gaps between American students and students in other countries (e.g., gaps of 1.5 standard deviations between American students and students in Singapore) with twelfth graders performing significantly below the international average. The 1999 and 2003 administrations of the TIMSS were conducted only in fourth and eighth grades, in part due to concerns about comparability at the twelfth-grade level across international school systems. The 2003 TIMSS shows American students in the fourth and eighth grades performing above the international average with no change for fourth graders between the 1999 and 2003 administration, but significant improvement for eighth graders.

Another national measure of student performance in math is the National Assessment of Educational Progress (NAEP). There are two types of NAEP assessments. The long-term trend assessment of the NAEP uses a set of questions developed in the early 1970s. In contrast, the main, or national, NAEP assessment is updated every decade to reflect more current classroom expectations. The national NAEP assessment is likely a better reflection of students' performance on contemporary mathematics (National Council of Teachers of Mathematics, 2000); however it does not allow for comparison over time.

Findings from the 2003 NAEP suggest that fourth and eighth graders improved in their mathematics performance and that this result was true for low, middle, and high performers (Braswell, Daane, & Grigg, 2003). Twenty-three percent of fourth graders, and 32 percent of eighth graders performed below basic level for their grades. Thirty-two percent of fourth graders and 29 percent of eighth graders scored at proficient or above.

The long-term trend assessment of the NAEP was administered in 2004 and shows that younger students continue to improve, while older students' scores have remained stable. Specifically, the trend for students at the ages of 9 and 13 has been positive at each measurement point (administered in 1973 and 1999), whereas 17-year-old students' scores have not changed measurably across those years. As Loveless and Diperna (2000) noted, "Clearly, the story is not one of disastrous decline. Slow and steady gains are being made. Nor is it cause for national celebration" (p. 6).

Unlike the area of beginning reading, where research findings have begun to coalesce enough to generate broad consensus (e.g., National Research Council, 1998), mathematics education lacks the research base to provide broadly generalizable answers. High quality research is particularly lacking on the topic of low-achieving learners who struggle to learn math (Baker, Gersten, & Lee, 2002). However, there is an increased focus on mathematics research and practice. For example, the National Research Council has published two summaries of mathematics research (Donovan & Bransford, 2005; Kilpatrick, Swafford, & Findell, 2001). In both documents, the authors reach similar conclusions about the need for a comprehensive approach to supporting students in achieving mathematical proficiency. Kilpatrick et al. (2001) suggest that proficiency develops out of five intertwining strands: (a) conceptual understanding, (b) procedural fluency, (c) strategic competence, (d) adaptive reasoning, and (e) a productive disposition. Donovan and Bransford (2005) condense this to three learning principles for teachers. First, teachers must be aware of students' preconceptions and be willing to activate those preconceptions and link them to new knowledge. Second, teachers need to understand that competence in an area requires both conceptual and factual knowledge. Finally, teachers need to provide assistance to students in developing the metacognitive strategies that support students in monitoring their learning and progress. These frameworks are consonant with the principles described in this book.

This chapter describes considerations for improving instruction for learners at diverse performance levels that are important for all teachers, regardless of the "tradition" they place themselves within. Many of the examples in this chapter are taken from a mathematics program designed to accommodate diverse learners, *Connecting Math Concepts* (Engelmann, Carnine, Kelly, & Engelmann, 1994). Others are taken from Liping Ma's (1999) recent text comparing the practices and knowledge base of American and Chinese educators: *Knowing and Teaching Elementary Mathematics*. Improved instruction alone cannot meet all the challenges that the needs of such learners present. However, the contribution of improved instruction can be enormous and plays a central role in any serious school improvement effort. While these considerations also contribute to the learning of average and above-average students, the considerations are particularly important for diverse learners. The first consideration—organizing content around big ideas—is particularly beneficial for all students, including high-performing students. The focus of this chapter, then, can be thought of as specific recommendations for developing instruction that meets the needs of diverse students.

PRINCIPLES FOR IMPROVING MATH INSTRUCTION STRATEGIES

Designing Instruction Around Big Ideas

Educational tools that are going to facilitate students reaching world-class standards should be organized around big ideas (or fundamental knowledge or root meanings) because these represent major organizing principles, have rich explanatory and predictive power, help frame significant questions, and are applicable in many situations and contexts. In their Principles and Standards in School Mathematics, the National Council of Teachers of Mathematics (NCTM) authors note, "Foundational ideas like place value, equivalence, proportionality, function, and rate of change should have a prominent place in the mathematics curriculum because they enable students to understand other mathematical ideas and connect ideas across different areas of mathematics" (p. 15).

Many of these big ideas are not complex, nor difficult to understand at face value. The difficulty comes in knowing when they apply and how their application changes over time. It is the interweaving of these ideas that provides mathematical power to students. For example, the four operations (addition, subtraction, multiplication, and division) rest upon a limited set of big ideas. These ideas include place value, the distributive, commutative, and associative principles, equivalence, and number sense (primarily the concept of composition and decomposition of numbers in a base 10 system [Ma, 1999]). These big ideas interweave through the teaching and learning of the operations. When they are clearly understood by teacher and student, they serve as the conceptual underpinnings for understanding the operations. In Table 6–1, we define and provide an example of each concept.

When the big ideas described in Table 6–1 are used together, they serve as powerful tools for learners to use in tackling the four basic operations ($+$, $-$, $\times$ and $\div$). For example, when students begin adding numbers in addition that require renaming, they engage in the process of composing numbers of higher value. For example, in the following problem students should understand several things. First, when they add the 7 ones from the top number to the 9 ones from the bottom number, they compose a number (i.e., 16) that is made up of one 10 and 6 ones. With their understanding of *place value*, they will know that the one 10 cannot assume the same place (i.e., column) as the 6 ones; rather it must be placed in the tens column. With their understanding of the commutative and associative properties, they will know that they can add the one 10 to the 3 tens in the tens column (i.e., $30 + (7 + 9) = 30 + 16$ and $30 + 16 = (30 + 10) + 6$).

$$\begin{array}{r} 37 \\ +9 \\ \hline 46 \end{array}$$

In subtraction, the inverse is true. In the following question, learners must note that they cannot take 7 ones away from 4 ones, but they can expand the number 34 into 3 tens and 4 ones, decompose the 3 tens by taking one of the tens and adding

TABLE 6–1
Big Ideas in Operations

Big Idea	Example
Place value: The "place" a number holds in a sequence of numbers gives information about that number.	In the number 265, the 2 at the beginning of the number is a hundreds number. We know that the placement of the 2 tells us that there are two units of 100, or two 100s, in that number. Similarly, the location of the 6 tells us that there are 6 units of 10 in the number.
Expanded notation: The reduction of a number to its constituent units.	The number 213 is composed of two 100s, one 10, and three 1s, which can be represented in an equation as $100 + 100 + 10 + 1 + 1 + 1 = 213$ or conversely as $200 + 10 + 3 = 213$.
Commutative property: The order in which numbers are placed in the equation can be changed without affecting the outcome. $a + b = b + a$	Addition and multiplication are commutative: In addition, $3 + 4 = 7$ and $4 + 3 = 7$ In multiplication, $4 \times 5 = 20$ and $5 \times 4 = 20$. Subtraction and division are not commutative: In subtraction, $5 - 3 = 2$ and $3 - 5 = -2$ In division, $6 \div 3 = 2$ and $3 \div 6 = 0.5$.
Associative property: The groupings in which numbers are placed in the equation can be changed without affecting the outcome. $(a + b) + c = a + (b + c)$	Addition and multiplication are associative: In addition, $(2 + 4) + 5 = 11$ and $2 + (4 + 5) = 11$ In multiplication, $(3 \times 2) \times 5 = 30$ and $3 \times (2 \times 5) = 30$. Subtraction and division are not associative: In subtraction, $(15 - 3) - 5 = 7$ and $15 - (3 - 5) = 13$ In division, $(32 \div 8) \div 2 = 2$ and $32 \div (8 \div 2) = 8$.
Distributive property: Numbers in an equation involving multiple operations can be distributed. $a \times (b + c) = (a \times b) + (a \times c)$ You can also distribute numbers in an equation that includes division and subtraction or addition. $(a + b) \div c = (a \div c) + (b \div c)$	$5 \times (3 + 2) = (5 \times 3) + (5 \times 2)$ $(8 + 4) \div 2 = (8 \div 2) + (4 \div 2)$

(continued)

TABLE 6–1 *(continued)*

Big Idea	Example
Equivalence: The quantity to the left of the equal sign (=) is the same as the quantity to the right.	$32 + 15 = 47$ $16 + 16 + 15 = 47$ $8 + 8 + 8 + 8 + (5 \times 3) = 20 + 20 + 7$ *Note:* Many students interpret the equal sign as an operation (e.g., "when I see the equal sign I add, subtract, etc.") rather than as a relationship (e.g., "when I see the equal sign I know that the quantity on one side must be the same as the other side").
Rate of composition/decomposition (Ma, 1999): A form of number sense. The rate of composition (or decomposition) of sets of numbers in our base 10 system is simply 10.	When you have accumulated 10 ones you have one 10. When you have accumulated 10 tens you have one 100 and so on. This concept is sometimes referred to as *unitizing*, that is, creating a tens unit from 10 ones. Similarly, when you remove a 1 from a 10 you have 9 ones, that is you have decomposed the 10.

it to the 4 ones (ideally with an understanding of the associative property, i.e., $(20 + 14) - 7 = 34 - 7$) and finally subtracting 7 ones from 14 leaving 7 ones.

$$\begin{array}{r} 34 \\ -17 \\ \hline 17 \end{array}$$

In multidigit multiplication, these ideas are most powerful in helping learners understand the commonly taught shortcut for multiplying larger numbers. Typically, students might be taught to simply cross multiply without a strong understanding of why they are using this strategy. In fact, in Ma's (1999) study, many U.S. teachers did not understand why the cross multiplication strategy worked. The answer, however, is quite simple if a learner comprehends the underlying concepts. First, learners need to understand the difference between multiplication and the problems they have been previously working in subtraction and addition. Whereas these latter two operations involve the removal of one set of numbers from another set or the combination of two sets together, multiplication is the combination of a number of sets each containing the same number of elements into a larger set. In the problems 345×32, a learner is combining 345 sets each containing 32 elements to identify one larger set of items. With smaller numbers, a learner could add the number of elements in a set for the number of sets (for example $3 \times 4 = 12$ could be translated into $4 + 4 + 4 = 12$). But with larger numbers, this approach rapidly becomes tedious. Because each of the 345 sets includes 32 elements, a student cannot simply multiply the number in the ones column vertically as they would have if they were adding them. Multiplying down the columns would result in an answer that would be far too small and inaccurate. With their understanding of place value and expanded notation, they can note that in this problem there are 3 tens and 2 ones in the multiplicand. Their understanding of the distributive property supports them in multiplying $(345 \times 2) + (345 \times 30)$ or conversely $(5 \times 2) + (40 \times 2) + (300 \times 2) + (5 \times 30) + (40 \times 30) + (300 \times 30)$.

$$
\begin{array}{r}
345 \\
\times 32 \\
\hline
10 \\
80 \\
600 \\
150 \\
1200 \\
+9000 \\
\hline
11040
\end{array}
$$

This strategy can be a helpful transition to the more commonly used multiplication strategy since it highlights the underlying logic of the algorithm. Notice that this strategy removes the need to rename. The more commonly taught algorithm is a simplification of this procedure. Students can use their understanding of the associative property to group the products together before adding them.

$$
\begin{array}{r}
345 \\
\times 32 \\
\hline
690 \\
+10350 \\
\hline
11040
\end{array}
$$

Division, of course, is the inverse of multiplication. Although the form of division problems is different, the underlying big ideas are consistent. Students must learn that division involves separating a larger set into equivalent sized subsets (i.e., measurement division) or conversely separating a larger set into a given number of sets (partitive division) (Stein, Silbert, & Carnine, 1997). In solving even simple multidigit division problems, students must integrate a number of different big ideas. In the following problem, for example:

$$
\begin{array}{r}
508 \\
9\overline{)4572} \\
45 \\
\hline
0 \\
72 \\
-72 \\
\hline
0
\end{array}
$$

The distributive property supports the understanding that $(4500 \div 9) + (72 \div 9) = 508$. Students understanding of place value helps them place numbers in the appropriate columns.

The big ideas discussed above are commonly known, although not frequently clearly taught. Often, however, big ideas in mathematics are not at all clear. For example, in geometry, students are typically expected to learn seven formulas to calculate the volume of seven three-dimensional figures:

Rectangular prism: $1 \times w \times h = v$
Wedge: $1/2 \times 1 \times w \times h = v$
Triangular pyramid: $1/6 \times 1 \times w \times h = v$
Cylinder: $\pi \times r^2 \times h = v$
Rectangular pyramid: $1/3 \times 1 \times w \times h = v$
Cone: $1/3 \times \pi \times r^2 \times h = v$
Sphere: $4/3 \times \pi \times r^3 = v$

These equations emphasize rote formulas rather than big ideas. An analysis based on big ideas reduces the number of formulas students must learn from seven to slight variations of a single formula—area of the base times the height ($B \times h$). This approach enhances understanding while simultaneously reducing the quantity of content to be learned, remembered, and applied. (See Figure 6–1.)

For the regular figures in Figure 6–1—the rectangular prism (box), the wedge, and the cylinder—the volume is the area of the base times the height ($B \times h$). For figures that come to a point—the pyramid with a rectangular base, the pyramid with

FIGURE 6–1
Volume as the "Big Idea" of Area of the Base Times a Multiple of the Height

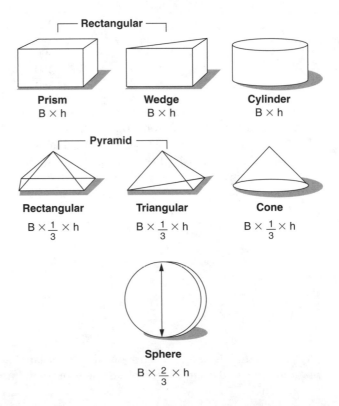

a triangular base, and the cone—the volume is not the area of the base times the height, but the area of the base times 1/3 of the height (B × 1/3 × h). The sphere is a special case: the area of the base times 2/3 of the height (B × 2/3 × h), where the base is the area of a circle that passes through the center of the sphere and the height is the diameter. This analysis of root meaning fosters understanding of the big idea that volume is a function of the area of the base times some multiple of the height. As Gelman (1986) stated, "a focus on different algorithmic instantiations of a set of principles helps teach children that procedures that seem very different on the surface can share the same mathematical underpinning and, hence, root meanings" (p. 350).

Designing Conspicuous Strategies

When students orchestrate multiple concepts in some fashion, they are executing a strategy. Any routine that leads to both the acquisition and utilization of knowledge can be considered a strategy (Prawat, 1989). While the ultimate purpose of a strategy is meaningful application, acquisition is most reliable for diverse learners when initial instruction explicitly focuses on the strategy itself, rather than its meaningful application.

Consider, for example, the following problem, presented to each fifth-grade class in a school:

> *At lunch, each student can choose a carton of white or chocolate milk. Estimate how many cartons of chocolate and white milk should be ordered for the entire school.*

For students to work such problems successfully, they must have both computational ability and well-developed strategies for data gathering, proportions, and probability that are relevant to a broad range of real mathematical problems.

In contrast to such well-developed strategies, strategies may be so specific and narrow in application that they are little more than a rote sequence for solving a particular problem or a very small set of highly similar problems. For example, in a study by McDaniel and Schlager (1990) on water-jar problem solving, students in one of the teaching conditions learned a rote formula for adding and removing amounts of water with different-sized jars (+1 −2 +1), which, predictably, did not transfer well to solving other water-jar problems.

Too often, mathematics knowledge appears to be rote. Davis (1990) points out that "traditional school practice" tests mainly the ability to repeat back what has been told or demonstrated. There are really two significant problems with the traditional school practice that Davis described. First, such practice is often directed toward *small ideas*—for example, arbitrary procedures such as cross multiplying to solve problems like x/a = b/c. Second, such procedures are frequently "repeated back" for rote recall, effectively preempting the possibility that students will even infer the important mathematical principles underlying them.

At the other extreme, a strategy may be so general that it is little more than a broad set of guidelines. Such strategies may be better than nothing, but they do not dependably lead most students to solutions for most problems. For instance, a broad strategy such as *draw a picture* or *read, analyze, plan, and solve* is probably far too general for reliably leading a majority of students to reasonable solutions for complex problems such as the milk-ordering problem above.

An important goal for strategy instruction is that the strategies taught are *good* in some sense. Some students develop strategies that are too narrow or too broad, while others develop strategies that are *just right*. A major challenge of instruction—perhaps *the* major challenge—is to develop just-right strategies for interventions with those students who do not develop strategies on their own, including, but not limited to, diverse learners.

Based on an exhaustive review of research, Prawat (1989) recommends that efficient strategy interventions should be intermediate in generality. That is, efficient strategies fall somewhere between the extremes of being narrow in application but, presumably, relatively easy to teach successfully, and being broad but not necessarily reliable or easy to teach. This suggests that the principal feature of a good strategy is that it adheres to the Law of Parsimony as it applies to evaluating competing theories: "That theory is best that explains the most in the simplest way" (Mouly, 1978). As applied specifically to evaluating strategies, the Law of Parsimony might read: The best strategy results in the greatest number of students successfully solving the greatest number of problems or completing the broadest range of tasks by applying the fewest possible strategic steps.

When experts implement strategies to acquire and utilize knowledge, only the result is overt; the steps in the strategy the experts follow are covert. The whole purpose of developing instructional strategies is to explicate expert cognitive processes so that they become visible to nonexpert learners. The research support for explicitly teaching conspicuous strategies is quite strong (Gleason, Carnine, & Boriero, 1990; Leinhardt, 1987; Resnick, Cauzinille-Marmeche, & Mathieu, 1987; Resnick & Omanson, 1987; Tournaki, 2003).

An example of a conspicuous strategy for the volume formula follows. Note that the first step prompts the connection with a more concrete representation of volume in which students can count the cubes in a figure. Step 2 introduces the strategy. In Step 3, the teacher does not assist the students because they have already been taught to compute the area of a rectangle. In contrast, Step 4 calls for a new calculation, so the teacher is more directive.

1. *Linkage to prior knowledge.* "Touch box A. You know how to figure out its volume. Count the cubes and write the volume. What did you write? Yes, 50 cubic meters."
2. *Introduction of new strategy.* "Touch box B. You're going to learn how to calculate the volume by multiplying the area of the base times the height."
3. *Computing the area of the base.* "First calculate the area of the base for box B."
4. *Computing the volume.* "To figure out the volume of the box, you multiply the area of the base times the height. What are the two numbers you will multiply? Yes, 6×7."
5. *Writing the complete answer.* Write the answer with the appropriate unit. What did you write? Yes, 42 cubic inches.
   a. Count the cubes:
   b. Multiply the area of the base times the height:

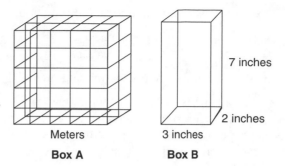

Box A   Box B

The applicability of the big idea for volume with variations of a single strategy for three-dimensional figures is obvious. In contrast, it is not at all obvious how a single big idea with variations of a strategy could link the following six problems:

1. Five packages of punch mix make 4 gallons. How many gallons of punch can Juan make for the party with 15 packages?
2. How long will it take a train to go 480 miles to Paris if it travels at 120 mph?
3. What is the average rate of a car that goes 450 miles in 9 hours?
4. How many pounds is 8 kilograms?
5. The oil transferred from the storage area has filled 44 tanks. There are 50 tanks. What percentage of the tanks are full?
6. There are 52 cards in a deck. Thirteen of them are hearts. The rest are not hearts. If you took trials (drew a card and then replaced it) until you drew 26 hearts, about how many trials would you expect to take?

However, it is with such seemingly unrelated problem types that a strategy based on a big idea is most valuable, particularly with learners for whom such connections usually remain elusive. The big idea that connects these different problems types is *proportions*. Proportion and ratio have been shown to be foundational concepts that support student learning in fractions, decimals, and percentages (Vergnaud, 1988). The strategy for proportions must be applied to each problem type in a systematic manner, to make clear that the same big idea underlies these very different problems. The application of proportions is most obvious in the first problem:

Five packages of punch mix make 4 gallons. How many gallons of punch can Juan make with fifteen packages?

A medium-level strategy for proportions might first have students map the units:

$$\frac{\text{packages}}{\text{gallons}}$$

Next, students insert the relevant information:

$$\frac{\text{packages}}{\text{gallons}} \quad \frac{5}{4} = \frac{15}{\square}$$

Finally, students solve for the missing quantity: *12 gallons*

Rate problems, which are not typically viewed as proportion problems, also can be solved through a proportion strategy. Note that the key to setting up rate problems as proportions is realizing that the ration in the proportion is a number of distance units over a single unit of time. This principle is applicable to solving the second problem:

How long will it take a train to go 480 miles to Paris if it travels at 120 mph?

First, map the units. The abbreviation mph can be represented as:

$$\frac{\text{miles}}{\text{hour}}$$

Next, insert the relevant information:

$$\frac{\text{miles}}{\text{hour}} \quad \frac{120}{1} = \frac{480}{\square}$$

Finally, solve for the answer: *4 hours*

In the next rate problem, students solve for the average rate:

What is the average rate of a car that goes 450 miles in 9 hours?

Map the units:

$$\frac{\text{miles}}{\text{hour}}$$

Insert the relevant information:

$$\frac{\text{miles}}{\text{hour}} \quad \frac{\square}{1} = \frac{450}{9}$$

Solve for the answer: *50 miles per hour*

Another application of proportions occurs with measurement equivalences. The key to this problem type is that students set up a ratio between the two units involved in the equivalence.

How many pounds is 8 kilograms?

Map the units:

$$\frac{\text{pounds}}{\text{kilograms}}$$

Insert the relevant information:

$$\frac{\text{pounds}}{\text{kilograms}} \quad \frac{2.2}{1} = \frac{\Box}{8}$$

Solve for the answer: *17.6 pounds*

Similarly, percent problems can be set up as proportions. For percents, the key to treating them as proportions is labeling the second ratio as telling about the percentage and pointing out that the denominator of the percentage ratio, which is almost always unstated, is 100.

The oil transferred from the storage area has filled 44 tanks. There are 50 tanks. What percentage of the tanks are full?

Map the units:

$$\frac{\text{filled tanks}}{\text{total tanks}}$$

Insert the relevant information:

$$\frac{\text{filled tanks}}{\text{total tanks}} \quad \frac{44}{55} = \overset{\text{percent}}{\frac{\Box}{100}}$$

Solve for the answer: *88 percent*

With the following, more difficult percentage problem, the proportion strategy makes the problem quite manageable, even for students with learning difficulties.

The oil transferred from the storage area filled 44 tanks. So far, 88% of the oil in the storage area has been transferred into tanks. How many tanks will be filled when all the oil is transferred from the storage area?

Map the units:

$$\frac{\text{filled tanks}}{\text{total tanks}}$$

Insert the relevant information:

$$\frac{\text{filled tanks}}{\text{total tanks}} \quad \frac{44}{\Box} = \overset{\text{percent}}{\frac{88}{100}}$$

Solve for the answer: *50 tanks*

The next problem type, illustrating odds and probability, also has a key for tying it to proportions: Setting up a ratio of one type of member to another type or to the total number of members. In the example that follows, the one type of winning trials is related to the total trials.

There are 52 cards in a deck. Thirteen of them are hearts. The rest are not hearts. If you took trials (drew a card and then replaced it) until you drew 26 hearts, about how many trials would you expect to take?

Map the units:

$$\frac{\text{hearts}}{\text{trials}}$$

Insert the relevant information:

$$\frac{\text{hearts}}{\text{trials}} \quad \frac{13}{52} = \frac{26}{\square}$$

Solve for the answer: *104 trials*

The next connection to be illustrated with proportions involves the coordinate system. Proportions can link simple proportion problems—rate, measurement equivalence, percentage, and probability—to the coordinate system. This linkage is illustrated in the graphs for each problem type in Figure 6–2. The concept of functions is also apparent in Figure 6–2. A function table accompanies each graph in the figure.

Finally, let's revisit the milk-ordering problem discussed previously. In this problem, students integrate the advanced proportion strategy with data gathering and probability-statistics strategies. (See Figure 6–3.) The students apply data gathering strategies—determining the ratio of chocolate milk to white milk for their class and finding out the total enrollment of the school. The students then invoke the advanced proportions strategy: mapping the relevant information. The fifth graders would need to assume that the preference for types of milk in their class represents the whole school's preference, which entails applying the concept of sampling from statistics and probability. Finally, the concept of missing addends is invoked to solve for the number for white milk.

Many subtle variations are possible with a problem like this, but all are accommodated through the integrated strategies illustrated in Figure 6–3. One variation might be to use average attendance instead of total enrollment, which would cut down on milk ordered (and wasted). In another variation, students might have reason to believe that the preferences in their own class would not be representative of the entire school. The students could gather data from different classes, work the problem, compare the results, and discuss variations in solutions based on different samples. As a final variation, the students could compare results with actual figures on milk ordered to predict shortages or excesses of each type of milk.

The milk-ordering problem and its variations illustrate how goals of the NCTM—working together to enhance understanding, engage in conjecture and invention, and connect mathematical ideas—can be effectively met for diverse learners through conspicuous instruction in medium-level strategies based on big ideas. As students discuss their options for selecting a sample group, they are working together to enhance their understanding of mathematics. As they weigh the relative merits of using total enrollment versus average attendance, they are engaging in conjecture and invention.

Five packages of punch mix make 4 gallons. Fifteen packages would make how many gallons of punch?

$$\frac{\text{packages}}{\text{gallons}} \quad \frac{5}{4} = \frac{15}{\square}$$

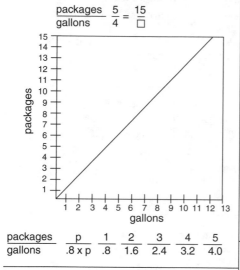

packages	p	1	2	3	4	5
gallons	.8 x p	.8	1.6	2.4	3.2	4.0

How many pounds is 5 kilograms?

$$\frac{\text{pounds}}{\text{kilograms}} \quad \frac{2.2}{1} = \frac{\square}{5}$$

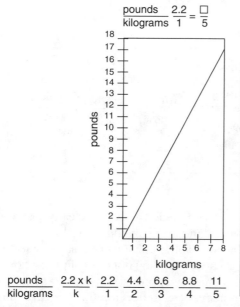

pounds	2.2 x k	2.2	4.4	6.6	8.8	11
kilograms	k	1	2	3	4	5

How long will it take a train to go 480 miles to Rome if it travels at 120 mph?

$$\frac{\text{miles}}{\text{hour}} \quad \frac{120}{1} = \frac{480}{\square}$$

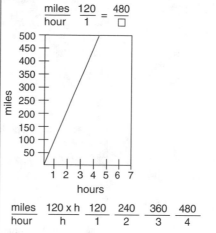

miles	120 x h	120	240	360	480
hour	h	1	2	3	4

There are 52 cards in a deck. Thirteen of these are hearts. The rest are not hearts. If you took trials (drew a card and then replaced it) until you drew 26 hearts, about how many trials would you expect to take?

$$\frac{\text{hearts}}{\text{trials}} \quad \frac{13}{52} = \frac{26}{\square}$$

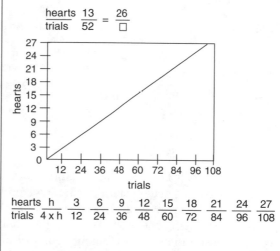

hearts	h	3	6	9	12	15	18	21	24	27
trials	4 x h	12	24	36	48	60	72	84	96	108

FIGURE 6–2
Using Proportions to Link Multiple Concepts to the Coordinate System

FIGURE 6–3
Data Gathering, Advanced Proportions, and Probability Statistics Strategies

Step 1: Data Gathering The students conduct a survey in their class to determine the preferences for white and chocolate milk. The students also find out from the office the total enrollment for the school.	There are 32 students in the class; 22 prefer chocolate milk and the rest prefer white. There are 479 students in the school.

Step 2: Advanced Proportions
The students map the units for the advanced proportions strategy and insert the relevant information.

	Fifth-grade class	*Entire school*
Chocolate	22	☐
White	10	☐
Total	32	479

Step 3: Probability and Statistics
The students solve a proportion to estimate the number of chocolate milk cartons to purchase for the entire school:

$$\frac{22}{32} = \frac{\boxed{329}}{479}$$

Chocolate	22	329
White	10	☐
Total	32	479

Step 4: Missing Addends
The students determine the estimate for white milk using their knowledge of missing addends:

$$479 - 329 = 150$$

Chocolate	22	329
White	10	150
Total	32	479

As they link their understandings of various strategies, they are clearly learning to connect mathematical ideas, solve problems, and apply mathematics broadly.

The application of the proportion big idea with variations of a strategy for these problem contexts will deepen the student's understanding not only of proportions but also of rate, measurement equivalencies, percentage, probability, the coordinate system, and functions. One of the most important ways to develop this understanding is through learning how various concepts are linked by a single strategy. In other words, a deep understanding of proportions is constructed by applying the strategy across many contexts. For this reason, the application of a strategy can be thought of as more important in developing understanding and proficiency than how the meaning of a strategy is initially constructed. These applications do far more to develop deep understanding than allowing students to initially construct their own meaning for proportions in authentic activities. Becoming proficient at authentic activities is far more important than starting out with authentic activities.

Designing Mediated Scaffolding

British educator A. J. Romiszowski has characterized traditional mathematics instruction as: "I'll work two on the board, then you do the rest." The "I'll work two" part of that approach can be thought of as a model, and the "you do the rest" is considered immediate testing. It has been said that the problem with learning from experience is that the lessons come too late. The same could be said of this traditional model of instruction. After *doing the rest,* students might receive feedback, ranging from right/wrong, to an explanation of how to do missed problems, and possibly a grade. The feedback is too late and the grade too early.

Scaffolding is a means by which students receive support in various forms along the path to full understanding and doing the rest successfully. Along the way, teachers would remove more bits of scaffolding, but in no instance would they abruptly remove all the scaffolding and, in essence say, "You do the rest." For example, after modeling the formula the teacher would not have the students do the rest. Instead, the teacher would scaffold the steps of the strategy, initially giving students feedback after every step. The steps for a scaffolded volume strategy involving a cone 5 inches tall with a radius of 1.6 inches might take this form:

1. "Write the formula for the volume of the figure."

   Students write: $B \times 1/3 \times h$

2. "Calculate the area of the base for that figure."

   Students write: $3.14 \, (1.6)^2 = 8.04$

3. "Calculate the volume."

   Students write: $8.04 \times 1/3 \times 5 = 13.4$

4. "Write the complete answer with the appropriate unit."

   Students write: 13.4 cubic inches.

This level of scaffolding is specific enough to be useful but general enough to be used flexibly with all three-dimensional figures. One test for flexibility is the degree to which the strategy can be applied to seemingly different problem types, as was illustrated earlier with proportions. This flexibility is also the means by which students come to understand how various big ideas can be linked, such as proportions, functions, and the coordinate system.

Clearly, an important part of scaffolding a task appropriately is to accurately determine students' prerequisite knowledge and target the task toward their instructional level. Vygotsky (1978) uses the term *zone of proximal development* to describe situations in which students' cognitive ability matches the cognitive requirements demanded by an instructional activity. The importance of designing educational strategies scaffolded to match students' zone of proximal development is critical to ensuring that students benefit from instruction and that the instructional experiences enhance the students' self-esteem.

Designing Primed Background Knowledge

In all of the proportion examples given in the conspicuous strategies section, a strategy is applied to a variety of concepts. The concepts to which the proportions strategy is applied—rate, percentage, measurement, probability—are assumed to have been introduced previously. Similarly, when proportions are linked to other big ideas—coordinate system and functions—these big ideas would need to have been taught. Without such prior knowledge, the application of proportions could be a rote activity, extending students' understanding of neither the proportions strategy, nor the concepts to which the strategy is applied, nor the other big ideas to which the strategy is linked. Similarly, the strategy for volume assumes certain prior knowledge on the part of the students: an understanding of the concept of area as well as computational proficiency, e.g., squaring a number and then multiplying by π.

Teachers and curriculum developers should also be aware of the need for important background knowledge to be *primed;* that is, students will need to be reminded of what they know and shown how and when previous knowledge supports the learning of new knowledge. This explicit linking of old to new knowledge is critical in helping students develop rich conceptual networks of mathematical knowledge.

Providing students with both the necessary background knowledge and flexible strategies based on big ideas that can link that knowledge is possibly the best way to prepare diverse learners for the challenges posed by the new NCTM *Standards.* Instruction should purposefully demonstrate a broad range of mathematics applications for students and enable them to successfully engage in such applications by providing the necessary prior knowledge.

Designing Strategic Integration

As the NCTM (2000) notes:

> In planning individual lessons, teachers should strive to organize the mathematics so that fundamental ideas form an integrated whole. Big ideas encountered in a variety of contexts should be established carefully, with important elements such as terminology, definitions, notation, concepts, and skills emerging in the process. (p. 15)

The previous discussion of the big ideas underpinning the four operations (rate, measurement equivalency, percent, and odds and probability) is a good example of how important ideas gain power when students learn how they are applied across the domain of mathematics. Students learn that the idea stays the same, but its implementation and use changes across the four operations.

The same concept is true for students' understanding and use of strategies. Students must not only understand important mathematical strategies as entities, but must also learn the relationships among strategies leading to an integrated, cohesive strategy (Nickerson, 1985; Prawat, 1989; Van Patten, Chao, & Reigeluth, 1986). It is conceivable that a student could learn several "good" strategies but not know when to apply them. However, instruction on individual strategies can be designed to anticipate situations in which several strategies are integrated, a practice also consistent with Piaget's (1973) model of assimilation of the new to the old and accommodation of the old to the new.

For example, if diverse learners are going to have opportunities to successfully engage in solving novel problems, they must not only be able to apply a strategy such as that for proportions but also be able to know when *not* to apply the particular strategy. Understanding involves knowing when a strategy applies and when it does not. Developing such understanding in diverse learners requires integrated teaching, not in the broad sense of interdisciplinary teaching, but within a discipline. Teaching for integration within mathematics can be illustrated with the proportion strategy. Problem A is a fairly straightforward proportion problem:

Problem A. A truck delivers cartons of juice to a store. Two sevenths of the juice is grape. The truck has 8400 cartons of juice. How many are grape juice?

Map the units: $\dfrac{\text{Grape}}{\text{Total}}$

Insert the relevant information:

$$\begin{array}{cc} & \textit{Ratio} & \textit{Juice Cartons} \\ \dfrac{\text{Grape}}{\text{Total}} & \dfrac{2}{7} = \dfrac{\boxed{}}{8400} \end{array}$$

Solve for the answer: *2400 cartons*

If students erroneously apply the same proportion strategy to the numbers in problem B, the answer will also be 2400.

Problem B. A truck delivers cartons of grape and apple juice to a store. Two sevenths of the juice is grape. The truck will deliver 8400 cartons of apple juice. How many cartons of grape juice will the truck deliver?

Map the units: $\dfrac{\text{Grape}}{\text{Total}}$

Insert the relevant information:

$$\begin{array}{cc} & \textit{Ratio} & \textit{Juice Cartons} \\ \dfrac{\text{Grape}}{\text{Total}} & \dfrac{2}{7} = \dfrac{\boxed{2400}}{8400} \end{array}$$

Solve for the answer: *2400 cartons*

FIGURE 6–4
*Advanced
Proportion
Strategy*

A truck delivers cartons of grape and apple juice to a store. Two
sevenths of the juice is grape. The truck will deliver 8400 cartons of
apple juice. How many cartons of grape juice will the truck deliver?

		Ratio	Juice Cartons
Step 1: The students map 3 units, not just 2, and insert the relevant information:	Grape	2	☐
	Apple	☐	8400
	Total	7	☐
Step 2: The students use their know- ledge of missing addends to come up with the unknown value in the ratio column: $7 - 2 = \boxed{5}$	Grape	2	☐
	Apple	$\boxed{5}$	8400
	Total	7	☐
Step 3: The students write and solve the proportion to determine the number of cartons of grape juice: $\dfrac{2}{5} = \dfrac{\boxed{3360}}{8400}$	Grape	2	$\boxed{3360}$
	Apple	$\boxed{5}$	8400
	Total	7	☐

For Problem B, the answer 2400 is *incorrect,* of course, because the 8400 does
not refer to the total number of cartons, but to apple juice cartons.

With integrated teaching, the students would be less likely to inappropriately apply the basic proportion strategy to problem B because an advanced proportion strategy would have been taught to "accommodate" these more complex problem types
that deal with not just two elements (total juice and grape juice), but with three elements (total juice, grape juice, and apple juice). Conversely, the new strategy for three
elements must be *assimilated* with the simpler strategy that handles only two elements.

This accommodation and assimilation is accomplished through an advanced
proportion strategy for three elements. This strategy illustrated in Figure 6–4.

The advanced proportion strategy in Figure 6–4 is in itself a medium-level strategy that can be flexibly applied to more complex mathematics problems, such as
those involving mixtures and discounts. Following is the map for the application of
the advanced proportion strategy to a discount problem:

FIGURE 6–5
Application of Advanced Proportion Strategy Applied to a Mixture Problem

Mixture Problem

A mix contains peanuts and almonds in a ratio of 4 to 3. If 35 pounds of mix are made, how many pounds of almonds will be used?

Step 1: The students map the units and write the known values:		*Ratio*	*Pounds*
	Peanuts	4	☐
	Almonds	3	☐
	Total	☐	35
Step 2: The students use their knowledge of missing addends to come up with the unknown value in the ratio column: $4 + 3 = \boxed{7}$			
	Peanuts	4	☐
	Almonds	3	☐
	Total	$\boxed{7}$	35
Step 3: The students write and solve the proportion to determine the number of pounds of almonds: $\dfrac{3}{7} = \dfrac{\boxed{15}}{35}$			
	Peanuts	4	$\boxed{20}$
	Almonds	$\boxed{3}$	$\boxed{15}$
	Total	7	35

A shirt was on sale. The discount was $2. The sale price was $18. What percent was the discount?

	Dollars	*Percent*
Sale Price	18	☐
Discount	2	☐
Original Price	☐	100

The application of the complete strategy to a mixture problem is illustrated in Figure 6–5.

Designing Judicious Review

The term "review" can be an emotive one in education, conjuring up images of endless (and, perhaps, mindless) drill and practice. Yet research strongly supports certain review practices as significantly effective (i.e., sufficient, distributed, cumulative, and varied). It can be said that one gets out of review what one puts into it; that is, the quality of instruction—principally in terms of big ideas and strategies—influences the value of review. Regardless of how much review is devoted to "small ideas" or marginally significant material, the ideas remain small and the material, marginally significant. These practices have been discussed in earlier chapters in this book and will not be addressed in detail here.

THE APPLICATION OF INSTRUCTIONAL DESIGN PRINCIPLES

Teachers and instructional developers both play a role in assuring that the tools for teaching mathematics to students are well designed around principles of effective instruction. Teachers primarily engage in the selection and modification of instructional materials. The choices they make in selection of materials and their demands and requests for improved materials create the incentive for those who develop materials to modify and upgrade the materials they produce. The following sections discuss suggestions for developing, selecting, and modifying materials.

Developing Instructional Tools

Instructional tools should be developed to allocate considerable time and space to teaching big ideas crucial to understanding mathematics, as opposed to giving approximately equal resources to the exposure of a multitude of topics or small ideas. Such big ideas would include number families, the identity principle, proportions, volume and area, estimation, and so on. These tools should be developed to provide explicit strategies for learning big ideas. Strategies should not be too narrow because they would likely result in rote learning. Neither should they be too broad, like some common "strategies" for solving verbal problems (e.g., draw a picture).

Some scaffolding, such as peer tutoring or instructional feedback, need not be built into instructional tools, but may instead be part of teachers' professional development training materials. Scaffolded *tasks*, however, should be built into tools. Such tasks are somewhat contrived versions of "outcome" tasks that help students achieve understanding at a reasonable pace. Here is a simple scaffolded task:

$$\_\_\_\_\_ + 2/3 = /12 + /12 = /$$

This task guides students through the strategy for converting fractions before adding.

Instructional tools that provide strong strategic integration do so by developing tasks and activities with a widespread potential for interrelating otherwise dissimilar-appearing mathematical concepts. For example, a well-designed tool might take a proportion strategy that can be applied variously to verbal problems involving rate, measurement equivalencies, percentages, probability, the coordinate system, and functions. The principal benefit of integrating conceptual knowledge this way is that it fosters deep understanding of problem solving. In addition, integrated tasks and activities are useful in relation to those mathematics topics that predictably cause confusion for students.

Developers should address background knowledge by creating assessment tools that determine whether students possess essential background knowledge for learning the strategies taught in a program and provide instruction on essential background knowledge for students with gaps in such knowledge. For diverse learners, it is risky to assume that material taught last year would be fully retained as essential background knowledge for strategies being taught this year.

Publishers do a great service to teachers when they provide plentiful review with instructional tools, because it is infinitely easier for teachers to simply skip review activities than create additional ones. Programs that include well-distributed review are far more efficient than those that do not, and programs with built-in cumulative review promote strategic integration as just described. Review should also be varied to promote transfer.

Selecting Instructional Tools

Teachers can examine mathematics tools to determine the extent to which the majority of time/space is allocated to teaching big ideas. Teachers should then examine tools to see whether conspicuous strategies exist to teach those big ideas. If conspicuous strategies exist at all, teachers should ask whether they generally appear to be intermediate in generality. Teachers should try to imagine themselves as a diverse learner who has to solve verbal problems presented by the tool based *solely* on the taught strategy.

Teachers can evaluate the extent to which scaffolded tasks are built into instructional tools by examining both *model* or *demonstration* tasks associated with a strategy and the tasks students eventually do independently. Are there "in-between" tasks that will help students gradually achieve independence and understanding?

To determine whether a tool strategically integrates important concepts, teachers can examine the scope and sequence of instructional tools, looking specifically to see whether some chapters (or units or lessons) are designated as "cumulative review" or "integration" or "consolidation." In a well-integrated tool the in-program assessments will include tasks representing all topics taught previously, not just those taught immediately preceding the assessment.

One way for teachers to assess the extent to which a tool relates prior information to new information is to dissect strategies for teaching important mathematics big ideas into their component parts. Then examine about 15 days worth of instruction *preceding* the introduction of the strategy to determine whether and how those components are handled. Ideally, components are taught or reviewed a few lessons preceding the introduction of the new strategy. Also, tools should be checked to determine the extent to which assessment tools are in place to identify important gaps in students' background knowledge. In addition, teachers can determine the extent to which a tool provides adequate review by locating a particularly difficult topic in mathematics, such as solving multistep verbal problems, then tracing the review throughout remainder of the program to determine whether review is plentiful, distributed, cumulative, and appropriately varied.

Modifying Instructional Tools

If a tool needs modification, teachers can identify the most important mathematics concepts and principles in existing tools and reallocate instructional time so that those concepts and principles can be taught thoroughly. Note that valid assessment should focus upon the important mathematics concepts selected for thorough instruction.

Teachers can help students who struggle with concepts and principles they are supposed to discover on their own by developing an explicit strategy for those concepts and principles. When strategies are too narrow, such as the "invert and multiply" rule to solve for x in problems of the form x/a = b/c, clearly and fully explain the underlying principles that make such a rule work. Without consuming too much time, teachers can convert independent tasks into scaffolded tasks by providing hints, cues, or prompts for some of the more difficult steps in the strategies associated with those tasks.

Teachers can also improve the effectiveness of tools by identifying common confusions, such as those identified previously and providing students with additional integrated practice centered on them. For instance, if a tool does not provide practice on a mixture of verbal problem types that have been taught previously, teachers can provide it using problems—or minor modifications of problems—from the instructional tool.

If teachers have the opportunity to analyze important strategies in advance of their introduction to students, they can provide some essential background knowledge based upon that analysis. For example, teachers can review the concept of area and make the connection between area and base before teaching a strategy for understanding volume. Teachers should also examine student errors carefully to determine whether they may be due largely to lack of background knowledge. If necessary, teachers can modify programs to improve the judiciousness of review principally by (a) taking a long set of tasks and distributing them over a period of days, and (b) making review cumulative. However, it can be quite time-consuming for teachers to modify programs to make review *appropriately* varied—that is, varied enough to avoid rote practice, but not so varied that it presses students to perform outside of the limits of strategies they have been taught.

SUMMARY

McCaffrey, Hamilton, Stecher, and Klein's (2001) work shows that teachers who used "reform" practices within traditional curricula were not as successful as teachers who used reform practices within reform curricula. "This finding suggests that efforts to provide professional development for teachers need to consider curriculum and instructional practices in combinations. Simple prescriptions for how to teach are unlikely to be effective" (p. 14). Instructional tools must be developed to assist teachers as they work to develop conceptual learning among students. Teachers who do not leave their preparatory programs with the depth of understanding needed for this task need the support and scaffolding provided by high quality, well-designed instructional materials.

The design considerations for mathematics presented in this chapter have significance for those working directly with students and for those developing and publishing mathematics instructional materials. Specifically, these individuals should develop or select tools for teaching mathematics in which:

- *Big ideas* are explicitly described and manifested through a wide range of appropriate content;
- *Strategies* are of an intermediate level of generality and explicitly described and utilized across a range of problem types;
- Tasks are flexibly *scaffolded* to provide students with support in learning new material and scaffolding is faded over time to lead students to independence;
- Important concepts are strategically *integrated* in ways that show the commonalities and differences between new and old knowledge;
- *Background knowledge* is primed before moving into new learning so students are prepared to make connections;
- *Review* opportunities are appropriately developed to be adequate, distributed, cumulative, and varied.

REFLECTION AND APPLICATION

Case Study

Allison has been hired to teach seventh- and eighth-grade mathematics. She recently completed a teacher training program, and her undergraduate emphasis in mathematics as well as a business background made her a good fit for a recent vacancy at Monroe Middle School. While generally enthusiastic about her new job, she realized that her low-ability, "remedial track" classes would be a challenge.

Half of the students in Math Applications, the lowest math track at Monroe, are mainstreamed special education students. The special education teacher doesn't assist in the instruction, but monitors each student's progress several times throughout the year. Instead, special education services provide Allison with a full-time aide.

The other half of the students in "Math Apps" are in the class for a variety of reasons. Some need just a little extra review before they enter the middle track, pre-algebra classes. Others seem apathetic about math and are taking the class because it is still a required subject. Still others have had a hard time with math since elementary school, but they just don't score low enough to qualify for special education services. As Allison quickly noted, "It really wouldn't make any difference. At this school, they'd still be in my class regardless of whether or not they qualified for special ed."

Allison started her Math Apps class using the district-recommended textbook — a widely marketed commercial basal that begins with a review of basic operations and quickly moves to its main concepts — fractions, decimals and percent, geometry, and negative numbers. In the beginning of the year, Allison thought she'd supplement the text with some daily living applications like learning how to balance a checkbook.

Sequence of District-Recommended Textbook

- Addition/subtraction of whole numbers
- Addition/subtraction of decimals
- Multiplication/division of whole numbers
- Multiplication of decimals
- Division of decimals
- Geometry
- Number theory and equations
- Addition/subtraction of fractions
- Multiplication/division of fractions
- Measurement: Metric units
- Ratio and proportion
- Percent
- Circles and cylinders
- Probability, statistics, and graphs
- Integers
- Measurement: Customary units

By the second week, however, Allison was overwhelmed. The range of academic abilities was too great, and the textbook material moved too quickly. Students were frustrated and bored with the introductory review chapter, and most seemed lost when fractions appeared in chapter 2 of the book. When Allison consulted the special education teacher, she offered her a highly sequenced set of skills worksheets. They were generally computational problems, from simple multiplication and division through decimals.

When Allison tried the worksheets for the majority of the class at the beginning of the third week, most students complained that the work was babyish and that "they'd seen this stuff before and they knew it already." Neither the prescribed textbook for the class nor a common remedial sequence seemed to be the answer. The text was too demanding cognitively, and the worksheets left students unmotivated and indifferent to mathematics.

Clearly, there was little in Allison's prior training that prepared her to teach these kinds of students. Most importantly, there seemed to be few, if any, resources in the school that could help her adjust the curriculum so that it would adequately meet the needs of her students. When she talked to more experienced faculty about the class, they shared her frustrations and were generally cynical about what could be accomplished with these students. Most felt that students in Math Apps would continue working at the sixth-grade level (at least as measured by district learning objectives) until they graduated from middle school. Allison found the thought of teaching many of these students for three years in a row too depressing.

- In what ways might the textbook have been inappropriate for Allison's students? How might the curriculum be modified to better meet the diverse learning needs of her students?

The conclusion of the case study can be found later in this chapter.

Content Questions

1. Describe the challenge in providing students with useful strategies.

2. What is the most valuable use of big ideas in mathematics instruction?

3. List seven applications of the proportions strategy.

4. What has been a problem with providing instructional feedback in traditional mathematics instruction?

5. Explain the authors' suggestions for scaffolding mathematics problems.

6. How can instruction prepare diverse learners for the challenges posed by the NCTM standards?

7. What behaviors must diverse learners perform in order to solve novel problems?

8. Name and describe two aspects necessary for the successful integration of problem-solving strategies.

Reflection and Discussion

1. Does there need to be a dichotomy between traditionalists who call for a return to "basics" in mathematics instruction and reformers who call for increased emphasis on conceptual skills, problem solving, and reasoning? What are the implications of these issue positions for students with diverse learning needs?

2. Given the increasing heterogeneity of achievement levels and learning needs in classrooms, how might effective teaching strategies and instructional principles be used to provide access to general education mathematics content for all students, including students with diverse learning needs?

3. A special educator is assigned to co-teach a tenth-grade math class with a general educator. When meeting to discuss the class, the math teacher says, "I'm not sure this will work; teaching math involves a great deal of content knowledge, and you aren't trained in mathematics." How should the special educator respond? What skills does a special educator or other education professional with expertise in instructional principles have that could benefit students in a higher level math class, both those with and without learning difficulties? Does the special educator need the same level of expertise in the content area of mathematics to effectively co-teach the class?

Application

1. Figure 6–6 shows an example of mathematics instruction that was designed using principles of effective instruction. Evaluate the instruction according to the following questions. What big idea does the instruction focus on? How is the instruction conspicuous? How is the instruction scaffolded? What background knowledge do students need to successfully complete the instruction? How could the instruction be extended to provide judicious review?

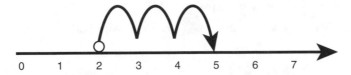

I'll show you how to write the equation for this problem. First, I'll see where the circle started. The circle started at two, so I'll write "2".

2

Now, I'll see how many places the circle moved forward by counting the loops with my finger ...1...2 ...3. So I'll write "plus 3".

2 + 3

Now, I'll see where the circle ended. The circle ended at five so I'll write "equals 5".

2 + 3 = 5

I'll read the whole equation for this problem. "Two plus three equals five."

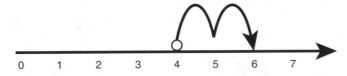

Now it's your turn to write the equation for a problem. First, you'll figure out where the circle started. Where did the circle start? (students respond) That's right! The circle started at four, so you'll write "4".

4

Now, you'll figure out how many places the circle moved forward by counting the loops with your finger. How many places did the circle move forward? (students respond) That's right! So you'll write "plus 2".

4 + 2

Now, you'll figure out where the circle ended. Where did the circle end? (students respond) That's right! The circle ended at six so you'll write "equals 6".

4 + 2 = 6

Read the whole equation for this problem. That's right! "Four plus two equals six."

FIGURE 6–6
Mathematics Instruction Example

Case Study (Conclusion)

Allison realized that she was confronted with several challenges. First, the textbook recommended by the district appeared poorly suited to the needs of her main-streamed special education students and other students with diverse learning needs. It presented a constant barrage of changing concepts that were briefly covered and poorly reviewed. Important ideas, such as proportionality, were not systematically integrated within the textbook and there were few visual displays to support these mathematical concepts.

A related challenge was the lack of adequate time for reorganizing and revising class materials, a problem compounded by the fact that Allison's preservice training had focused primarily on the needs of students with average or above average learning abilities. Additionally, she found that the available opportunities for professional development were not helping her to develop instructional strategies to accommodate the diverse learners in her Math Apps class.

Fortunately, Allison was able to take advantage of a district initiative that offered support from educators with extensive experience in adapting curricula to meet the needs of students with diverse learning needs. In collaboration with these specialists, Allison decided that adapting the original math textbook to meet the needs of her Math Apps students would prove too time-consuming. Therefore, the original text was replaced with innovative materials that had previously proven successful with diverse learners. Importantly, the new curriculum was designed around a *few big ideas,* rather than the myriad concepts presented in the old curriculum. The revised curriculum also aligned well with the district's essential learnings and the state framework in mathematics.

Sequence of New Curriculum

1. Proportions
   - Representing common fraction
   - Transforming fractions
   - Understanding decimals
   - Percents
   - Ratios
2. Common measurements
   - Using fractions
   - Metrics
3. Geometry
4. Charting numbers and modeling data

Allison used several instructional strategies to reinforce the big ideas in the new curriculum. Instruction was made more *conspicuous,* for example, by emphasizing graphic displays and other visual supports to illustrate concepts such as fractions and ratios. She explicitly taught steps for solving geometry problems, initially modeling the application of sequential steps for her students. After they had worked through several examples together, Allison utilized *mediated scaffolding* by gradually fading the level of guidance and feedback that she provided for her students.

With the assistance of colleagues available through the district initiative, Allison systematically designed opportunities for *strategic integration, primed background knowledge,* and *judicious review.* The steps used to find the area of a circle, for example, were reviewed prior to introducing the concept of a cylinder and computation of its volume. Allison was careful to make direct links between the concepts of circles and cylinders, rather than assuming that her students would implicitly make these connections. She also used concrete props to demonstrate how these concepts are similar and different, explaining that the volume of a cylinder represented a measurement of space in three dimensions.

The students in Allison's class responded favorably to this adjusted curriculum. Within a few weeks of initiating these changes, her Math Apps students appeared appropriately challenged by their instruction and demonstrated improved performance on quizzes and homework assignments. Allison eventually decided to apply these instructional principles in her other mathematics classes in order to promote effective learning experiences for *all* of her students.

- How might Allison extend principles of effective instruction to daily living applications, such as balancing a checkbook?
- Would it be realistic to expect all students, including those in upper track math classes, to benefit from the effective teaching strategies that Allison employed successfully in her Math Applications class?
- Would Allison be able to incorporate these instructional strategies in other mathematics classes in the absence of a district initiative and assistance from curriculum specialists?

The Reflection and Application section of this chapter was written by John P. Woodward of the University of Puget Sound and Richard P. Zipoli, Jr. and Maureen F. Ruby from the University of Connecticut.

REFERENCES

BAKER, S., GERSTEN, R., & LEE, D. (2002). A synthesis of empirical research on teaching mathematics to low-achieving students. *Elementary School Journal, 103*(1), 51–73.

BRASWELL, J., DAANE, M., & GRIGG W. (2003). *The nation's report card: Mathematics highlights 2003.* Washington, DC: National Center for Education Statistics. Retrieved August 11, 2005 from http://nces.ed.gov/pubsearch/pubsinfo.asp?pubid=2004451

DAVIS, R. B. (1990). Discovery learning and constructivism. In R. B. Davis, C. A. Maher, & N. Noddings (Eds.), *Constructivist views on the teaching and learning of mathematics.* Reston, VA: National Council of Teachers of Mathematics.

DEPARTMENT OF DEFENSE. (2005). *National Defense Act: Ensuring national security tomorrow through education today.* Retrieved October, 11, 2005 from http://www.dod.mil/ddre/text/t_ndea.html

DONOVAN, M. S., & BRANSFORD, J. D. (2005). *How students learn: History, mathematics, and science in the classroom.* Washington, DC: National Research Council.

ENGELMANN, S., CARNINE, D., KELLY, B., & ENGELMANN, O. (1994). *Connecting math concepts, A through F.* Columbus, OH: SRA.

GATES, W. (2005). *National Education Summit on High Schools.* Retrieved October 10, 2005 from http://www.gatesfoundation.org/MediaCenter/Speeches/BillgSpeeches/BGSpeechNGA-050226.htm

GELMAN, R. (1986). Toward an understanding-based theory of mathematics learning and instruction, or in praise of Lampert on teaching multiplication. *Cognition and Instruction, 3,* 349–355.

GLEASON, M., CARNINE, D., & BORIERO, D. (1990). Improving CAI effectiveness with attention to instructional design in teaching story problems to mildly handicapped students. *Journal of Special Education Technology, 10*(3), 129–136.

KAZMIERCZACH, M. F., JAMES, J., & ARCHEY, W. T. (2005). *Losing the competitive advantage? The challenge for science and technology in the United States.* Retrieved August 16, 2005 from http://www.aeanet.org/publications/idjj_CompetitivenessMain0205.asp.

KILPATRICK, J., SWAFFORD, J., & FINDELL, B. (Eds.). (2001). *Adding it up: Helping children learn mathematics.* Washington, DC: National Research Council.

LEATH, A. T. (2005). Hearing examines science and math education competitiveness, *FYI, The AIP Bulletin of Science Policy News, 84.* Retrieved August, 15, 2005 from http://www.aip.org/fyi/2005/084.html

LEINHARDT, G. (1987). Development of an expert explanation: An analysis of a sequence of subtraction lessons. *Cognition and Instruction, 4*(4), 225–282.

LOVELESS, T., & DIPERNA, P. (2000). How well are American students learning? Focus on math achievement. *The Brown Center Report on American Education, 1*(1).

MA, L. (1999). *Knowing and teaching elementary mathematics: Teachers' understanding of fundamental mathematics in China and the United States.* Mahwah, NJ: Erlbaum.

McCAFFREY, D. F., HAMILTON, L. S., STECHER, B. M., & KLEIN, S. P. (2001). Interactions among instructional practices, curriculum, and student achievement: The case of standards-based school mathematics. *Journal for Research in Mathematics Education, 32*(5), 493.

McDANIEL, M. A., & SCHLAGER, M. S. (1990). Discovery learning and transfer of problem solving. *Cognition and Instruction, 7*(2), 129–159.

MOULY, G. J. (1978). *Educational research: The art and science of investigation.* Boston: Allyn & Bacon.

NATIONAL CENTER FOR EDUCATION STATISTICS. (2003). Trends in International Mathematics and Science Study Retrieved August 11, 2005 from http://nces.ed.gov/timss/Result303.asp

NATIONAL CENTER FOR EDUCATIONAL STATISTICS. (2005). *NAEP 2004 trends in academic progress three decades of student performance in reading and mathematics.* Retrieved from http://nces.ed.gov/pubsearch/pubsinfo.asp?pubid=2005464

NATIONAL COUNCIL OF TEACHERS OF MATHEMATICS. (2000). *NAEP: Understanding the headlines.* Retrieved August 16, 2005 from http://www.nctm.org/news/articles/2000-12naep.htm

NATIONAL COUNCIL OF TEACHERS OF MATHEMATICS. (2000). *Principles and standards for school mathematics.* Retrieved August 16, 2005 from http://standards.nctm.org/index.htm

NATIONAL RESEARCH COUNCIL. (1998). *Preventing reading difficulties in young children.* Washington, DC: National Academies Press.

NICKERSON, R. S. (1985). Understanding. *American Journal of Education, 93,* 201–239.

PIAGET, J. (1973). *The child and reality: Problems of genetic psychology.* New York: Viking Press.

Prawat, R. S. (1989). Promoting access to knowledge, strategy, and disposition in students: A research synthesis. *Review of Educational Research, 59*(1), 1–41.

Resnick, L. B., Cauzinille-Marmeche, E., & Mathieu, J. (1987). Understanding algebra. In J. A. Sloboda & D. Rogers (Eds.), *Cognitive processes in mathematics* (pp. 169–203). Oxford: Clarendon Press.

Resnick, L. B., & Omanson, S. F. (1987). Learning to understand arithmetic. In R. Glaser (Ed.), *Advances in instructional psychology* (pp. 41–95). Hillsdale, NJ: Erlbaum.

Stein, M., Silbert, J., & Carnine, C. (1997). *Designing effective mathematics instruction: A direct instruction approach* (3rd ed.). Upper Saddle River, NJ: Merrill.

Tournaki, N. (2003). The differential effects of teaching addition through strategy instruction versus drill and practice to students with and without learning disabilities. *Journal of Learning Disabilities, 36*(5), 449–458.

Van Patten, J., Chao, C., & Reigeluth, C. M. (1986). A review of strategies for sequencing and synthesizing instruction. *Review of Educational Research, 56*(4), 437–471.

Vergnaud, G. (1988). Multiplicative structures. In J. Hiebert & M. Behr (Eds.), *Number concepts and operations in the middle grades* (pp. 141–161). Reston, VA: NCTM.

Vygotsky, L. S. (1978). *Mind in society: The development of higher psychological processes.* (M. Cole, V. John-Steiner, S. Scribner, & E. Souberman, Eds. & Trans.). Cambridge, MA: Harvard University Press.

CHAPTER 7

Effective Strategies for Teaching Science

Bonnie J. Grossen
University of Oregon

Douglas W. Carnine
University of Oregon

Nancy R. Romance
Florida Atlantic University

Michael R. Vitale
East Carolina University

THIS CHAPTER PARALLELS the other chapters in this book by illustrating the same six key principles in designing educational tools for enabling teachers to accommodate a wide range of students, including diverse learners (children of poverty, children with disabilities, linguistically different and minority children).

The purpose of this chapter is to illustrate the six principles in designing or selecting effective tools in the area of science education. These principles derive from a thorough review of the educational research literature, described in Chapter 1. This chapter is not a research review; it is an illustration of the implications of that research review. The illustrations are directed toward the needs of both educational practitioners (e.g., teachers and supervisors) and designers of new instructional tools (e.g., publishers and developers).

CURRENT ISSUES IN SCIENCE INSTRUCTION

Meeting the needs of all students, including diverse learners, is a purpose that is entirely consistent with recent efforts to reform science education. Two major national efforts to reform science curriculum were initiated in the 1990s: Project 2061 of the American Association for the Advancement of Science (AAAS), and the National Committee on Science Education Standards and Assessment of the National Research Council (1995). The emphasis of both groups was on a commitment to "science for all" that is highly significant for diverse learners. For example, the National Science Education Standards (National Research Council [NRC], 1995) asserts:

> The intent of the *Standards* can be expressed in a single phrase: Science standards for all students. The phrase embodies both excellence and equity. The *Standards* apply to all students, regardless of age, gender, cultural or ethnic background, disabilities, aspirations, or interest and motivation in science. Different students will achieve understanding in different ways, . different students will achieve different degrees of depth and breadth of understanding depending on interest, ability, and context. But all students develop the knowledge and skills described in the *Standards,* even as some students go well beyond these levels. (p. 2)

There are a number of common perspectives on problems in teaching science that have bearing on the present chapter. Among the most important are guidelines for teaching the fundamental concepts, principles, facts, laws, and theories that exemplify scientific literacy by providing a foundation for understanding and applying science. The AAAS refers to these fundamental understandings as the "big ideas" of science. In keeping with the NRC standards (1993, p. 4), a big idea is one that:

1. "represents central scientific ideas and organizing principles."
2. "has rich explanatory and predictive power."
3. "motivates the formulation of significant questions."
4. "is applicable to many situations and contexts common to everyday experiences."

The present chapter adopts a curricular emphasis on "big ideas" as a fundamental characteristic for all effective science instructional tools.

Another important concern addressed in the research is the role of textbooks as the most commonly used tool for teaching science, and as the determiners of as much as 70 percent of the instructional activity in science (Raizen, 1988; see also Wood & Wood, 1988). A recent AAAS Project 2061 study examined the most widely used textbooks to determine how well they helped students learn key science ideas in the middle grades and high school (AAAS 1999, 2000). The in-depth study of middle-school texts, including the most recently published "new crop" of texts, found that "most textbooks cover too many topics and don't develop any of them well. All texts include many classroom activities that either are irrelevant to learning key science ideas or don't help students relate what they are doing to the underlying ideas" (AAAS, 1999, p. 1). Not one text was rated satisfactory at any level. The evaluation of high school biology texts found that "Big Biology Books Fail to Convey Big Ideas" (AAAS, 2000, p. 1). Four major problems described are as follows:

1. Research shows that essentially all students—even the best and the brightest—have predictable difficulties grasping many ideas that are covered in the textbooks. Yet the textbooks fail to take these obstacles into account in designing activities and questions.

2. For many biology concepts, the textbooks ignore or obscure the most important ideas by focusing instead on technical terms and trivial details (which are easy to test).

3. While most of the books are lavishly illustrated, these representations are rarely helpful, because they are too abstract, needlessly complicated, or inadequately explained.

4. Even though several activities are included in every chapter, students are given little guidance in interpreting the results in terms of the scientific concepts to be learned.

Other studies echo these criticisms, including that science texts contain too many concepts, present ideas in a list-like rather than an integrated fashion, have unclear prose and illustrations, and are generally ineffective in effecting conceptual change for meaningful learning (Lloyd, 1989; McCarthy, 2005; Newport, 1990; Osborn, Jones, & Stein, 1985; Smith, Blakeslee, & Anderson, 1993).

Although the admittedly poor design of current science texts has caused many educators to totally reject their value, the view expressed in this chapter is that properly designed (or properly augmented) textbooks can be useful learning tools in science classrooms.

The poor design of science textbooks not only has caused many educators to reject textbooks, but also has led some educators to reject instruction in science subject matter as a reasonable goal for pre-university science instruction (Shaw, 1983; Staver & Small, 1990; Yager & Penick, 1987; Yeany, Yap, & Padilla, 1986). These educators recommend instead that proficiency in science inquiry skills be the primary goal of science education, so that student-directed inquiry methods can be used exclusively, rather than the explicit, teacher-directed presentations that typify textbook-based instruction. Apparently, explicit instruction for content understanding has been denigrated because it is done so poorly in science texts.

However, in keeping with national science standards, stepping back from the challenge of effectively teaching science subject matter would be incompatible with the nation's emerging goals to achieve world-class standards in science. Toward that end, the new science content standards include, along with science inquiry, science subject matter (the concepts and principles of science) as a critical component in both the reform of science education and the achievement of scientific literacy for all students. Two additional goal areas addressed by the new national science education standards are scientific connections and science in human affairs.

The reader should view each of the following design principles as the focus of efforts to develop, select, or enhance instruction so that it accommodates a broad range of students, including diverse learners:

1. Does the instruction focus on teaching the "big ideas" of science?
2. Does it make the strategies for using the big ideas conspicuous?
3. Are important component concepts of big ideas and component steps of strategies taught?
4. Does mediated scaffolding provide a smooth transition to independent success?
5. Is judicious review provided?
6. Is the content strategically integrated for greater efficiency in learning?

In the first part of this chapter, the first three highly interdependent design considerations—big ideas, strategies, component steps and concepts—are discussed, and examples from science inquiry and from subject matter knowledge are given. The sequence of illustrations models the order in which the development of an instructional sequence occurs—starting with the desired student outcome and analyzing back to a reasonable starting point for instruction—rather than the reverse order, which would more closely correspond to the actually teaching of the instructional sequence. In the second part of this chapter, the remaining three considerations—scaffolding, judicious review, and strategic integration—are discussed. These design considerations apply to the design of the communication.

PRINCIPLES FOR IMPROVING INSTRUCTIONAL STRATEGIES IN SCIENCE

Designing Instruction Around Big Ideas in Science Inquiry

Science inquiry—the process of truth-seeking—is perhaps the "biggest" idea of science. The classic approach to science inquiry—the scientific method—consists of several well-accepted steps: observing patterns or discrepancies, forming hypotheses to explain these observed patterns or discrepancies, controlling and manipulating variables, planning investigations to test hypotheses, and interpreting the resulting data.

Science inquiry—the ability to test hypotheses—is a crucial truth-seeking skill in both formal scientific and informal contexts. Kuhn (1993) found that few adults have the minimal truth-seeking skills required to confront their informal beliefs in an honest manner. For example, only 40 percent of her subjects could describe the nature of the evidence that would cause them to falsify their theories for such questions as: What causes prisoners to return to a life of crime after they are released? What causes children to fail in school? What causes unemployment? Many adult subjects claimed that they did not have to consider any evidence because their opinion was their opinion and they were entitled to it.

The processes needed to establish and evaluate everyday beliefs and theories are essentially the same processes used in formal scientific hypothesis testing. For this reason, science inquiry (or the scientific method) is truly a big idea that is relevant to a much larger range of human affairs than simply the domain of science, and is one that connects across a wide range of disciplines.

Component Steps and Concepts in Science Inquiry

One component skill of science inquiry that is also a big idea in the science education of younger children is the ability to identify a pattern in observations. Once a scientist observes a pattern, then the scientist can form a hypothesis to explain or predict the noted pattern. Very young children begin to develop the skill of identifying patterns in their study of the classification system of plants and animals. The common features of the categories represent a pattern in the observations. When teachers make these patterns explicit and engage children in classifying organisms according to the features of the categories, of mammals for example, children are developing their observation skills and their ability to see recurring patterns across several examples or observations.

A second key component of science inquiry is effectively controlling variables (Ross, 1988). As an inquiry skill, controlling variables means that in order to isolate the effect of a variable, students must be able to identify all other relevant variables and then design an experiment that keeps unchanged all but the variable being tested. This critical strategy component—controlling variables—is illustrated in the following section as an example of making a strategy conspicuous.

Designing Conspicuous Strategies in Science Inquiry

A fairly common hypothesis in science education is that "inquiry" instructional methods (also sometimes called nonexplicit, activity-based, student-centered, or discovery methods) are preferable to explicit instructional methods for teaching students how to *do* science inquiry. However, this hypothesis seems generally contradicted by experimental research. Research comparing "inquiry" (nonexplicit) methods with instruction that makes the strategies for carrying out science inquiry explicit finds that the latter results in better learning, especially for students with low academic achievement levels who do not already possess an understanding of inquiry (Klahr & Nigam, 2004; McCleery & Tindal, 1999; Ross, 1988; Rubin & Norman, 1992; Zohar & Aharon-Kravetsky, 2005).

In spite of these findings, the hypothesis that persists is that inquiry instructional methods work better than explicit instruction for teaching science inquiry skills. A second group of studies are often cited to support this hypothesis (e.g., Shymansky,

Kyle, & Alport, 1983; Staver & Small, 1990). However, the conclusions from this group of studies are misleading because the "explicit" treatments in these studies teach only scientific principles and do not explicitly teach the skills of science inquiry at all. For example, several studies compare an explicit treatment designed to teach the displacement principle (i.e., the amount of liquid displaced by an object is equal to the volume of the object) with inquiry instruction designed to teach students to derive the principle of displacement through their own inquiry (e.g., Bay, Staver, Bryan, & Hale, 1992). None of the explicit treatment conditions was designed to teach science inquiry skills.

It is not surprising that studies with this design generally find that inquiry teaching methods result in better science inquiry performance than "explicit" instruction (Bredderman, 1983; Shayer & Adey, 1993; Shymansky et al., 1983; Staver & Small, 1990). However, conclusions about explicit instruction for teaching science inquiry cannot be made on the basis of explicit treatments designed to teach only scientific principles. Studies that compare inquiry instruction with instruction designed to make the strategy for science inquiry explicit generally conclude that explicit instruction is more effective. Explicit methods that teach what students are expected to learn usually result in better learning than inquiry (nonexplicit) teaching methods. The conclusions to be drawn from such research are: If students are to learn science inquiry, make the strategy for science inquiry explicit. Similarly, if students are to learn scientific principles, it is important to make the scientific principles explicit.

Our interpretation of this research is that effective instruction makes significant strategies "conspicuous" rather than simply "explicit." We make this distinction because educators often interpret "explicit instruction" to mean simply "verbalized instruction." However, the effective treatments in the first group of studies involved much more than simply teacher verbalization, and, in effect, they made the strategies for science inquiry very conspicuous.

To illustrate a conspicuous strategy that accommodates the needs of *all* learners, we present a modified activity from *Elementary Science Study* (1974), a popular inquiry-based curriculum of the 1970s. In the original inquiry activity, students viewed a row of figures called mellinarks and a second row of figures that were not mellinarks. The students then viewed a third row of mellinarks and nonmellinarks and identified which figures would be classified as mellinarks. The instruction did not model or describe any strategy for controlling variables that the students could use to think about the examples in order to figure out the concept of mellinark. Students continued the activity with similar concepts until they themselves discovered or "self-learned" the inquiry skill needed to derive a concept from examples and nonexamples. Therefore, the instruction was described as an "inquiry" method.

Although this activity may seem quite simple, Lawson et al. (1991) found that only 22 percent of high school chemistry and biology students possess the science inquiry skills to successfully identify a mellinark and other such imaginary concepts. These findings indicate that nearly *all* students would benefit from a teacher-directed experiential activity designed to teach a conspicuous strategy for controlling variables.

The instruction begins with the presentation of only one figure, Drawing A in Figure 7–1. The students' goal is to determine with some certainty what it means to

FIGURE 7–1
*Controlling Variables
to Define a Concept*

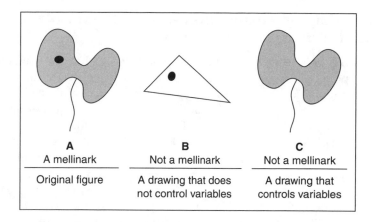

A	B	C
A mellinark	Not a mellinark	Not a mellinark
Original figure	A drawing that does not control variables	A drawing that controls variables

be a mellinark by designing (drawing) additional examples, each of which the teacher identifies as mellinark or nonmellinark. For these examples to be most informative, students must control the possible variables; that is, they must design each example so that it is exactly the same as the original figure except for the one feature that students want to test. For example, Drawing B in Figure 7–1 is not very informative because it does not control many variables; that is Drawing B differs from Drawing A in more than one way. On the other hand, Drawing C is quite informative because it controls for all variables except the spot, so the information that Drawing C is not a mellinark would allow students to conclude that a mellinark must have a spot.

The activity continues with students designing more figures that change only one of the other variables listed on the board, or the drawings could test additional variables, such as the range of acceptable sizes for the spot, or even whether more than one spot is possible on a mellinark. The variable list is potentially endless. (This conspicuous strategy with additional scaffolding is illustrated later in this chapter under the topic, scaffolding.)

The steps made conspicuous in the strategy for identifying mellinarks form a generic strategy for controlling variables—a strategy that students can learn and apply not only to the mellinark problem, but to any problem requiring systematic scientific investigation. These elements are: Design the figure (the experiment) so that the new figure (the experimental treatment) differs from the original figure (the control treatment) in only one feature (the independent variable) and all the other features (variables) are kept the same (controlled). Gather information about whether each figure is a mellinark to identify whether the feature that was changed is critical to the figure's being a mellinark (interpret the results).

In the initial instruction, the teacher should not use the sophisticated vocabulary that is normally used to describe these steps (e.g., independent and dependent variable). The teacher's goal should be to make the actual *strategy* conspicuous. Vocabulary words can be taught later, after students have acquired the meanings that go with them. The mellinark activity is easily managed and could readily teach most students, including diverse learners, science inquiry strategies by making them conspicuous to learners.

Designing Instruction Around Big Ideas in Science Subject Matter

As noted earlier, both the NRC and the AAAS science standards emphasize the importance of teaching the big ideas of science subject matter. For purposes of illustration, some significant big ideas in science subject matter include the nature of science, energy transformations, gravity, flow of matter and energy in ecosystems, and the interdependence of life. Such big ideas and their component concepts clearly cut across the science domains (e.g., physics, earth science, biology) and are essential in building a level of scientific literacy among all students that is necessary for understanding and problem solving within the natural and created world.

The AAAS's Project 2061 is analyzing the major big ideas in science in a publication called *Atlas of Science Literacy* (in press). A preview of the contents of this publication can be found on the web at http://www.project2061.org/.

Convection: An Example of a Big Idea. The principle of convection is a good example of a big idea that both explains and unifies many of the dynamic phenomena that occur within the earth (geology), oceans (oceanography), and atmosphere (meteorology)—three domains of science usually associated with earth science. For example, in the area of geology, plate tectonics, earthquakes, volcanoes, and the formation of mountains are all influenced by convection in the mantle. Global and local convection patterns influence the dynamics of the atmosphere. Similarly, the ocean currents, thermohaline circulation, and coastal upwelling are influenced by global and local convection. In turn, the interaction of these phenomena in the earth and the atmosphere results in the rock cycle, weathering, and changes in landforms. The interaction of these phenomena in the ocean and in the atmosphere influence the water cycle, wind-driven ocean circulation, El Niño, and climate in general.

As is the case for many currently evolving big ideas, alternative and variant explanations for these phenomena have been offered, and the fact that competing theoretical explanations often exist is an aspect of science of which students should be made aware. However, not all the alternative and variant explanations need to be taught, particularly in initial instruction. Figure 7–2 illustrates the core principle of convection and the various phenomena it explains.

Benefits of an Analysis of Big Ideas. By design, big ideas have the potential to transfer or apply more widely to other areas (domains) of science and everyday phenomena than small (or less general) ideas. For example, as discussed previously, the principle of convection can be used to explain dynamic natural phenomena in geology, meteorology, and oceanography. Also, well-designed instruction in big ideas allows for more efficient use of time. Because of the foundational understanding and connections established with big ideas, the teacher can cover a greater amount of meaningful content while teaching fewer principles. And, as students apply big ideas across other domains of science, these big ideas function as prior knowledge within which students can easily assimilate new learning with appropriate elaboration rather than learning everything as if it were new. (While the use of big ideas is an effective

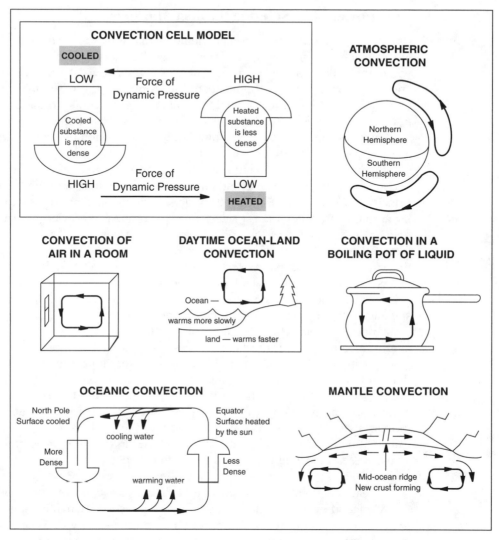

FIGURE 7–2
The Big Idea of Convection and Simple Visual Maps of Some of Its Applications

and efficient strategy, other characteristics of instructional delivery, such as scaffolding and review, determine the extent to which students actually learn the big idea.)

In general, big ideas represent an adaptive curricular solution that amplifies meaningful understanding in a fashion that is of particular importance to diverse learners, rather than encouraging mere memorization of an array of disconnected facts, as too often occurs. This approach provides diverse learners with the opportunity to learn that scientific concepts and "real world" science phenomena are both understandable and logically related.

Components in Science Subject Matter

Component concepts are essential elements that must be identified when attempting to teach any big ideas, including those identified as benchmarks or standards within the national science reform initiatives of the NRC or AAAS. In order to explain and meaningfully apply a big idea such as convection, for example, students must understand and use its component or underlying concepts. In the case of convection, in-depth understanding depends on students' prior understanding of concepts such as cause-and-effect relationships between and among the phenomena of heating and cooling, density, force, and pressure.

By designing instruction to teach the component concepts conspicuously (in this example, a network of cause-and-effect relationships that underlie the larger causal principle of convection), a deeper understanding of the principle can be achieved by all students rather than a select few. In turn, the knowledge resulting from a deeper understanding of the underlying causes of convection (density, heat, the effect of heat on density and pressure, and so on) provides a meaningful foundation that can be used to explain everyday phenomena as well as more abstract phenomena, such as novas and black holes in the universe.

In fact, unless students have extensive specialized prior scientific knowledge, specific instruction in the component concepts is necessary in order to build understanding of convection. For example, students must understand that heat causes a substance to expand and become less dense, and that substances move from a place of high pressure to a place of low pressure. Simultaneously, in order to understand and apply the underlying component concepts and principle of convection, specific facts about the solar system, the ocean, the solid earth, and the atmosphere must be known. For example, students must know that the sun is the primary external source of heat, that the tilt of the earth as it orbits around the sun causes variations in the amount of heat received in different areas of the earth (i.e., changing seasons), that the core of the earth is hot, that the ocean is very, very deep, and so on.

As students learn to integrate the component concepts with other relevant knowledge, they gain an understanding analogous to a dynamic mental model of a generic convection cell (upper left box in Figure 7–2). By conspicuously teaching component concepts, understanding and application of the convection process becomes accessible to a wider range of diverse students.

Designing Conspicuous Strategies in Science Subject Matter

Better problem solving in the form of applications of scientific knowledge is a major goal of science education reform. To solve problems, students need to learn strategies for using and applying the big ideas of science and their component concepts in a variety of contexts. The big ideas and component concepts represent scientific knowledge that, of necessity, must be brought to bear in the problem-solving process. Thus, the design of instructional tools and classroom instruction around big ideas is a critical dimension underlying the degree to which students can understand and apply the knowledge they have learned. Students should learn important big ideas in a form that optimizes their explanatory and predictive power, along with the kinds of problems to which the big ideas apply.

In fact, the strategies necessary for effective problem solving and learning in science are literally the applications of big ideas. For example, instructional strategies that connect component concepts to a big idea or scientific principle (such as convection) can be applied by students to predict the location of and movement in a substance given the placement of the heat source. Such knowledge becomes dynamic whenever it helps students interpret events in the world or make more accurate predictions about what is likely or not likely to happen. Knowledge of big ideas and their component concepts forms the basis for meaningful conceptual learning and effective problem solving in science. Within this context, science learning for students is analogous to the current problem faced by scientists of predicting earthquakes and volcanoes given prior factual knowledge in conjunction with the conceptual understanding of the location of plates in the earth and their significance.

Building Understanding Through Wide Application of Big Ideas.

Once the big idea of convection and the component concepts underlying it are understood in simple forms and are used to explain and predict common experiences, they can then be broadened to explain more abstract phenomena, such as convection in the atmosphere and in the earth's mantle. Given these two applications, the big idea of convection is important to the meaningful understanding of each, for two reasons. First, the common convection models amplify their similarity: The source of heat is at the bottom of the convection cell in both cases because the sun heats the surface of the earth, which causes convection in the atmosphere, and the heated core of earth causes convection in the mantle. Second, aspects of the models amplify their differences: One convection model involves gases, the other involves solids. At a more abstract level, using the convection model to understand that movement in the mantle is similar to movement in the atmosphere and is similar to common experiences prevents a possible misconception that convection does not occur in solids.

Explaining the application of the big idea of convection to the ocean would best be taught after the mantle and atmosphere because it requires more complex understanding beyond convection. In oceans, the source of heat is at the top of the convection cell: The sun heats the surface of the ocean. This is only a minor elaboration of the convection model. However, convection in the ocean also interacts with convection in the atmosphere (i.e., winds), so that the surface currents of the ocean must be explained by both ocean and air convection patterns. Finally, an even more complex process is the interaction of local convection patterns in the atmosphere with global convection in the atmosphere. This interaction can be quite complex, which is why weather prediction is usually very difficult. However, an awareness of the problems involved in using an understanding of convection to make accurate predictions can add a final touch of realism to the instruction.

While other factors are important in these applications (such as the rotation of the earth), the important point is not only that teacher-directed sequences involving the wide application of big ideas can enhance the understanding of big ideas for all students, but also that these forms of adaptation are of great importance in the success of diverse learners in science instruction.

Using Visual Maps to Model Strategies for Organizing Concepts and Big Ideas.   Science subject matter content, as represented by big ideas and component concepts, should be presented in such a way that the instruction facilitates the application of big ideas, which often manifest themselves in problem solving. To accomplish this, instruction can use visual maps (i.e., concept maps, pictures, diagrammatic sketches) to emphasize the explanative nature of science and the organization of science's big ideas. This approach will further improve problem-solving performance (Guastello, Beasley, & Sinatra, 2000; Mayer, 1989; Mayer & Gallini, 1990; Woodward, 1994). Ideally, such illustrations should correspond with how an expert organizes and uses the information in applying science concepts to solve problems. This requirement is important because in science, expert problem solvers differ from novice problem solvers in three important ways: Expert problem solvers have more knowledge; the knowledge is better organized in a hierarchical structure; and good problem solvers seem to organize this hierarchy around explanatory principles that function as big ideas.

As an illustration, Figure 7–2 shows a hierarchical organization around an explanative principle: convection. The central concept is a generic convection model (upper left box in Figure 7–2.) The other figures illustrate the various applications or effects of convection. The generic convection model—the big idea—can be used by students to explain everyday occurrences such as the movement of air currents in a room and the movement of water in a heated pan. Each application of the strategy is not unrelated but forms part of a unified, structured schema related to the principle of convection.

In general, visual maps of big ideas add to the overall "considerate" quality of an instruction tool. A considerate tool is one that eases comprehension in a supportive manner (Armbruster, 1984; Armbruster, Anderson, & Ostertag, 1987; Guzzetti, Snyder, Glass, & Gamas, 1993; Yates & Yates, 1990). In addition to visual maps, considerate communication uses cues in the text or textual elements such as headings and signal words to make the structure of the knowledge being communicated as clear and coherent as possible. Considerations of the structure, coherence, unity, and audience appropriateness (Kantor, Anderson, & Armbruster, 1983) and even accuracy (Champagne & Bunce, 1989) have been found to contribute to understanding. Clearly showing useful perspectives on how knowledge is best organized can provide important benefits to diverse learners.

Adding a "Refutational" Aspect to Communication of a Big Idea.   In addition to conspicuous strategies for visually representing concept relationships and applications, adding a "refutational" aspect to the communication can further facilitate understanding and conceptual change for students (Guzzetti et al., 1993; Muthukrishna, Carnine, Grossen, & Miller, 1993; Niedelman, 1992; Smith, Blakeslee, & Anderson, 1993). Along with conspicuously presenting a coherent new strategy, a refutational text anticipates

FIGURE 7–3
*Strategy Example
with Density*

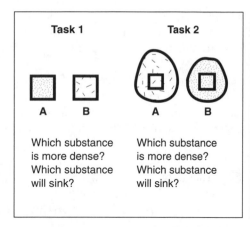

The first step in teaching students to understand density is to have them compare the masses of substances of equal volume and predict which substances will sink when mixed. Two same-sized cubes with differing numbers of dots can be used to teach this step, as in Task 1 in Figure 7–3. In the figure, each dot represents 1 gram of mass. In this case, the more dots there are inside a cube (the greater the mass), the greater the density of the cube.

common misconceptions and builds into instruction examples that directly confront such misconceptions. Because students have many preconceived notions or misconceptions about science (e.g., "big objects float and small objects sink"), it is important that instruction clearly confront common misconceptions in a conspicuous manner. Many studies have found that a refutational, considerate, explicit text is very successful in achieving conceptual change; some studies have shown that student performance reaches a ceiling of conceptual change (e.g., Guzzetti, 1990). The following example illustrates how conceptually based strategy instruction can be designed to refute misconceptions.

The first step in teaching students to understand density is to have them compare the masses of substances of equal volume and predict which substances will sink when mixed. Two same-sized cubes with differing numbers of dots can be used to teach this step, as in Task 1 in Figure 7–3. In the figure, each dot represents 1 gram of mass. In this case, the more dots there are inside a cube (the greater the mass), the greater the density of the cube.

Next, students can learn to identify equivalent volumes of substances of unequal sizes and predict which will sink when the substances are mixed. In Task 2 of Figure 7–3, figures of different sizes are shown, with empty cubes placed over segments of equal size to confront the misconception that more size means greater density. By looking at the number of dots in the equal-sized cubes, students can tell that substance B is more dense than substance A, although substance B is smaller in size. Students are able to compare the density of a series of substances like those in Task 2 where the size and number of dots varies.

Next, as students form a conceptual understanding of mass and volume, such understanding can provide a foundation for subsequent activities using actual substances in a naturalistic environment in which (in conjunction with appropriate measurement skills) students predict which substance will sink when the substances come together (Task 3 in Figure 7–3).

Research has shown that planned refutations (built-in teaching examples that counter commonly observed misconceptions) were more effective in changing students' naive conceptions to scientific understandings than instruction that left the teacher to provide refutational material spontaneously during instruction. The teachers using the curricular material with planned refutations achieved better learning outcomes than the teachers who introduced refutations spontaneously (Smith et al., 1993).

Because curricular materials are designed before they reach the classroom, they must necessarily incorporate planned refutation if they are to include any refutation at all. As an illustration, Task 2 in Figure 7–3 is a planned example that refutes the common misconception that density is the same as weight. Having all students respond to this example reduces the likelihood that this misconception will occur. By anticipating predictable misconceptions such as this, instruction can be more effective for all students, particularly diverse learners, than instruction that relies on the teacher to respond spontaneously to presumably unpredictable misconceptions that might differ from individual to individual, and then design the teaching examples on the spot.

Providing Relevant Experiential Learning.   It is often falsely assumed that if knowledge is conspicuously introduced, it must be in a lecture setting in which the teacher is active (i.e., telling) and the students are passive. Similarly, it is falsely assumed that in order to involve students actively in learning, science instruction must utilize hands-on experiences and the teacher should not communicate information conspicuously. Neither of the preceding assumptions is valid because the initial communication of scientific concepts to naive learners can be very interactive and conspicuous. With this in mind, Table 7–1 contrasts traditional telling methods, inquiry methods, and conspicuous communication methods.

Conspicuous communication methods are interactive and experiential, just as inquiry methods are. However, conspicuous communication methods include only learning experiences that are relevant to understanding big ideas. In this regard, "hands-on" learning experiences may or may not be relevant. Certainly, simple mechanical participation in a hands-on activity without conceptual understanding is analogous to the meaningless memorization of facts. In many cases, it is often impossible to design relevant hands-on activities that effectively communicate underlying

TABLE 7–1
Features of Traditional Telling Methods and Inquiry Methods Contrasted with Conspicuous Communication Methods for Initially Teaching Naive Learners

Traditional Telling Methods	Inquiry Methods	Conspicuous Communication Methods
Traditional	Innovative	Innovative
Teacher-directed	Student-directed	Teacher-directed
Nonexperiential	Experiential	Experiential
Noninteractive	Interactive	Interactive

causal big ideas. For example, students would have difficulty discovering an acceptable theory of electricity from a pile of wires, batteries, and switches, or from operating the lights and electrical appliances in their homes. Students may believe that a wire that is cut through cannot carry electric current and therefore is safe to touch, when in fact it can still deliver quite a shock if it is still connected to the power source. This is not to say that hands-on activities for applying electricity concepts are inappropriate; they would, for example, be very appropriate for applying strategies about electrical circuits. The important distinction is that students could not be expected necessarily to derive or construct a reliable understanding and explanation of electricity solely from hands-on experiences.

To avoid misconceptions, hands-on activities should be used in initial instruction only when they are concretely relevant to the concept being taught. Hands-on experience would certainly be relevant where physical texture is an important feature of understanding, as it is in most identification and categorization activities, such as the identification of rocks, leaves, or flowers. In most cases, hands-on experience seems to detract from initial learning when texture is not a key feature of meaningful learning, as in learning about electricity, for example (Hider & Rice, 1986).

Designing Mediated Scaffolding in Science Inquiry and Subject Matter Instruction

The Concept of Scaffolding in Instruction.   The emphasis of scaffolding is that, to be effective, instruction must always be adapted to the initial level of student proficiency. It is important to stress that scaffolding addresses and operates on the processes (or means) through which desired instructional goals are accomplished, not on changing (and in particular not simplifying or not limiting) achievement goals. Scaffolding, then, emphasizes dynamic efforts that provide initial learners with substantial support early in learning, support that is then purposively reduced as they gain additional proficiency. Because of its importance in supporting initial learning, scaffolding is also of great importance to ensuring the success of instruction with many diverse learners. The implication of scaffolding is that educators must strive to design, select, or adapt instruction in order to make the goals of science literacy available to all students.

Illustrations in the preceding section characterized ideal initial instruction as being interactive, conspicuous, and teacher-directed. In this context, the notion of scaffolding applied to initial instruction assumes that students are faced with learning instructional content that is new to them. Whenever students experience the key features of a new science concept or inquiry strategy, scaffolding stresses that the initial presentations should strive to make all key features conspicuous through a variety of techniques that include explicit verbal prompts or very clear representational models and examples that provide guidance and support.

When the idea of scaffolding (e.g., through prompts) is combined with other instructional design characteristics, such as a focus on big ideas and conspicuous strategies, the result is effective initial learning in which students are actively and meaningfully involved in experiential learning. In this sense, teacher-directed (or

FIGURE 7–4
*Continuum of
Effective
Instructional
Practices as They
Relate to the
Learner's Level of
Performance in the
Specific Type of
Learning Activity*

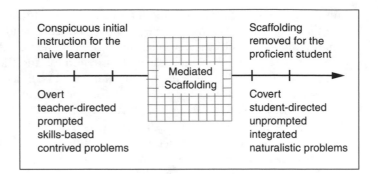

teacher-supported) initial instruction is far more powerful for initial learning than independent, student-directed activities. However, as initial learning activities evolve and students become more proficient, the reduction of support purposefully eliminates teacher direction until learning is, in fact, independent and student-directed. The purpose of scaffolding, thus, is to allow *all* students to become successful in independent activities, not just the select few who do not require initial learning support.

Figure 7–4 shows additional aspects of initial instruction that work to create a supportive learning environment that can enable naive students to enter into new learning successfully. In this sense, the term "scaffolding" is an apt metaphor for describing this dynamically supportive environment. As students, with the support of a scaffold, progress toward proficiency in a learning objective, the scaffolding is removed and the instructional activities become less teacher-directed and more student-driven.

Understanding the Two Categories of Scaffolding Techniques. There are at least two distinct ways to scaffold instruction. The first is through teacher assistance and the second is through the design of the examples used in teaching. Both assume that the student is actively involved in learning tasks rather than being a passive learner.

Scaffolding Teacher Talk. As illustrated in Figure 7–5, the initial presentation of the conspicuous strategy for controlling variables (at the top of the figure) involves more telling, while the later scaffolding (at the bottom of the figure) involves more questioning or scaffolding. In the example, the conspicuous steps of the initial strategy and of the scaffolded strategy are: (1) select one variable (hypothesis) to test; (2) vary the tested variable only and keep the other variables the same; (3) interpret the results. Only the degree of teacher guidance varies. As noted earlier, students will eventually be expected to control variables as they direct their own projects.

Scaffolding Examples. The example presented previously in Figure 7–3 illustrates a way to scaffold instruction through the design of sequences of teaching examples. In the example, each task corresponds to a step in a strategy for applying the concept of density. Task 1 requires students to compare the masses in an equivalent volume and predict which substance will sink. Task 2 requires students to identify equivalent volumes in two unequal-sized substances and predict which substance will sink. Task 3 (with some additional assumptions) requires application of the strategy to real examples.

Initial Conspicuous Strategy Presentation

Step 1: (*Introduction*) You're going to figure out what a mellinark is by drawing pictures that might be mellinarks.

Step 2: (*Generating hypotheses*) This is a mellinark. (Teacher makes Drawing A in Figure 7–1.) What variables might be important in determining whether something is a mellinark or not? (As students name possibilities, the teacher lists them on the board: the barbell shape of the body, the curved shape of the body, the presence of a dark spot, the position of the spot, the presence of a tail, the size, the color, and so on, with the list of features [variables] representing a list of hypotheses.)

Step 3: (*Controlling variables*) The best way to figure out what a mellinark is, is to draw a new figure that changes only one variable. The first variable I want to test is whether a mellinark needs a spot. Watch. (Teacher draws Drawing C in Figure 7–1.)

Step 4: (*Interpreting data*) This figure is not a mellinark. From that information you can figure out one variable that defines a mellinark. What variable is that? (A spot.) After you draw a figure, I will tell you if it is a mellinark or not. From what I tell you, you should be able to figure out more about the variables that tell about a mellinark.

Later Scaffolded Instruction

Step 1: (*Hypothesis*) (Point to this figure.) This is a glerb. ⎯⎯⎯⎯⎯→ Pick a feature to test to see if it defines a glerb. What feature did you select?

Step 2: (*Controlling variables*) Draw a figure that allows you to test for that feature.

Step 3: (*Interpret data*) (For example, if the student ⎯⎯⎯⎯⎯→ drew this figure.)

This is not a glerb. Now, what do you know about glerbs? . . .Yes, they need an opening. (Corrective feedback for drawings that do not control variables, such as this one, for example.) ⎯⎯⎯⎯⎯→

You did not draw a glerb. But there are a lot of reasons why this is not a glerb. It could be too big; it could be the wrong shape; it could have the wrong number of sides; it could be the wrong color. You can't tell why because you changed too many things from the original figure. When you test a variable, you must keep all the other variables the same.

What variable were you trying to test?	What about the other variables?
Whether it needs straight sides.	*Keep them the same.*

So what variable would you change?
The straight sides.

FIGURE 7–5
Using Teacher Assistance to Scaffold Instruction

Because scaffolding is a dynamic process, as learners become more competent, the scaffolding is removed by purposively moving slightly ahead of the learner on the continuum of instructional practice shown in Figure 7–4. As learners grow in competence and independence, effective instruction moves forward on the continuum. This process is illustrated as follows, using activities presented earlier in the chapter.

1. Progress from overt descriptions of the thinking strategies to covert practice of those strategies.

   Example: In initial instruction, the teacher states and/or models overtly the thought process involved in drawing a mellinark to test whether it needs a spot. With covert practice, the teacher says nothing. Students carry out a single step by drawing a figure that changes only one variable.

2. Progress from teacher-directed to student-directed activity.

   Example: When students first begin testing variables, the teacher directs students by telling them which variable to control for (e.g., the spot), how to control for that variable, and so on. When students are proficient, the directions for the activity become more general and students select their own variables (hypotheses) and control for them without assistance.

3. Progress from prompted to unprompted assistance.

   Example: The teacher initially prompts students as they work by giving specific feedback on their mellinark drawings or specific instructions that prompt better control of the next variable. As students become more proficient at controlling variables, the prompts are no longer needed, and students successfully control the variables without teacher prompts.

4. Progress from instruction in component concepts to instruction that integrates the concepts into a whole.

   Example: The instruction in the convection cell begins with instruction in the components of the convection cell, including concepts of density and pressure; understanding of the source of heat; the cause-and-effect relations of heat, density, and pressure; and the effects of these on the movement of cells. Later instruction in the convection cell presumes knowledge of these components and provides an integrated model explaining their interactions.

5. Progress from more contrived problems to naturalistic ones using real objects.

   Example: The density drawings in Tasks 1 and 2 of Figure 7–3 are contrived in order to scaffold the strategy for using density. When students are proficient in the strategy, they can then use it in Task 3 to predict which of two real substances will sink or float.

An example of an activity that incorporates all of these unscaffolded features for students who are more proficient at science inquiry would be a lab activity in which students identify rules that will predict which of various tubes—some made of iron, others aluminum; some hollow, others solid; some short, others long—will roll faster down a ramp (as described in Main & Rowe, 1993). Students will need to apply their knowledge about controlling variables to determine which variables increase the speed of the tubes. The students would need to select appropriate pairs of tubes to roll down the ramp to test possible variables. The variables might include hollow versus solid, large versus small, heavy versus light, short versus long, and so on. Similar experiences with varied unscaffolded applications such as this provide opportunities for details in understanding to be further clarified.

It seems generally that the more the teacher interacts with the students by scaffolding important content, the more effective the instruction. Teacher-directed instruction that is characterized by frequent interactions (i.e., checks for understanding and applications) can scaffold content-specific instruction so that students with learning disabilities acquire an understanding of scientific concepts that Harvard graduates frequently do not have (Muthukrishna et al., 1993).

Designing Judicious Review

Science is a difficult subject for most students. Therefore, review is essential. However, when the instruction focuses on developing an understanding of big ideas, review consists of applications of these big ideas in different contexts, rather than rote recitation of memorized facts. Ample opportunities to apply the concept are necessary if students are to fully understand the relevance and utility of a concept or big idea.

Review can also incorporate new learning as students apply a known concept in a new context. For example, after intensive study of density in a series of introductory lessons, density can be reviewed sporadically as it is applied in the context of learning about pressure, the effects of heat on density and pressure, the effects of changes in density on movement and pressure, and so on.

Over time as a concept is reviewed, the scaffolding is gradually removed and the context of the application becomes more complex, making the application just a bit more challenging each time for the students. From the initial presentation, students can acquire only a basic understanding of concepts. For example, after learning about density, students may not realize that relative density holds for fragments from a piece of substance. Students might predict that a large glob of mercury would sink, but when asked about a tiny ball from that glob, they might predict that it would float. Similarly, after the initial presentation in controlling variables, students will need much more practice in a wide variety of contexts.

Varied practice contributes to students' generating more ideas for solving problems, having higher quality ideas, asking better questions, and more successfully solving problems (Covington & Crutchfield, 1965; Schmidt & Bjork, 1992; Wardrop et al., 1969). When real-world application practice follows instruction using contrived examples, students are able to apply the strategies to different types of problems, and retention improves (Olton & Crutchfield, 1969). When students fail to use knowledge, it is usually associated with very few practice examples (Gick & Holyoak, 1980; Lesgold & Perfetti, 1978) or examples from an overly limited context (Bransford, Vye, Adams, & Perfetti, 1989; Levin, 1979; Nitsch, 1977; Schmidt & Bjork, 1992).

Designing Strategic Integration

In a domain that is hierarchically organized, such as science, review can be designed in such a way that all four of the above review dimensions—sufficient, distributed,

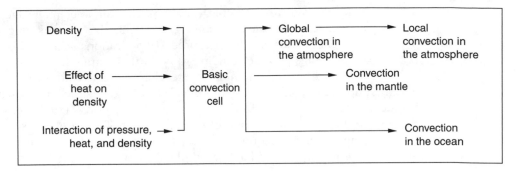

FIGURE 7–6
A Strand Design

varied, and cumulative—are incorporated almost automatically in the design of the curriculum. Instruction can be organized so that new learnings provide a new context for old learnings. In addition, review naturally occurs as subordinate concepts and strategies are incorporated in more complex, integrated concepts and strategies. Figure 7–6 illustrates a strand design that can provide this built-in practice and review. Designing instruction in overlapping strands (topics) facilitates the naturalness of integrated review. The strands that teach the concepts of density, heat, and pressure overlap until they are integrated in the model of the basic convection cell. The concept of density is taught first, then the scaffolding is removed and unscaffolded practice using the concept of density is provided in the context of teaching about the effects of heat on density. Similarly, in initial instruction about pressure, unscaffolded practice with density and heat are provided in the context of learning the interaction of heat, density, and static and dynamic pressure. All of these concepts are further reviewed when they are integrated in the basic convection strategy.

This basic strategy is then applied to explain global convection in the atmosphere, the earth's mantle, and the ocean. Each of the applications provide review of the convection cell and its related concepts. In this way, one of the central goals of the new science standards—connectedness—can be achieved.

THE APPLICATION OF INSTRUCTIONAL DESIGN PRINCIPLES

Developing Instructional Tools

One possible application of the six instructional design principles is in developing instructional tools in the area of science education. First, identify the most important scientific principles and reallocate instructional time so that those concepts and principles are taught more thoroughly. For example, rather than simply have students memorize all the different types of rock, have them apply their understanding of the rock cycle (convection) to predict the next form the rock would take.

Teach explicit steps for applying big ideas. Such steps are an approximation of the steps experts follow covertly (and, perhaps, unconsciously) while working toward similar goals. Strategies for using the big ideas of science should initially be made overt and conspicuous for students through the use of visual maps and models that represent expert knowledge and refute common misconceptions. Wide-ranging application of big ideas facilitates strategy acquisition. Experiential application opportunities should be relevant to better understanding of the instructed big idea and its use.

For example, a strategy for using density could require students to:

1. Identify equivalent volumes in two substances
2. Compare the masses within those volumes
3. Predict which substance will sink

The fundamental steps in the strategy for science inquiry are:

1. Identify the variable to test
2. Create a condition that changes that variable
3. Keep the other variables the same
4. Gather data
5. Interpret the outcome

Good strategy instruction starts with teaching a well-organized knowledge base of component concepts and their relationships. Provide specific instruction in difficult component concepts to achieve an in-depth understanding of the big idea or strategy. For example, the component concepts of the relationship between mass and volume are particularly important in understanding convection. Other component concepts of convection that also relate to density include the effect of heat on density and dynamic pressure. Instruction in these component concepts and their cause-and-effect relationships is crucial to an in-depth understanding of convection.

Similarly, the component step of controlling variables is crucial to effective use of the scientific method. This difficult step requires specific, explicit instruction and practice in varying only the variable under examination and keeping all the other relevant variables the same.

Scaffolded practice, which should follow the introduction of big ideas, strategies, and component concepts, provides a systematic transition from the initial teacher-directed, modeled, structured, prompted practice within defined problem types to a more naturalistic environment of student-directed, unstructured, unpredictable problems that vary widely across all problem types.

Scaffolding can be provided through the design of the tasks or examples or through teacher talk. For example, initial scaffolded instruction in controlling variables could model the procedures for controlling for one variable, then direct and prompt students as they control for a second variable, reminding them to change only the variable they are testing and keeping all the others the same. Finally students can control variables on their own.

All of the previous principles of effective instruction can be integrated in such a way that their incorporation seems natural in the development of understanding. Organize the topics for instruction into overlapping strands so that the connections of science are more easily communicated, the big ideas are more easily built, and scaffolding can build new learning on top of a foundation of prior learning.

Selecting Instructional Tools

A second application of the six instructional design principles is in selecting instructional tools in the area of science education. For this purpose, evaluate tools for important big ideas that are well taught. Look for conspicuous models for using scientific principles (and content) and for conspicuous illustrations of the steps students should use in scientific inquiry. More students become proficient in scientific reasoning (i.e., scientific inquiry) when it is explicitly taught. Many currently popular programs use activity-based instruction to teach the scientific method but do not conspicuously focus instruction on this important strategy. The amount of review provided in a text should be appropriate for the slowest learner. From a teacher's standpoint, dropping review is substantially easier than adding review for diverse learners. Review should be distributed rather than massed. (Ten opportunities over ten days can be more effective than ten opportunities within a single class period.) All that is taught in a program should accumulate within review. That is, review should include not only the most recently learned material, but material from throughout the program. This is particularly true for material that is potentially confusing. Examine the initial instruction and the independent application to see if the tool provides "in-between" application tasks that are scaffolded. Finally, review should include new examples, but new examples of the same type as those used during initial instruction.

Many current science materials are organized around units that can be taught in almost any order. While this design allows flexibility in choice of topics, it encourages a fragmented understanding of science content. Curricular materials that use strategic integration to build an integrated understanding around underlying causal principles, such as convection, rather than around more superficial units, such as geology, meteorology, or oceanography, cannot be rearranged so easily.

Researchers and developers affiliated with the University of Oregon have developed some science curricula that exemplify the design principles described in this text. These materials were not evaluated in the AAAS materials evaluations because they are not a full-year curriculum published by a mainstream publisher. The following materials incorporate many of the design principles described in this chapter: *The Earth Science* (1987) and *Understanding Chemistry* (1989) Core Concepts videodisc science programs marketed by BFA Phoenix Film, and *Reasoning and Writing* published by SRA (Engelmann & Grossen, 2001). *Understanding Life Science* (Carnine, Vachon, Carnine, & Shindledecker, 2001), *Understanding Physical Science* (Steely & Carnine, 2001), and *Understanding Earth Science* (Miller & Carnine, 2001), full-year texts either for middle school or for at-risk high school students struggling to meet standards are currently in development but have no publisher as yet.

Modifying Instructional Tools

A third application of the six instructional design principles is in modifying instructional tools. To emphasize big ideas, develop a course or unit outline identifying the 10 most important concepts or principles for students to learn. Focus instruction and testing on these few concepts or principles. To make strategies conspicuous, model each step and verbalize the thinking that accompanies each step.

Teachers can analyze the important big ideas to identify key component concepts. These concepts will answer the question "why?" For example, a thorough understanding of density and its interaction with heat explains in large part "why" convection occurs. Instruction in key concepts requires more than just a teacher explanation. It also requires the other features of instruction described here: mediated scaffolding and judicious review.

After providing the initial model, teachers can provide scaffolding by using prompts and cues borrowed from the model that assist the students in difficult parts of the strategy or concept, gradually removing the prompts and cues until students are able to use the knowledge accurately and without assistance. Such prompting and cueing would be appropriate for any students whose performance on independent tasks indicates that more work is needed before they can successfully perform independently.

Cut back review for students who need less. If not enough review is provided, then design additional review. Consider that the review should be (1) sufficient, (2) distributed, (3) varied, and (4) cumulative.

Sequence topics so that component concepts are taught first and subsequent material builds on earlier learning. Provide the additional instruction to link the old learning with the new learning for deeper understanding.

SUMMARY

This chapter illustrates six instructional design principles that can improve science instruction and result in higher achievement, particularly for diverse learners. Higher achievement for *all* learners is a national goal in four areas of science: science as inquiry, science subject matter, scientific connections, and science and human affairs.

The big ideas of science inquiry can be applied to any domain of study. The big ideas of science subject matter can be linked with the measurement skills of mathematics to add precision to the predictions of science. Furthermore, the relevance of science to human affairs is a fairly natural consequence of selecting big ideas based on their explanative quality, which in part depends on their utility in human affairs. To enable better problem solving, the structure of science knowledge should be clearly communicated using considerate, user-friendly tools, including visual maps, to illustrate the connections of science. Instruction should teach carefully the component concepts that underlie big ideas, build understanding by showing the utility of strategies in problem solving, include examples that confront common misconceptions, and provide relevant experiences.

For initial learning, teacher-directed experiential methods that scaffold the acquisition of meaningful learning are superior to teacher-directed, passive learning methods and also seem superior to student-centered, experiential methods, particularly for diverse learners. As learners become more proficient, scaffolding should be removed. Whether students should work under close teacher direction or independently depends on careful consideration of the learner's proficiency level in the desired learning objective. Review can be organized into overlapping strands so that all the component concepts are consistently reviewed and then integrated into the larger models.

These six principles can be evaluated in the context of student performance using guidelines developed by Romance, Vitale, and Widergren (1996). If the principles illustrated in this chapter are applied to the design of science instruction, better problem solving and higher level thinking for all learners will result. In addition, the instruction can provide the opportunity for diverse learners, not just university-bound students, to acquire a usable knowledge base in the content and reasoning of science. Providing educational opportunities for diverse learners requires more than simply placing these students in a science class typically earmarked for university-bound students and adding a few teaching tips for making the content accessible to diverse learners (Parmar & Cawley, 1993).

If the only instructional methods used are those that seldom work for diverse learners, the opportunity to learn science remains denied. Considerate, user-friendly instruction in the big ideas of science is most likely to open the doors to understanding science. Diverse learners who receive the instruction described previously in convection may not become expert meteorologists, but they will be able to explain scientific principles such as why mountains form or why seasons change (Muthukrishna et al., 1993). Certain aspects of user-friendly tools and approaches that make science accessible to less able students can also make science accessible to more able students. In contrast, an approach that is designed only for more able students is difficult to modify so that less able students can also learn, because the teacher must design and create the needed missing components.

REFLECTION AND APPLICATION

Case Study

Marielle is in her first year as a kindergarten teacher at Marshall Elementary. All of Marshall's classes are characterized by the school as "inclusion classes." Marielle has a kindergarten class of 17 students. Five of the students have IEPs (three children have speech and language concerns, one child has Down's syndrome, and one student is identified with an emotional and behavioral disorder).

Marielle was a biology major and stated in her job interview that her personal goal was to insure that kindergartners learned science. One of her most meaningful learning experiences as a preservice teacher was participating in the New Century Museum of Natural History's "Virtual Science Seminars." These summer seminars were designed to provide elementary science teachers with a deeper understanding of science content through interactive learning experiences.

For example, one unit entitled "Frames of Reference" was designed to support teachers' understanding of Einstein's theory of relativity and the position and motion of objects through hands-on and virtual experiences. During this unit, Marielle observed a computer simulation in which a basketball, which was glowing, was bounced up and down against a dark backdrop by a moving basketball player. Marielle had to answer questions about the relative position of the ball, basketball player, and background by manipulating components of the simulation.

Marielle was eager to use her learning experiences to create a community of "kinderscientists." As an adult learner, she recognized how much she valued the hands-on learning that she was exposed to in Virtual Science Seminars and was determined to design her instruction so that it emphasized student-centered learning. If this was important and successful in her own learning, certainly it was essential for her kindergarten students.

After consulting with the district science frameworks and the state standards, Marielle decided to begin the year by focusing on her state's "Conceptual Theme 2— Properties of Matter." The goal for kindergarten students within this theme was to understand that "objects have properties that can be observed and used to describe similarities and differences." Marielle thought that this "big idea" would be a perfect overarching concept for kindergarten students. Marielle began brainstorming and exploring ways in which she could use this concept as a cohesive thread to organize her first few weeks of school.

A week before school began, Marielle mailed a welcoming letter to her students and their families. In the envelope she included four buttons of different sizes, shapes, colors, and materials. Additionally, she included a small, snack-sized zip-lock baggie with the child's name written on it. The information in the letter, among other things, instructed the children to talk with their family members about the buttons and then place them into the baggie, zip it tightly, and bring it to school for use in an exciting activity.

On the first day of school, Marielle engaged in the typical first day of kindergarten routines. After the children enjoyed some "getting to know you" activities, she asked the children to bring their baggies to morning circle. She then read *The Button Box* by Margaret Reid to the children. Later in the morning Marielle had learning centers set up for the children. Each of the four stations had a bowl of 30 assorted buttons. Marielle instructed the students to bring their buttons to the centers and sort them with the other buttons by how they looked and felt. She set the timer for 7 minutes.

At first, Marielle was encouraged by what she observed. The children went quietly to their stations and began to examine the buttons. However, within a few minutes, many of the children began to play with the buttons and after about four minutes had lapsed, the noise level in the room had risen dramatically. At the end of the seven minutes many of the buttons were on the floor and those that had been sorted into piles seemed to lack any observable organization. When she questioned her students about the strategy they had used to sort the buttons, only a few were able to answer.

Marielle was surprised by the students' difficulty with this seemingly simple activity. She had done much careful planning in designing similar types of interactive learning activities for her students and hadn't ever considered the possibility that her students might not respond to or learn from this hands-on approach. She felt like she had already failed and was unsure what to do next.

- Why might Marielle's students have had difficulty with this activity? What instructional principles and teaching strategies might Marielle have utilized to make her instruction more likely to result in student success?

The conclusion of the case study can be found later in this chapter.

Content Questions

1. Describe the big ideas of science according to NRC standards.

2. List four commonly cited criticisms of science texts.

3. Name and describe the steps of the scientific method.

4. What have been the findings of research comparing nonexplicit inquiry strategies with explicit methods of instruction?

5. List five examples of big ideas in science subject matter.

6. What are three benefits of presenting big ideas in science curricula?

7. Provide three examples that contribute to the "considerate" quality of an instructional tool.

8. Describe the continuum of instructional scaffolding in science.

9. List each of the four components of judicious review and their benefits for science students.

Reflection and Discussion

1. Imagine that you are listening to a lecture or discussion or attempting to read an article on a scientific subject that assumes an understanding of essential concepts or sophisticated terms that are beyond your present level of training. How might this affect your learning and your motivation to learn? What are the implications of this thought exercise for all students of science, including those with diverse learning needs?

2. In your opinion, should the goal of science education in the primary through secondary grades be the development of subject matter knowledge, inquiry skills, or both? How can effective teaching strategies be utilized to achieve these goals? How can these strategies be used to support the additional goals of understanding scientific connections in human affairs?

3. Should explicit, teacher-directed instructional methods and science inquiry be seen as mutually exclusive? Please explain your answer.

Application

1. Review a science textbook with the following questions in mind. Does the textbook focus on big ideas in science or does it cover numerous concepts and details that tend to vary across domains? Are the important ideas clearly

presented, well developed, and integrated throughout the book? Are student activities explicitly linked to big ideas in science? Develop an example of how principles of effective instruction might be applied to section of this science textbook in order to better support student learning.

Case Study (Conclusion)

Marielle was exhausted by the time she arrived home after that first day. Determined to identify what went wrong with her lesson, she sat down to peruse the course materials from her science seminar. She reviewed her notes from all of the assignments and activities that initially encouraged her to embark on the hands-on button activity. What had made her own experience so instructionally powerful and engaging? Reflecting upon her own question, she realized that her seminars had set her up for success in the hands-on activities through careful and intentional planning. For example, the course provided background readings outlining foundational concepts that were prerequisites for understanding the simulations. Additionally, instructors provided direct explanations and demonstrations of the processes and strategies that participants would need to use to complete the interactive activities. Finally, the activities were sequenced in such a way that the insights that participants gleaned in the initial activities were directly supportive of the more complex learning that took place later in the summer. The "ah-ha" moments that excited Marielle during her hands-on experiences resulted from the sequential building and mediation of her learning experiences. Her learning experiences was so seamless that she had failed to think through the work that had preceded her connection.

Marielle saw the children's faces in her mind's eye as she replayed the lesson in her head. The children's quiet wandering to the centers may have been a sign of uncertainty or disorientation as they probably had little understanding of the task they faced. The rising noise level was likely additional evidence of their confusion. Marielle realized that the students' inability to articulate any sorting strategies was probably related to her oversight in neglecting to *teach* any strategies conspicuously. Marielle decided to revisit and plan her lesson again.

Marielle realized that in selecting *The Button Box,* she had been distracted by the title. In the book, the boy describes various buttons from the perspective of what he imagines and knows about them in relation to his family history. Marielle decided that her literature introduction should be more closely related to the learning goal of the lesson (i.e., properties of objects). She also decided that for this initial lesson, she should scaffold the instruction so that students would be initially working with only one type of attribute. She hoped that this would help ensure student success and provide a framework for future learning.

She decided to focus first on color. *Is It Red? Is It Yellow? Is It Blue?* by Tana Hoban would be much more supportive to the children in learning about color. After reading the book, and modeling the activity for the children, Marielle would provide them with sets of buttons that were identical in all ways except color. They would engage in sorting buttons by color in their learning centers, followed by a rich discussion designed to process the students' experience with the hands-on activity. It would also allow Marielle to support their developing vocabulary related to sorting and color. Once Marielle was comfortable with the student's grasp of the concept of sorting the buttons by color, she would build upon this understanding and introduce new attributes such as size, shape, and texture. She planned to continue to provide students with interactive learning activities, but not before she was sure that students had the skills and strategies to be successful. Marielle felt more confident that her revised lesson plan would better meet the needs of her students through conspicuous instruction and modeling of effective strategies along with realistic and scaffolded supports for the follow-up hands-on activity.

- How could a teacher who provides conspicuous and scaffolded science instruction respond if a parent expressed concern that students were not being given an "opportunity to discover" science principles on their own?

The Reflection and Application section of this chapter was written by Maureen F. Ruby and Richard P. Zipoli, Jr., both of the University of Connecticut.

REFERENCES

AMERICAN ASSOCIATION FOR THE ADVANCEMENT OF SCIENCE. (1993). *Benchmarks for science literacy: Project 2061.* Washington, DC: Author.

AMERICAN ASSOCIATION FOR THE ADVANCEMENT OF SCIENCE. (1999). *Heavy books light on learning: Not one middle grade science text rated satisfactory by AAAS's Project 2061.* Washington, DC: Author.

AMERICAN ASSOCIATION FOR THE ADVANCEMENT OF SCIENCE. (2000). *Big biology books fail to convey big ideas, reports AAAS's Project 2061.* Washington, DC: Author.

AMERICAN ASSOCIATION FOR THE ADVANCEMENT OF SCIENCE. (in press). *Atlas of science literacy.* Washington, DC: Author.

ARMBRUSTER, B. (1984). The problem of "inconsiderate text." In G. G. Duffy, L. R. Roehler, & J. Mason (Eds.), *Comprehension instruction* (pp. 202–217). New York: Longman.

ARMBRUSTER, B., ANDERSON, T. H., & OSTERTAG, J. (1987). Does text structure/summarization instruction facilitate learning from expository text? *Reading Research Quarterly, 22,* 331–346.

BAY, M., STAVER, J., BRYAN, T., & HALE, J. (1992). Science instruction for mildly handicapped: Direct instruction versus discovery teaching. *Journal of Research in Science Teaching, 29* (6), 555–570.

BRANSFORD, J. D., VYE, N. J., ADAMS, L. T., & PERFETTI, C. A. (1989). Learning skills and the acquisition of knowledge. In A. Lesgold & R. Glaser (Eds.), *Foundations for a psychology of education* (pp. 199–249). Hillsdale, NJ: Erlbaum.

BREDDERMAN, T. (1983). Effects of activity-based elementary science on student outcomes: A quantitative synthesis. *Review of Educational Research, 53* (4), 499–518.

CARNINE, D., VACHON, V., CARNINE, L., & SHINDLEDECKER, K. (2001). *Understanding life science.* Unpublished manuscript.

CHAMPAGNE, A., & BUNCE, D. (1989, April). *Electricity in 6th grade tests: Too much, too fast.* Paper presented at the American Educational Research Association Conference, San Francisco.

CORE CONCEPTS. (1987). *Earth science.* St. Louis, MO: BFA Phoenix Film.

CORE CONCEPTS. (1989). *Understanding chemistry.* St. Louis, MO: BFA Phoenix Film.

COVINGTON, M. V., & CRUTCHFIELD, R. S. (1965). Facilitation of creative problem solving. *Programmed Instruction, 4,* 3–5, 10.

ELEMENTARY SCIENCE STUDY. (1974). *Attribute games and problems: Teacher's Guide.* New York: McGraw-Hill.

ENGELMANN, Z., & GROSSEN, B. (2001). *Reasoning and writing.* Blacklick, OH: Science Research Associates.

GICK, M. L., & HOLYOAK, K. (1980). Analogical problem solving. *Cognitive Psychology, 12,* 306–355.

GUASTELLO, E. F., BEASLEY, T. M., & SINATRA, R. C. (2000). Concept mapping effects on science content comprehension of low-achieving inner-city seventh graders. *Remedial and Special Education, 21,* (6) 356–365.

GUZZETTI, B. J. (1990). Effects of textual and instructional manipulations on concept acquisition. *Reading Psychology, 11,* 49–62.

GUZZETTI, B., SNYDER, T. E., GLASS, G. V., & GAMAS, W. S. (1993). Promoting conceptual change in science: A comparative meta-analysis of instructional interventions from reading education and science education. *Reading Research Quarterly, 28* (2), 116–159.

HIDER, R. A., & RICE, D. R. (1986). *A comparison of instructional mode on the attitude and achievement of fifth and sixth grade students in science.* Technical research report. Mobile, AL: University of South Alabama.

KANTOR, R. N., ANDERSON, T. H., & ARMBRUSTER, B. B. (1983). How inconsiderate are children's textbooks? *Journal of Curriculum Studies, 15,* 6–72.

KLAHR, D., & NIGAM, M. (2004). The equivalence of learning paths in early science instruction. *Psychological Science, 15* (10), 661–667.

KUHN, D. (1993). Science as argument: Implications for teaching and learning scientific thinking. *Science Education, 77* (3), 319–337.

LESGOLD, A. M., & PERFETTI, C. A. (1978). Interactive processes in reading comprehension. *Discourse Processes, 1,* 323–336.

LAWSON, A., MCELRATH, C., BURTON, M., JAMES, B., DOYLE, R. WOODWARD, S., ET AL. (1991). Hypothetico-deductive reasoning skill and concept acquisition. Testing a constructivist hypothesis. *Journal of Research in Science Teaching, 28* (10), 953–970.

LEVIN, T. (1979). Instruction which enables students to develop higher mental processes. *Evaluation in education: An international review series, 3* (3), 174–220.

LLOYD, C. V. (1989, December). *The relationship between scientific literacy and high school biology textbooks.* Paper presented at the annual meeting of the National Reading Conference, Austin, TX.

MAIN, J., & ROWE, M. (1993). The relation of locus-of-control orientation and task structure to problem-solving performance of sixth-grade student pairs. *Journal of Research in Science Teaching, 30* (4), 401–426.

MAYER, R. E. (1989). Models for understanding. *Review of Educational Research, 59* (1), 43–64.

MAYER, R. E., & GALLINI, J. (1990). When is an illustration worth ten thousand words? *Journal of Educational Psychology, 82* (4), 715–726.

MCCARTHY, C. (2005). Effects of thematic-based, hands-on science teaching versus a textbook approach for students with disabilities. *Journal of Research in Science Teaching, 42* (3) 245–263.

McCleery, J., & Tindal, G. (1999). Teaching the scientific method to at-risk students and students with learning disabilities through concept anchoring and explicit instruction. *Remedial and Special Education, 20* (1), 7–18.

Miller, S., & Carnine, D. (2001). *Understanding earth science.* Unpublished manuscript.

Muthukrishna, A., Carnine, D., Grossen, B., & Miller, S. (1993). Children's alternate frameworks: Should they be directly addressed in science instruction? *Journal of Research in Science Teaching, 30* (3), 233–248.

National Research Council. (1993). *National science education standards: A sampler.* Washington, DC: National Academy Press.

National Research Council. (1995). *National science education standards.* Washington, DC: National Academy Press.

Newport, J. F. (1990). Elementary science texts: What's wrong with them? *Educational Digest, 59,* 68–69.

Niedelman, M. (1992). Problem solving and transfer. In D. Carnine & E. Kame'enui (Eds.), *Higher order thinking: Designing curriculum for mainstreamed students* (pp. 137–156). Austin, TX: Pro-Ed.

Nitsch, K. E. (1977). *Structuring decontextualized forms of knowledge.* Unpublished doctoral dissertation, Vanderbilt University.

Olton, R. M., & Crutchfield, R. S. (1969). Developing the skills of productive thinking. In P. Mussen, J. Langer, & M. Covington (Eds.), *Trends and issues in developmental psychology* (pp. 68–91). New York: Holt, Rinehart and Winston.

Osborn, J. H., Jones, B. F., & Stein, M. (1985). The case for improving textbooks. *Educational Leadership, 42,* 9–16.

Parmar, R. S., & Cawley, J. F. (1993). Analysis of science textbook recommendations provided for students with disabilities. *Exceptional Children, 59* (6), 518–531.

Raizen, S. (1988). *Increasing educational productivity through improving the science curriculum.* Washington, DC: The National Center for Improving Science Education.

Romance, N. R., Vitale, M. R., & Widergren, P. (1996). *Student conceptual understanding in science: Knowledge-based perspectives for enhancing teaching practices.* Monograph series. Washington, DC: National Science Teachers Association.

Ross, J. A. (1988). Controlling variables: A meta-analysis of training studies. *Review of Educational Research, 58* (4), 405–437.

Rubin, R., & Norman, J. (1992). Systematic modeling versus the learning cycle: Comparative effects on integrated science process skill achievement. *Journal of Research in Science Teaching, 29* (7), 715–727.

Schmidt, R., & Bjork, R. (1992). New conceptualizations of practice: Common principles in three paradigms suggest new concepts for training. *Psychological Science, 3* (4), 207–217.

Shaw, T. (1983). The effect of a process-oriented science curriculum upon problem-solving ability. *Science Education, 67* (5), 615–623.

Shayer, M., & Adey, P. (1993). Accelerating the development of formal thinking in middle and high school students IV: Three years after a two-year intervention. *Journal of Research in Science Teaching, 3* (4), 351–366.

Shymansky, J., Kyle, W., & Alport, J. (1983). The effects of new science curricula on student performance. *Journal of Research in Science Teaching, 20* (5), 387–404.

Smith, E., Blakeslee, T., & Anderson, C. (1993). Teaching strategies associated with conceptual change learning in science. *Journal of Research in Science Teaching, 30* (2), 111–126.

Staver, J. R., & Small, L. (1990). Toward a clearer representation of the crisis in science education. *Journal of Research in Science Teaching, 27* (1), 79–89.

Steely, D., & Carnine, D. (2001). *Understanding physical science.* Unpublished manuscript.

WARDROP, J. L., GOODWIN, W. L., KLAUSMEIER, R. M., OLTON, R. M., COVINGTON, R. S., CRUTCHFIELD, et al. (1969). The development of productive thinking skills in 5th-grade children. *Journal of Experimental Education, 37,* 67–77.

WOOD, T. L., & WOOD, W. L. (1988). Assessing potential difficulties in comprehending fourth-grade science textbooks. *Science Education, 72* (5), 561–574.

WOODWARD, J. (1994). Effects of curriculum discourse style on eighth graders' recall and problem solving in earth science. *Elementary School Journal, 94* (3), 299–314.

YAGER, R. E., & PENICK, J. E. (1987). Resolving the crisis in science education: Understanding before resolution. *Science Education, 71* (1), 49–55.

YATES, G. C. R., & YATES, S. (1990). Teacher effectiveness research: Towards describing user-friendly classroom instruction. *Educational Psychology, 10* (3), 225–238.

YEANY, R. H., YAP, K. C., & PADILLA, M. J. (1986). Analyzing hierarchical relationships among modes of cognitive reasoning and integrated science process skills. *Journal of Research in Science Teaching, 23* (4), 277–291.

ZOHAR, A., & AHARON-KRAVETSKY, S. (2005). Exploring the effects of cognitive conflict and direct teaching for students of different academic levels. *Journal of Research in Science Teaching, 42* (7), 829–855.

CHAPTER 8

Effective Strategies for
Teaching Social Studies

Donald B. Crawford
Western Washington University

Douglas W. Carnine
University of Oregon

Mark K. Harniss
University of Washington

Keith L. Hollenbeck
University of Oregon

Samuel K. Miller
University of Oregon

EQUAL ACCESS TO an education should not simply entail using the same instructional strategies with all children; the goal is to use strategies that are effective for every child. This chapter discusses how the six important principles for improving instructional strategies presented in earlier chapters can be applied to social studies education. The six principles are derived from a comprehensive review of the education research literature (National Center to Improve the Tools of Educators, 2001). The chapter purpose is to illustrate how the six principles can be used to modify or develop educational strategies to be effective for teaching social studies to students with diverse learning needs (refer to Chapter 2 for a discussion of diverse learning needs).

CURRENT ISSUES IN SOCIAL STUDIES INSTRUCTION

Current reforms within social studies education require us to begin with a discussion of its fundamental issues. The field of social studies is among the most complex and fractious of all academic fields and classroom subjects. It is based on a loose confederation of disciplines that include anthropology, archaeology, economics, geography, history, law-related education, philosophy, political science, psychology, religion, and sociology. Educators and curriculum designers have struggled for years over the relative weight to give the various disciplines and over which disciplines to include under the social studies umbrella. The struggle to agree on national standards in the area of history was so contentious that the effort has essentially been abandoned (Ravitch, 2000).

A second struggle over expectations seemingly has been resolved. There is now widespread agreement that competency in social studies is essential for everyone. This goal is exemplified by the recommendation of the Multicultural Education Consensus panel discussing social studies instruction: "Schools should ensure that all students have equitable opportunities to learn and to meet high standards" (Banks et al., 2005, p. 36).

This new emphasis means that social studies teachers face increased expectations for teaching a diverse student population with a wide range of cognitive abilities. The challenge for students is that many of the changes associated with the "new social studies" of the 1960s—inductive teaching, discovery learning, and content drawn from the newer social sciences—continue to influence social studies reform today. These programs were of great interest to scholars and university professors but were not a great success in the classroom and "emphasized the brightest students without much consideration of other students" (Hertzberg, 1981, cited in Brophy, 1990, p. 359). Clearly, yesterday's instructional strategies will not be adequate for teaching today's diverse learners.

In recent years the debate about what social studies education should stress has prompted a series of recommendations from national commissions, task forces, and professional organizations—e.g., the National Council for the Social Studies, the Bradley Commission, the National Commission on Social Studies in the Schools, and the National Center for History in the Schools. The recommendations generally advocate that the purpose of social studies education is to develop well-educated citizens who share a common body of knowledge drawn in a coordinated and systematic way from a range of disciplines and that content knowledge from the social studies should not be treated as knowledge to memorize, but as knowledge through which important questions may be explored.

As an example of these recommendations, the National Council for the Social Studies (NCSS) articulated a set of 10 thematic strands that form the basis of the social studies standards. The scope of the social studies curriculum remains disconcertingly broad, as one can see from the 10 NCSS strands:

Social studies should include experiences that provide for the study of . . .

1. Culture and cultural diversity
2. The ways human beings view themselves in and over time
3. People, places, and environments
4. Individual development and identity
5. Interactions among individuals, groups, and institutions
6. How people create and change structures of power, authority, and governance
7. How people organize for the production, distribution, and consumption of goods and services
8. Relationships among science, technology, and society
9. Global connections and interdependence
10. The ideals, principles, and practices of citizenship in a democratic republic (National Council for the Social Studies, 1994, pp. 365–368)

Developers of state standards for social studies have the difficult task of translating these recommendations into meaningful benchmarks for learning while struggling to reconcile problems associated with content selection and an overloaded curriculum. In general, elementary grade social studies instructional materials are criticized for teaching too little content, and secondary level materials are viewed as two-minute reviews of the earth's history, which emphasize coverage rather than depth. United States history curricula exemplify these problems:

The typical American history survey course . . . comprises everything from Mayans to moon landings. We are, as far as I know, the only country in the Western world that tries to teach the whole of our history to students in a single year. It's just insane. (Gagnon in O'Neil, ASCD Update, 1989, p. 5)

From this discussion it is clear that an ongoing concern about social studies centers on what content is worthwhile to teach and how it can be taught effectively. The challenge of teaching social studies is to provide students with both breadth and depth. In response to this problem, many social studies educators advocate the development of curriculum and instruction around selected concepts, rather than the superficial parade-of-facts approach (Twyman & Tindal, 2005). Some of the national recommendations for teaching social studies reflect a sentiment that can be characterized as "pausing for depth":

There is the ever-present problem of time. Social history, no less than political history, requires careful selection from among the numberless topics available. The sheer scope of the historical record requires the imaginative synthesis of political and social, cultural, economic, and religious history around central, significant themes and questions. (National Center for History in the Schools, 1992, p. 17)

Taking the time to teach depth of knowledge has its cost, and as yet there has been no consensus on content that can be left out to give time for more depth of study. Unfortunately, state officials who write the various state standards do not share the educators' notion of the perspective of "less is more" (Placier, Walker, & Foster, 2002). Students who learned about one particular theme, culture, region, or historical era in depth would likely do poorly on state performance assessments that sample broadly from the lengthy lists of state social studies standards. For this reason teachers feel considerable pressure to cover all of the material listed in the various state social studies standards. This increasing pressure from state level standards-based accountability has overwhelmed any other perspectives on what should be taught in social studies classes. For teachers currently, all instruction must be directly and explicitly aligned with specifics in the state standards (Kauffman, Johnson, Kardos, Liu, & Peske, 2002; Sandholtz, Ogawa, & Scribner, 2004; Twyman & Tindal, 2005). Given that much of this instruction must be designed by the individual teacher, instructional strategies to do so effectively assume ever greater importance.

PRINCIPLES FOR IMPROVING INSTRUCTIONAL STRATEGIES IN SOCIAL STUDIES

One challenge specific to improving the instructional strategies for teaching social studies has to do with how to assist diverse learners in identifying and remembering what is truly important to learn. Social studies teachers widely recognize the difficulties that diverse learners experience when attempting to garner the critical information from textbooks (Twyman & Tindal, 2005). Considerable research has shown that employing a variety of mediators of content such as advance organizers, study guides, interspersed questions, concept maps and other graphic organizers can greatly improve the ability of diverse learners to successfully acquire the essential content. These various forms of content mediation have three basic functions. One, they direct students' attention to the most important ideas in the textbook. Two, they focus attention on the organizational structures of the texts. Three, they require rehearsal by asking students to recite or write down critical information (see Figure 8–1).

Rich, authentic learning experiences are not sufficient for eliminating the difficulties that diverse learners experience in acquiring knowledge by reading textbooks. The same mediators of content needed by diverse learners when they are expected to learn from textbooks are also needed if they are to successfully learn from nontextbook sources such as watching videos, interviewing adult informants,

FIGURE 8–1
Basic Functions of Mediational Materials

1. ***Direct student's attention*** to the most important ideas in the textbook.

2. ***Focus attention*** on the organizational structures of the text.

3. ***Require rehearsal.*** Students recite or write down information.

listening to plays, going on field trips, having discussions, or participating in simulations. Even when the source of information is more user friendly than the typical textbook, teachers must still create mediational materials that insure that diverse learners attend to the most important concepts, understand the organization of the information, and have an opportunity to recite or write down the key ideas. Teacher creation of mediational materials that assist diverse learners in acquiring, comprehending, and remembering social studies content demands a critical analysis of the curriculum, and admittedly, can be very time consuming. Ellis and Sabornie (1990) found that teachers trained in creating these kinds of mediational materials were concerned about the extra time required to prepare them. Currently, the demand that all social studies lessons meet specifically delineated state standards has generally relegated textbooks to the status of an occasionally-used reference. Many new teachers attempting to design instruction aligned with state standards, without the ability to rely on a textbook for assistance, are completely overwhelmed (Kauffman et al., 2002).

A second challenge facing efforts to improve instructional strategies for teaching social studies has to do with how to assess student outcomes. The multiple-choice tests traditionally associated with social studies texts are increasingly coming under attack, as are the somewhat similar multiple-choice national norm-referenced tests in social studies. Recommendations for replacing these with performance assessments of projects, essays, oral reports, simulation activities, and the like have yet to be accompanied by stringent assessment criteria that would help identify students who have not learned what was expected. In addition to lack of stringent assessment criteria, performance assessments have been very difficult to score reliably. Further, when diverse learners lack skills in writing or public speaking, it is often impossible to discern what they have learned from their low scores on performance assessments. Without assessment criteria that can discriminate between successful and unsuccessful student results, teachers receive minimal useful feedback on the effectiveness of their social studies teaching. Without useful feedback on the effectiveness of such teaching efforts, it is very difficult for teachers to improve their instructional strategies.

Designing Instruction Around Big Ideas

Rather than sacrificing breadth of coverage in an effort to make sense of social studies, one approach for bringing order to a breadth of social studies content is to organize it around *big ideas*. Big ideas are important concepts or principles that are more specific than the thematic strands recommended by NCSS and fundamentally different from traditional social studies concepts such as democracy or community. Not all big ideas in social studies are equally useful. Big ideas must be chosen that facilitate efficient and broad acquisition of knowledge. To be instructionally effective, big ideas in social studies must be chosen which enable learners to organize, interrelate, and apply information so that meaningful connections can be made within social studies, and between social studies content and their own lives. Only a few big ideas need to be developed to adequately organize a year's worth of instruction in social studies because these ideas have repeated applicability. Choosing big ideas requires a thorough reading of the material with an eye to recurrent relationships and patterns. The following sections describe several examples of big ideas and discuss their value for preparing meaningful social studies curriculum and instruction. This handful of ideas was enough to organize instruction in U.S. history through the Civil War (Carnine, Crawford, Harniss, & Hollenbeck, 1994).

Problem–Solution–Effect. The problem–solution–effect structure is one example of a big idea. When applied to the study of social studies, it has the potential to help students understand that individuals, groups, and governments tend to react to common problems with identifiable causes and solutions. At the same time, the elements of the problem–solution–effect analysis can have great relevance to the daily lives of students. The structure and examples described are based on a United States history text (Carnine et al., 1994).

Problems. Common problems in social studies can be attributed to the following economic or human rights issues:

1. Economic problems can generally be linked to conditions that create difficulty for people trying to acquire or keep things they need or want. At a basic level, people need and want to maintain the availability of food, clothing, and shelter. In their personal lives students can identify the struggle with economic problems—trying to acquire or keep things they need or want—and have an intuitive understanding of the motivational power of economic issues.
2. Human rights problems in social studies are usually linked to groups of people trying to achieve rights associated with religious freedom, freedom of speech, equal protection under the law, equal rights for women, minorities, different social classes, and so forth. Adolescents are especially concerned about issues related to equal rights and freedom of expression in their own lives.

Solutions. When students can classify common historical problems, they can relate this knowledge to recurring actions people use to solve problems. Recurring solutions to historical problems can be categorized as attempts by individuals or groups to either move, invent, dominate, tolerate, or accommodate. These five solutions are described as follows:

1. *Move.* When people move to solve a problem, they hope to find a new place where the problem does not exist. United States history is filled with examples of immigrants and pioneers who moved in response to problems. While students seldom have the option of moving themselves to solve problems, they all are acquainted with family members or friends who have moved to solve problems as well as the limitations of this type of solution to problems.
2. *Invent.* Throughout history people have tried to solve problems by inventing new ways or abilities to do things they could not do before. For example, people could not farm on the Great Plains because the soil was too heavy to plow. The invention of the steel plow solved this economic problem. Students' experience with inventions rarely extends to seeing them as solutions to problems, but through an examination of historical examples they can develop this understanding.

3. *Dominate.* Another way people historically have solved problems involves controlling or dominating other people. The United States and its allies fought against Germany, Japan, and Italy in World War II. The opposing sides tried to dominate each other in response to economic problems such as inflation, unemployment, and limited natural resources. From personal experience, students know that attempting to dominate others can result in a fight in which both sides lose. Students can apply this knowledge to understand historical events involving domination.

4. *Accommodate.* When people accommodate each other, they adjust or adapt to solve a problem. Historically, people have accommodated each other by negotiating or compromising. For example, delegates from the Northern and Southern states effected a series of compromises that enabled passage of the Constitution despite their serious ideological differences. Young people are aware of the power of negotiations in their dealings with adults and that understanding can be applied to historical situations as well.

5. *Tolerate.* When one group of people decides not to move, invent, dominate, or accommodate, they tolerate a problem. Sometimes this solution is applied because there is no other choice. Before 1863, although many African Americans escaped slavery or fought against it, many others had to tolerate the problems of being slaves and of not having equal rights. Again, students can use their own lives to appreciate the connection between power and one's choice of solution. Adolescents know they only tolerate a situation when they do not have the power to change it.

Understanding the relationship between common problems and solutions can help students view social studies as a dynamic subject. Common solutions to problems in one era often become less viable as times change. Today, moving to solve the problem of acquiring land to grow food is less practical than it was 150 years ago when territory could still be taken from the Native Americans. Moving to acquire land to grow food has been replaced by the invention of new ways to grow more food on land that has already been settled.

Effects. Solutions to problems produce consequences or effects. One effect is that a problem may cease to exist, but an examination of social studies shows that solutions to problems often create new problems. For example, tribes of the Pueblo culture in the Southwest desert solved the problem of building shelters in an environment where wood was hard to find. Their solution was to build the walls of their homes with stones and use logs only to support the roof.

Building the walls with stone had the effect of creating a new problem—the extreme amount of hard work required to carry heavy stones for constructing shelters. The Pueblo tribes solved this problem by eliminating the space between homes so they shared a common wall.

The problem–solution–effect big idea can be useful to teachers as a framework for helping students organize their thinking during oral reading, classroom discussions, and written essays. Such big ideas can be especially useful to students in reading both textbooks and primary source documents.

Figure 8–2 is an excerpt from a social studies textbook (Carnine et al., 1994) which uses the big idea of problem–solution–effect to describe how the Chinook tribe solved problems related to food, clothing, and shelter and the effects of those solutions. Note, however, that a different big idea could have been used to present the same material. For example, an alternate big idea that could be used in this instance is, "People's cultures reflect aspects of their environment."

This narrative is also an example of clearly written text students can easily comprehend. It is important for teachers and authors of instructional materials to understand that improving social studies curricula requires more than simply changing the length of words and sentences. For an instructional tool to do more than provide information, every aspect of its design must be carefully engineered to bring about understanding.

Multiple Perspectives. Another big idea in social studies is the notion that events can be viewed from more than one perspective and that these different perspectives are important to fully understanding social events. The following discussion of multiple perspectives is placed within the context of the problem–solution–effect big idea.

Something that will be a problem from one perspective may not be a problem from another perspective. In fact, what is a solution from the perspective of one person or group may actually create problems for another person or group. Understanding this relationship can help students recognize that groups of people often have different perspectives about the same event. Figure 8–3 illustrates the big idea of multiple perspectives at an elementary level.

A related big idea that could be used at an elementary level is, "There are always two sides to every story (or argument)." This idea is closely related to multiple perspectives and it could be used both to structure the solving of disagreements and social problems within the classroom as well as to prompt students to look for an opposing point of view when doing research in the newspaper, for example. An instructional tool that consistently presented both sides of each "story" would go a long way toward developing critical thinking skills in students.

Factors of Group Success. Another big idea is that the success of group efforts, such as wars or the establishment of colonies, are frequently associated with the following four factors:

1. *Motivation.* Successful groups have group members or supporters who are committed to a common goal.
2. *Leadership.* Successful groups have highly qualified, knowledgeable, and effective leaders.
3. *Resources.* Successful groups have sufficient resources (usually money) to accomplish their goals.
4. *Capability.* In addition to resources and leadership, successful groups have a sufficient quality of know-how and appropriate tools to accomplish their goals.

The Chinook Culture's Solutions to Basic Problems

The Chinook and the Problem of Food. The Chinook found plenty to eat. The rivers of the Pacific Northwest Coast were a great place to catch fish. The Chinook knew that the best time to catch fish was during the runs when the salmon left the ocean to go up the rivers to spawn. The Chinook would work so hard during the salmon runs that the tribe would catch enough salmon to last all year. They took so many salmon at one time that it was more like harvesting a crop than it was like fishing. The salmon were cleaned and then smoked or dried to preserve them as food for the rest of the year.

In general, Native American tribes had to meet their basic needs by adjusting and adapting to use the natural resources and their environment. The Chinook also had to use the solution of accommodating to their environment in order to survive. The Chinook accommondated to the generous supply of salmon in their environment by making salmon a main staple of their diet.

However, the Chinook wanted to have something to eat besides fish all the time. Another way the Chinook got food was by gathering food from edible plants in the forests, especially blackberries which grow wild in the region.

There was a third way of getting food, besides fishing and gathering, on the Northwest Coast. The men also hunted game, but that was a much less important source of food than fishing.

The Chinook would also go out to sea and bring back other kinds of fish and even whales to eat. The Chinook were the same as the Inuit because they both needed boats of some kind to use to go out to fish in the sea and also travel from village to village. The Chinook were different from the Inuit because they had plenty of trees in their environment. Because they had trees the Chinook did not need to make boats and canoes out of animal skins. The Chinook used the plentiful forests along the Northwest Coast to make their canoes and boats out of wood. The largest boats were 60 to 70 feet long. These huge boats were hollowed out of a single trunk of one of the huge cedar trees in their forests.

The Chinook and the Problem of Clothing. The northernmost tribe in the Northwest Coast, the Tlingit (tling-git, rhymes with fling kit), made use of tailored garments of deerskin, with leggings (pants) and moccasins, a style of clothing that was common throughout North America.

The milder temperature of the rest of the Northwest Coast region meant that the Chinook did not need as much clothing as the Tlingit. South of the Tlingit, the Chinook wore minimal clothing, usually a deerskin leather shirt and breechcloth, which is like the bottom part of a bikini. However, in rainy weather, the deerskin leather clothing became wet and uncomfortable. The Chinook found a way to make use of their plentiful forests to provide clothing that was cooler and more comfortable to wear than deerskin leather. The soft, stringy inner bark of cedar trees was softened and then woven into cloth to make cooler clothes. The tribes south of the Tlingit, where the climate was more rainy and warmer, preferred clothing made of shredded and woven bark. This softened cedar bark was also used to make blankets.

The Chinook and the Problem of Shelter. Because of the plentiful forests in the Northwest Coast region, the Chinook made many things from the trees in the forest. They used wood to construct buildings that were large enough for several families to live in at the same time. The wooden buildings were organized into villages of as many as 1,000 people.

The Effect of the Chinook Solutions. The Chinook accommodated to the plentiful supply of salmon by making salmon their main food. As a result of adapting to their environment the needs of the Chinook were well met. The effect was that the Chinook had more free time for celebrations and for artistic works. The art of the Chinook is still prized today. These are the effects of making good use of the abundant natural resources of the Northwest Coast.

FIGURE 8–2

Example of Problem–Solution–Effect Passage from Textbook

From: Carnine, D., Crawford, D., Harniss, M., & Hollenbeck, K. (1994). *Understanding U.S. History. Volume 1: Through the Civil War.* Eugene, OR: Considerate Publishing. Reprinted by permission.

Perspective of Local Community	Perspective of People Who Live Near the Airport

Problem: Not enough jobs.	
Solution: Build an airport.	**Problem:** Airplanes cause a lot of noise.
Effect: People get jobs at the airport.	**Solution:** People try to sell their houses.
	Effect: The noise of the airplanes makes it difficult for people to sell their houses and they lose money.

FIGURE 8–3
Graphic Representation of an Example of Multiple Perspectives

These factors can help explain why different groups throughout history either succeeded or failed in reaching their goals. For example, when the Constitution was first proposed, many Americans were reluctant to support its passage. They saw no need to change from the voluntary form of cooperation that had worked for the colonies up to that time. Initially, only wealthy, established leaders known as the Federalists supported establishing the Constitution. The Federalists supported the Constitution because they were convinced a stronger federal government was in their best interest.

The four factors associated with group success can help students understand why the Federalists were able to get the Constitution ratified despite widespread opposition:

1. *Motivation.* The Federalists were motivated to secure passage of the Constitution because they strongly believed it would help protect their considerable business interests. Their desire for success was much greater than that of their opposition, who simply did not like the idea of a federal government.

2. *Leadership.* Both the Federalists and their opponents had capable leaders who were able to persuade followers to support their position.
3. *Resources.* The Federalists had superior monetary resources compared to the anti-Federalists. This gave the Federalists an advantage in organizing and mobilizing their followers.
4. *Capability.* The Federalists had carefully planned and organized how to achieve their goal during, and possibly even prior to, the Constitutional Convention. They knew what they were doing and how to do it. This provided the Federalists with a head start over their opponents and ultimately led to passage of the Constitution.

Problem–solution–effect, multiple perspectives, and the four factors of group success are three examples of big ideas in social studies instruction. When social studies is taught in this way, it becomes possible for students to comprehend historical events as an interrelated network.

Big ideas enable relevance-making activities. At one level big ideas are useful because their explanatory power can help students more easily understand content material. Equally important is that big ideas can help students recognize connections between the content of social studies and their personal lives.

A big idea such as the four factors of group success can provide students with a tool for applying what they learn during social studies to current events and their own lives. Through repeated exposure, students can learn how to use the four factors to analyze the strengths and weaknesses of group efforts in almost any realm. An elementary teacher might use this framework to discuss plans for a fund drive for playground equipment. A high school teacher might use this big idea to lead students to discuss their high school football team in terms of the motivation, leadership, resources, and capability of the team. A political science instructor might use it to analyze and predict the outcome of an upcoming general election.

The problem–solution–effect analysis is another big idea students can apply to their own lives. For example, two eighth-grade boys who had learned this big idea in social studies class got into a fight and were sent to the office. While the boys were awaiting their fate outside the principal's office one of the authors stopped to ask what happened. When they explained they got into a fight, the author remarked, "I guess someone was trying to dominate, eh?" One of the boys replied, "Yeah, next time we ought to try accommodating."

Designing Conspicuous Strategies

Teaching higher order thinking (i.e., problem solving, decision making, analysis, and critical thinking) is another highly valued goal of social studies education reform. Although social studies educators tend to distinguish among the terms *problem solving, decision making, analysis,* and *critical thinking,* they all require students to apply an organizational strategy to understand and apply content knowledge. Extensive empirical evidence suggests that all students benefit from having such organizational strategies made conspicuous for them, and that diverse learners are especially in need of conspicuous presentation of the organization of knowledge. In practice, however, social studies curricula and materials rarely include explicit organizational strategies designed to help students understand and apply content knowledge.

A strategy is a general set of steps used to solve a problem or analyze content. Very often in the social studies, effective strategies are literally the application of a big idea. Higher-performing students are more likely to invent their own useful organizational strategies, given adequate time. The purpose of explicit strategy instruction is to ensure that all learners have equal and timely access to the details that lead to success in solving a problem. The emphasis in social studies on critical thinking provides a natural context for including strategies in instruction on social studies content.

Teaching students to apply the big idea of problem–solution–effect when examining the behavior of groups would be an example of a conspicuous strategy that could be profitably taught initially in the early grades. Problem–solution–effect develops naturally out of the narrative text structure with which students are familiar. Given social studies passages that used problem–solution–effect as an expository text structure, students could learn to anticipate and predict the elements of social studies material as well as they do stories. Looking for the motivating problems, attempts at solutions, and the effects of those attempts could serve as a heuristic strategy for initial efforts at research.

A second strategy for relating historical conditions to group behavior could be taught to students who understand that group cooperation evolves in identifiable developmental stages. Students at a young age can be taught the specific features of this big idea as a strategy for examining group cooperative activities. Figure 8–4 summarizes four common conditions and their relationship to the development of group cooperation.

In a multiyear social studies curriculum designed around big ideas and conspicuous strategies, young learners could begin by learning a basic strategy in social studies

FIGURE 8–4
Stages of Group Cooperation

1. **Gather together and discuss common problems**
   IF some members agree on a solution to a common problem, THEN people will begin occasional voluntary cooperation.

2. **Occasional voluntary cooperation**
   IF cooperative solutions are effective and the problems recur, THEN people will begin to cooperate regularly.

3. **Regular voluntary cooperation**
   IF the need for cooperation continues but voluntary cooperation fails, THEN people may agree to legally binding cooperation.

4. **Legally binding cooperation**
   The group is forced by rules to cooperate.

of looking for identifiable patterns in human behavior. Then they could be taught the developmental stages of cooperation in the context of a problem they were likely to encounter in their own lives, such as what to do after school. Students could learn the stages of cooperation in the context of a story about how the occasional after-school baseball games of a group of children became more regular and finally became organized into a league with rules. Later, the curriculum could use the stages of group cooperation as a strategy for organizing the study of the how the local city government became organized. In another year it could be applied to the development of the state. Students would learn that the strategy of looking for identifiable patterns of human behavior pays off. The power of a conspicuous strategy in social studies is heuristic—it helps students anticipate what questions to ask and what information is important. At a lower level, students who learned the *two-sides-to-every-story* big idea would know to keep researching until they find the opposing viewpoint.

For example, the application of the strategy of looking for the stages of cooperation can be even more powerful in deriving political science principles from history. The stages of cooperation can help explain why the Second Continental Congress gave almost no power to the central government in the Articles of Confederation. Students often regard the Articles of Confederation as somehow being imperfect because they failed to give the government essential powers needed to run the government. Instructional materials often do not explain that, when the Articles of Confederation were conceived, voluntary cooperation between the states had successfully resulted in the elimination of British taxes and a Revolutionary War victory. Without a strategy for understanding the development of group cooperation, even capable students have difficulty understanding that the weak nature of the Articles and the government were due to the level of cooperation between the states at that time.

However, if students acquire the big idea that groups who regularly cooperate with success are not compelled to adopt legally binding agreements until it is necessary, this knowledge becomes a sophisticated strategy for understanding history and its application to other social sciences at a deeper level. Using the stages of cooperation, students can relate their understanding of the Articles and the weak role of a central government to political science questions, such as the current struggle for cooperation among the republics of the former Soviet Union, rather than being dependent on the teacher for that insight.

Designing Mediated Scaffolding

Temporary assistance along the path to self-regulated learning can help students become independent learners. In social studies this support, or *scaffolding*, is often necessary for diverse learners to comprehend what they read, whether a textbook or primary source document. Ideally, instructional materials should provide carefully designed sequences of tasks that involve concept organizers such as maps, time lines, and study guides. However, if materials do not present such techniques, then the teacher must provide supplemental instruction. Although it is not often provided, scaffolding is also needed for diverse learners to comprehend the critical concepts and ideas of nontextbook sources of social studies information, such as discussions, videos, interviewed informants, and simulation activities. The process of designing scaffolding can be divided into teacher activities done *before, during,* and *after* reading the text, viewing the video, or playing the simulation.

Before Instruction. Supplementing instruction requires a careful analysis of the content aimed at identifying what concepts and ideas are critical for all learners to acquire. Because preparation time for teachers is a scarce commodity, this content analysis should focus on methods for scaffolding instruction that are achievable. One reasonable approach to scaffolding is for a teacher to prepare questions prior to a lesson, which then are interspersed during reading, viewing, or discussing the topic at hand. Interspersed questions prepared in advance can help reduce the number of irrelevant or obscure questions posed by a textbook or by the teacher at the spur of the moment. Carefully chosen questions will help students identify critical information and relationships needed for conceptual understanding. Preparation of graphic organizers that identify the key concepts and fundamental relationships are very helpful. Another important aspect of scaffolding that needs to be accomplished prior to instruction is identifying essential prerequisite information to present to students prior to reading a social studies selection. The value of readings, discussions, video viewings, or simulations that are prefaced in this manner is greatly enhanced for diverse learners, who often have limited background knowledge of common social studies content.

During Instruction. Interspersed questions are more helpful if they are posed in close proximity to the material that answers them. In other words, if a question is widely separated from its answer, the question changes from a facilitator of understanding to a test of memory or a test of searching strategies. It is critical to interrupt reading, lectures, videos, and discussions to intersperse carefully prepared questions that help insure that students capture, express, and summarize the ideas and concepts that they are expected to glean from the activity.

Another useful and common technique for scaffolding students' comprehension of social studies texts is oral reading. When students read the text aloud, it provides an opportunity for teachers to correct decoding and comprehension errors, prevents students from skipping material, and provides sufficient time for all students to process information.

After Instruction. The same graphic organizers, concept maps, and outlines that were used to assist organization of the ideas as presented can be reused as ways to scaffold students' attempts to articulate in review the ideas presented. When given the scaffold of the key points to cover, many students are still challenged to write or explain the whole idea. However, far more material is learned and articulated than when students are left on their own to remember and organize the information. Students can eventually be moved into more self-regulated learning by, for example, gradually reducing the quantity of information provided on a graphic organizer. This strategy provides the teacher with a means of taking down the scaffold while still holding students to a high standard of explanation and understanding.

While it is possible for teachers to apply these scaffolding techniques to primary source documents and their existing social studies textbooks, the effort is considerable. Figure 8–5 presents an example appropriate to an elementary textbook that carefully presents the big idea of economic problems as a component of the problem–solution–effect big idea. The excerpt supports students' understanding of economic problems through a clearly written narrative and interspersed questions in close proximity to new concepts. Figure 8–6 demonstrates how a middle-school level U.S. history textbook (Carnine et al., 1994) applies the big idea of economic problems to different groups (e.g., families, businesses, governments, and other organizations) and scaffolds the concept by relating it to a graphic model that uses a balance scale. Figure 8–7 shows an example of how an elementary level textbook could conclude its initial presentation of economic problems with scaffolded application questions; i.e., the problem is already set up so the focus is on the implications of the answer rather than on the set-up of the problem.

The amount of scaffolding a teacher or instructional material provides will vary depending on the difficulty level of a concept and the needs of the students. Diverse

---

Introduction to Problem–Solution–Effect

Studying history is like looking back in time through a window. When we look through this window, we can relive important problems and the solutions people used to solve them.

Sometimes these solutions cause positive effects. Often, however, solutions have unintended effects that create new problems.

Problems faced by large numbers of people together are usually *economic problems* or *people's rights* problems. People have problems when they are unable to get things they want or need.

ECONOMIC PROBLEMS
An economic problem involves difficulty in getting and keeping items that people need or want.

- *What is an economic problem?*

  At a basic level, people need three things: (a) food to eat, (b) shelter to keep them dry and out of the weather, and (c) clothing to keep them warm. People require these three basic items to live. For centuries, people have found ways to meet these basic needs.

- *What three basic things must people have to live?*

FIGURE 8–5
Example of Textbook Introduction to Problem–Solution–Effect

Over the past 400 years, the way people have met their basic needs has changed dramatically. Four hundred years ago, Native American families grew crops, hunted and killed their own food, helped build their own shelters, and made their own clothes. Now not many people grow their own food, build their own shelters, or make their own clothes. Today, families earn money by working. When members of a family work, they exchange their time and skills for money. The money they earn is spent on food, shelter, clothing, and things such as entertainment. If a family earns more money than it spends, the family will have extra money. When a family saves money, they are accumulating wealth. If a family spends more money than they earn, they would end up in debt. A family that gets too much into debt has an economic problem. They cannot afford the things they want and need.

Larger groups also can have economic problems. Factory owners, for example, earn money by selling their products. Some factories make and sell clothes, while others make and sell computers. A factory spends money for many things, such as paying for materials, machines, buildings, and workers' salaries. Factory owners have economic problems if they spend more money making things than they receive by selling those things.

Governments can have economic problems, too. Governments receive money by collecting taxes from their citizens. Governments spend money to pay for protection by the military, education, social services, and many other services. They have problems if they spend more money than they receive from taxes.

Businesses and governments are like families. When businesses and governments save money, they are accumulating wealth. When they spend more money than they earn, they have economic problems and cannot get all the things they want and need.

The figure below shows three different economic situations that families, businesses, governments, and other organizations may experience.

1. If families, businesses, governments and other organizations earn as much as they spend, they will be **economically balanced**. This situation is shown in box A. For example, if a family earns $4000 a month and spends $4000 a month, then it is economically balanced.

2. If a group earns more than it spends, the group will **accumulate wealth**. This situation is shown in box B. For example, if a business earns $50,000 a month and only spends $30,000 a month, then it is accumulating wealth.

3. If a group spends more than it earns, it will have an **economic problem**. This situation is shown in box C. For example, if a government takes in one billion dollars in taxes a month but spends two billion dollars a month, then it has an economic problem.

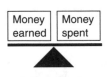

A. Balanced

B. Accumulating Wealth

C. Economic Problem

FIGURE 8–6
Graphic Representation of Economic Problems Analysis
From: Carnine, D., Crawford, D., Harniss, M., & Hollenbeck, K. (1994). *Understanding U.S. History. Volume 1: Through the Civil War.* Eugene, OR: Considerate Publishing. Reprinted by permission.

Economic Problems Activity

1. Darleen's parents give her $5.00 a week as her allowance. She spends $2.50 a week to buy candy.

> 5.00
> − 2.50
> ——

Will Darleen have a balance of money earned and spent, be accumulating wealth, or have an economic problem?

2. Roy earns $2,500.00 a month as a bank teller. He borrows from his parents and spends $2,700.00 a month on car and house payments.

> 2,500.00
> − 2,700.00
> ————

Will Roy have a balance of money earned and spent, be accumulating wealth, or have an economic problem?

3. Larry earns $1,300.00 a month as a radio announcer. He spends $1,300.00 a month on rent and groceries.

> 1,300.00
> − 1,300.00
> ————

Will Larry have a balance of money earned and spent, be accumulating wealth, or have an economic problem?

FIGURE 8–7
Examples of Math Practice for Learning Economic Problems Analysis

learners typically require more scaffolding, while more able students are able to develop effective comprehension strategies independently. Regardless of a student's instructional level, scaffolding must be gradually withdrawn over time. It makes little sense to develop learners who can understand social studies only with textbook or teacher-mediated support.

Designing Strategic Integration

Big ideas and strategies related to problem–solution–effect, factors of group success, and the stages of group cooperation should initially be presented as discrete concepts. However, instructional materials should go on to help students integrate this knowledge. The goal of integration is to help students achieve a deeper understanding of social studies by providing them with opportunities to apply several big ideas and strategies to previously introduced topics. Practice in the application of big ideas and strategies can best be achieved through careful selection and sequencing of material. Following are principles for integrating big ideas and strategies in social studies instruction.

Integrating Several Big Ideas and Strategies.   Students can integrate their knowledge of problem–solution–effect and the stages of group cooperation to analyze historical events such as the Federalists' effort to get the Constitution ratified and the resistance to the new Constitution.

Voluntary cooperation between the states after the Revolutionary War could not prevent interstate taxation, which was limiting trade between the states, nor could it raise a peacetime navy to protect shipping activities or raise enough money to pay off debts incurred by the war. These problems led to economic chaos and a general insurrection in Massachusetts (Shay's Rebellion), which in turn convinced the wealthy colonial establishment that voluntary cooperation defined by the Articles of Confederation needed to be replaced by a stronger central government, via a constitution. Understanding these relationships requires students to apply and integrate their knowledge of problem–solution–effect and the stages of group cooperation.

Integrating Potentially Confusing Concepts.   Lower-performing students often become confused when exposed to similar ideas. McKeown and Beck (1990), in a study of elementary students' knowledge of United States history after a year of instruction, found students could no longer discriminate between the Declaration of Independence and the Constitution. The students had a "document stew" level of understanding because the textbook did not anticipate that students would need help remembering important facts about each document.

Thus, well-designed knowledge integration in instructional materials or a teacher presentation involves the initial separation of similar ideas to reduce confusion. Later, however, the potentially confusing concepts must be carefully integrated and explicitly contrasted.

Integrating a Big Idea Across Multiple Contexts.   A third aspect of integration involves providing students with opportunities to establish connections between recently and previously introduced topics. An example of this type of integration involves having students throughout all levels of social studies use the four factors of group success to analyze and understand why some group efforts fail. Elementary studies of Roanoke, Jamestown, the Pilgrims, and the Puritans could use the four factors to see why some colonies failed and others succeeded. These factors also can be used to analyze middle-school studies of the changes Britain made during the French and Indian War, which resulted in victory after an initial series of defeats. And, as previously noted, at a high school level the factors can help students analyze the efforts of the Federalists to ratify the Constitution. The application of a big idea across multiple contexts can help students understand their usefulness for comprehending social studies. It also models for students the process of making connections between seemingly diverse content.

Designing Primed Background Knowledge

Research has shown that students with diverse learning needs have less background knowledge of social studies content than their normally achieving peers

(Lenz & Alley, 1983). This lack of knowledge impedes comprehension of social studies instructional materials, and the extent of knowledge influences the quality of understanding that a student can construct (McKeown et al., 1992). In order to be effective with diverse learners, instructional tools must provide adequate background knowledge so that all students are able to understand. If not, teachers must provide the requisite information and explanations before students encounter the material.

The components of big ideas and the steps that constitute strategies often require explicit instruction. For example, to understand the following primary source material from the writings of Geronimo, students must have prerequisite knowledge about the world views of the Apache and of Native Americans in general:

> For each tribe of men Usen [Apache word for God] created, He also made a home. In the land created for any particular tribe He placed whatever would be best for the welfare of that tribe.
>
> When Usen created the Apaches He also created their home in the West. He gave them such grain, fruits, and game as they needed to eat. To restore their health when disease attacked them He taught them where to find these herbs, and how to prepare them for medicine. He gave them a pleasant climate and all they needed for clothing and shelter was at hand. (McLuhan, 1971, p. 154)

In preparation for reading this passage, students need to know that Native American tribes had, over thousands of years, evolved very intimate and unique relationships between themselves and their local environments. Far from being one Indian culture, the tribes living in different ecological environments solved their basic needs in very different ways.

This background knowledge would enable students to apply one component of the problem–solution–effect big idea (i.e., Native Americans *accommodated* their environment) to comprehend the deeper meaning of the primary source material. Additionally, having learned the big idea of accommodating versus dominating, students are prepared to understand fundamental differences between how Native Americans and Western cultures relate to the environment. This knowledge can also be used to examine the impact of humans on ecological systems and events associated with the environmental movement's desire of citizens to accommodate the environment.

Without prerequisite knowledge, full application of a big idea or strategy is not possible and students are not prepared to make sophisticated connections between seemingly diverse content.

Designing Judicious Review

A major goal for all students is to remember what they have learned. Retention of social studies content can be especially difficult for diverse learners especially if the instruction they receive covers too many topics superficially. Retention is dependent on the use of effective review practices that are widely supported by research. Reviewing the same or nearly same material ad nauseam promotes rote learning; however, effective review can lead to long-term retention and generalization.

It is easy to confuse the "delivery vehicles" of review—concept maps, mnemonic graphics, study guides, tests—with the attributes of effective review. Social studies programs sometimes include these instructional aids but do not often incorporate effective review principles.

Effective review is achievable when the guidelines pertaining to big ideas, strategies, and scaffolding are inherent in the design of instruction for social studies. In other words, if the presentation (either from the textbook or from a nontextbook source) lacks clarity and coherence, it will also lack a foundation for providing effective review. However, if instructional presentations are designed using big ideas, then principles of effective review can be applied. For example, after the big idea of problem–solution–effect is introduced and subsequently used in a variety of contexts, then the four factors of group success can be introduced and used in a variety of contexts until it too is mastered. Once students learn the four factors that determine group success, the factors can be reviewed through an analysis of various group efforts such as the settlement of Jamestown, the Federalist drive for ratification of the Constitution, and the Civil War. After the two ideas are used separately, then in new contexts both big ideas are reviewed and used together. Varied review of this sort also preempts the possibility of students resorting to shallow, rote recall. Varied review is also linked to big ideas that can be related to current events. In the absence of an understanding of the stages of cooperation, for example, it is difficult for students to recognize connections between events in the former Soviet Union and the events leading up to the adoption of the U.S. Constitution.

THE APPLICATION OF INSTRUCTIONAL DESIGN PRINCIPLES

Developing Instructional Tools

One use of the foregoing six major principles of effective instruction would be to inform the design and development of instructional tools in social studies. Instructional tools could include textbooks, workbooks, video lessons, Web-delivered distance learning, and many other examples. The next section talks about how one could use the six principles of big ideas, conspicuous strategies, mediated scaffolding, strategic integration and judicious review when developing an instructional tool.

One approach for bringing understanding to social studies without sacrificing breadth of content is to develop instructional tools around big ideas. Several of the big ideas applicable to history have been described in this chapter: (a) problem–solution–effect, (b) multiple perspectives, (c) every story (argument) has two sides, (d) four factors of group success, (e) developmental stages of cooperation, and (f) a people's culture is influenced by their environment. Using one or more of these big ideas is a good way to begin developing an instructional tool in social studies. Developing additional big ideas requires fairly extensive reading in the discipline, with an eye for patterns and recurring relationships. However, a developer might only need a handful of big ideas for a year's program. In addition, big ideas are most effective when used repeatedly, rather than relying on new ideas for every topic under examination.

Students with diverse learning needs often have less background knowledge of social studies content than their typically-achieving peers. Therefore, instructional tools that will be used with diverse learners should be designed for students who lack essential background knowledge.

Social studies instructional tools should provide students with scaffolding of key relationships through graphic organizers and explicit explanation of the big ideas until their learning becomes self-regulated. In addition, interspersed questions located close to the content targeted are needed to facilitate identification of important material and ideas during initial input of information.

Instructional tools for use with diverse learners need to provide ample review in a variety of formats. An instructional tool with many review exercises gives teachers the option of using or skipping the exercises depending on the needs of their students. It is far easier for teachers to skip unneeded review exercises than to create additional ones. Integrating such things as graphic organizers, outlines, and semantic webs into the review process enables teachers to incorporate meaningful review. Effective review using big ideas promotes transfer of learning by requiring application of content at different times and in different contexts. Review questions ought to focus on the most important ideas identified. Cumulative review of key material will assist in learning.

Testing materials are most effective when they stimulate study of the material. Production responses such as fill-in-the-blank, short answer, and essay responses require more thorough learning of the material than multiple-choice response formats. Students can more easily remember and make use of more thoroughly learned material. An effective instructional tool in social studies should emphasize knowledge that can be integrated and applied in multiple contexts. The goal is to promote understanding about when to use specific knowledge by providing students with opportunities to apply several big ideas and strategies to new material.

Selecting Instructional Tools

A second use of the six major principles of effective instruction for teaching social studies would be in the process of selecting instructional tools. As noted earlier, teachers who learn how and why to develop strategic supplemental materials to enhance the content of textbooks are critical of publishers' failures to include this essential material in the first place. Once these six principles are learned they can then be used to evaluate the potential for instructional efficacy of textbooks being considered for adoption. The following section describes how this process might occur.

First, examine social studies tools to determine whether the use of big ideas lends cohesion to adequate breadth of coverage. Neither of two extremes is acceptable. Does the tool strike you as a series of unrelated facts rather than an interrelated network of information? Or does the tool strike you as providing depth in only a few areas at the expense of adequate breadth?

Examine several big ideas presented in a tool to assess the degree to which they are explicitly interrelated. This evaluation can be achieved by comparing the development of knowledge presented early in a tool with knowledge presented in subsequent sections.

Examine tools first to see what forms of scaffolding (graphic organizers, concept maps, highlighting, bolded information) are present to help students identify critical information and relationships needed for conceptual understanding. When evaluating a social studies tool for review, *more* is preferable to *less,* provided the review is distributed, cumulative, and varied. It is far easier for teachers not to use the review when it is provided than to prepare the review if it is needed.

Evaluate instructional tools to determine what provisions are made to teach students with limitations in important prerequisite knowledge. If students have gaps in their knowledge, does the tool make provisions to introduce or review important background information several lessons *prior* to introduction of the target knowledge?

Examine instructional tools to determine what explicit strategies associated with the big ideas are described. If strategies are present, determine if they: (1) are clearly described, (2) have narrow or broad application, and (3) are an integral part of the tool or just optional. Try to imagine yourself as a diverse learner who must analyze a problem based solely on a suggested strategy.

Modifying Instructional Tools

The third use of these six major principles of effective instruction, modifying instructional tools, is the biggest chore for the teacher. Modifying instructional tools to make them instructionally effective usually means the teacher will be creating a good deal of supplementary material. This activity must necessarily be extra work, above and beyond normal teaching responsibilities, but can often pay large dividends in the form of increased learning. The following section offers some suggestions on that process.

Identify several big ideas to incorporate into existing instructional materials either through supplemental materials or extensive revision of the tool. Select big ideas that (a) have rich explanatory and predictive power, (b) are a point of departure for posing significant questions, and (c) are generalizable to many situations and contexts.

Preparing interspersed questions in advance can help reduce the number of irrelevant or obscure questions posed in instructional tools or by a teacher on the spur of the moment. Well-chosen questions should help students identify critical information and relationships needed for conceptual understanding. Another example of scaffolding is for students to read social studies material aloud. Oral reading allows teachers to correct decoding and comprehension errors, prevents students from skipping material, and provides sufficient time for all students to process information. Oral reading and interspersed questions can be applied as scaffolding for instructional tools.

Teachers can also provide scaffolding with supplemental materials (e.g., graphics, concept maps, study guides, or outlines). In general, it is difficult for teachers to modify existing tools to accommodate background knowledge. Such modification requires the development of new instruction and affects the sequence of existing instruction. To some extent, teachers can review important big ideas, events, or important prerequisite vocabulary to help students make connections with new information. This requires a thorough analysis of the component skills and concepts needed to understand new knowledge.

Teachers can develop integration activities in which several important concepts are included. Such activities should be preceded by instruction that teaches component concepts first, so the integrated material builds on earlier learning. A more extensive implementation of integration can be achieved through the application of several big ideas to analyze events. Teachers can prepare review activities before instruction begins. This can be accomplished by evaluating the important information presented in a tool that is likely to cause students difficulty. Ask yourself if such information is needed for understanding subsequent material and the extent to which the tool provides sufficient review in anticipated problem areas. Review can also be prepared after instruction takes place and students' knowledge deficiencies become evident. Again, such review should be ample and provide opportunities for practice that can be applied at different times and in different contexts.

SUMMARY

Many of the guidelines for improving instructional strategies for teaching social studies to diverse learners apply to other learners as well. Understanding the guidelines can help teachers determine how best to attempt program modifications and what principles characterize an effective social studies program for diverse learners.

- Organizing social studies curriculum around big ideas is essential to help learners make connections among the facts and concepts they learn in social studies.
- Some big ideas in history are: (a) problem–solution–effect; (b) the developmental stages of group cooperation; (c) multiple perspectives; (d) two sides to every story (argument); (e) a people's culture is influenced by their environment; and (f) the four factors of group success.
- The important ideas that are essential for high-performing students to know arc csscntial for *all* other students.
- Big ideas facilitate the process of making what students learn from content area instruction meaningful and appropriate to their own lives.
- In social studies the strategy is often simply the application of the big ideas to the content.
- Mediated scaffolding in social studies includes oral reading, interspersed questions, concept organizers of various sorts, and application questions.
- Strategically integrated curriculum will offer students an opportunity to successfully integrate several big ideas.
- Big ideas learned in one context must be applicable in multiple contexts.
- Strategic integration of content within the curriculum can help students learn when to use specific knowledge.
- The concepts unified by a big idea or strategy must be explicitly introduced in advance.
- Teachers must make certain that all students possess the requisite background knowledge for deep understanding of the content.

- Effective review of social studies content must be designed to be an integral and meaningful part of later lessons.
- All students require cumulative review to achieve transfer and generalize information.

REFLECTION AND APPLICATION

Case Study

Mario teaches social studies to tenth- and eleventh-grade students in an urban priority school district. His three general World History courses are composed of heterogeneous groups of students, which include several students receiving special education services as well as many other students with diverse learning needs.

Mario recently attended a professional development conference that included presentations and workshops on integrating effective teaching strategies, including big ideas, into social studies curriculums to enhance learning outcomes for all students. Exploring historical events through the framework of problem–solution–effect analysis was among the more prominent big ideas in social studies covered during this training. Mario believed that this strategy was particularly well suited for his Western Civilization courses and he enthusiastically planned to emphasize this important big idea during an upcoming unit.

Shortly after completing the conference, Mario incorporated explicit and clear explanations of problem–solution–effect analysis into a unit on the Age of Revolutions. He demonstrated this process to his students, for example, by applying problem–solution–effect analysis during presentations on Napoleon's invasion of Russia. Mario started with a description of problem–solution–effect analysis, explaining this big idea with language that was clear, concise, and consistent. He then modeled how this analysis could be applied to Napoleon's invasion, using graphic organizers to scaffold instruction.

The results of an examination on this unit were encouraging to Mario. He noted that his best students seemed to demonstrate a deeper understanding of the content than usual. Somewhat more surprisingly, several of his students with diverse learning needs also performed strongly. He also noticed that these students seemed to be more engaged during whole class discussions during the unit.

Based on student success with the problem–solution–effect framework, Mario decided to shift his emphasis to another big idea in social studies during the next unit. He believed that the content in the unit on the Industrial Age was ideal for emphasizing the big idea of environmental influences. Mario continued to provide conspicuous instruction and scaffolding. During an initial presentation, he discussed the importance of environmental influences, and then carefully explained how an increased demand for raw materials contributed to colonialism. Mario also organized a student discussion focusing on the effects that pollution had on ecosystems. In an attempt to scaffold instruction, he posited initial questions and supported student dialogues with occasional comments and feedback.

Once again, Mario's students did well on the exam and were able use the big idea of environmental influences to make meaningful and insightful observations about the unit content. Mario was disappointed, however, that many students failed to apply the problem–solution–effect analysis on one of the examination questions for this unit. He was initially puzzled by the finding that many of his students with diverse learning needs had difficulty utilizing the problem–solution–effect analysis to answer a question on the Industrial Age. Like the other students in his classes, these learners had demonstrated an understanding of this *big idea* during the previous unit on the Age of Revolutions. Moreover, he had used *conspicuous strategies* and *mediated scaffolding* to present this strategy.

- Why might Mario's students have had difficulty applying the big idea of problem–solution–effect to the unit on the Industrial Age? What instructional principles and teaching strategies might Mario have utilized to more effectively address the learning needs of all of the students in his classes?

The conclusion of the case study can be found later in this chapter.

Content Questions

1. Describe two different struggles over expectations for teaching social studies.

2. What is the purpose of social studies education, according to the recommendations of the National Council for Social Studies (NCSS)?

3. Identify the problems associated with the instructional materials of elementary and secondary level social studies.

4. How are big ideas identified in social studies instruction?

5. Identify three examples of big ideas for social studies curriculum.

6. Describe the components of problem–solution–effect as a big idea in social studies.

7. Define what is meant by a strategy and provide an example of a conspicuous strategy.

8. Provide three examples of content organizers that can be used to scaffold social studies instruction.

Reflection and Discussion

1. Have you ever taken a social studies course in which you felt overwhelmed by having to memorize facts? What was your response to this course? Would your response have been different if the course content had been organized around big ideas?

2. Why might some methods that were utilized for social studies instruction in the past, such as inductive teaching and discovery learning, have been less successful for students with diverse learning needs?

3. Given the variety of disciplines in the field of social studies (e.g., history, economics, philosophy) and the amount of content teachers are expected to cover, how might educators use principles of effective instruction to balance breadth and depth of instruction?

Application

1. In small groups, generate a list of current issues in the news. Design an instructional activity for students in the primary grades that applies the big idea of problem–solution–effect to a current issue. Next design an activity for older students in which the problem–solution–effect analysis is applied to another current issue.

2. Use the six principles of effective instruction to evaluate the following section from a chapter on "Exploration" taken from a fifth-grade social studies textbook (Figure 8–8). How might this section be reorganized or rewritten to reflect effective teaching strategies?

FIGURE 8–8
Columbus Discovers America

Columbus Discovers America

Marco Polo, a traveling merchant from the city of Venice, ventured from Italy to the East in the late 1200s. He visited China, Japan, and India and returned home with intriguing stories of Asia. These later became his book *The Travels of Marco Polo*. Reading about the riches of the East—perfumes, spices, gold, and silk—enticed European fortune seekers to search for an easier route to Asia than the treacherous land journey Marco Polo had taken.

The sailors and mapmakers of Portugal were students of navigation and cartography. These two sciences deal with the guiding of sea travel and the making of maps. Maps are used in navigation and are often called charts. Prince Henry of Portugal owned the school and directed his men, including Bartholomew Diaz and Vasco de Gama, as they explored the west coast of Africa in the caravels built by his Portuguese navigators. It took years to travel around the southern tip of Africa and arrive in India. Christopher Columbus thought he could find a shorter route.

1271: Marco Polo left Venice
1488: Bartholomew Diaz sails to Cape of Good Hope
1495: *Travels of Marco Polo* published
1498: Vasco de Gama sails to India

Sailors discovered how to make compasses. Compasses use magnetic iron that points to the north by using the earth's magnetic field.

Technology advanced exploration.

Case Study (Conclusion)

After reviewing notes from the professional development conference, Mario realized that he had not applied the instructional principles of *judicious review* and *strategic integration* during his recent World History classes. Although some students had demonstrated an ability to generalize the problem–effect–solution analysis to the unit on the Industrial Age, many of his students with diverse learning needs had not transferred this big idea in the absence of judicious review and strategic integration. Mario decided to apply these additional instructional strategies during the next several units in an attempt to better meet the needs of his students with diverse learning needs. Specifically, he planned to reinforce the big ideas in social studies that he had already introduced by designing opportunities for judicious review and strategic integration during the next unit, which covered the era of the two world wars.

Prior to discussing the invasion of Russia by Axis troops, Mario reviewed the problem–solution–effect strategy that had previously been used to analyze Napoleon's invasion of Russia. He then guided the students through a discussion of historical parallels between these two invasions, with continued emphasis on the problem–solution–effect framework. During a subsequent class, Mario attempted to facilitate his students' integration of problem–solution–effect analysis with the big idea of environmental influences. He asked the students to discuss the impact of geographic and climatic conditions on Axis troops at the Russian front. Mario was particularly pleased with the responses given by Janet, a student with a learning disability who often appeared withdrawn and unengaged during class discussions. Janet appeared animated and confident when noting how Russia's large land mass and cold winters had also weakened Napoleon's army.

With increased emphasis on judicious review and strategic integration, most of the students with diverse learning needs demonstrated an improved ability to analyze historical events using the problem–solution–effect approach during ongoing class discussions and the unit test. Additionally, Mario was already planning to systematically apply another instructional principle during the next section. The students' recent analysis of two large-scale invasions of Russia would surely afford an excellent opportunity to build on *primed background knowledge* while studying the Cold War.

- Would it be realistic to assume that a teacher could incorporate principles of effective instruction into social studies units after attending a professional development conference? What challenges might a teacher face in attempting to do this? What are potential resources and solutions that could facilitate a teacher's successful integration of instructional principles into his or her social studies teaching?
- Would it be challenging to organize social studies content around big ideas, such as problem–solution–effect within a social studies textbook or

curriculum that was not specifically organized to facilitate these concepts? How might an instructor successfully incorporate these big ideas into a social studies curriculum?

The Reflection and Application section of this chapter was written by Richard P. Zipoli, Jr., and Maureen F. Ruby, both of the University of Connecticut.

REFERENCES

BANKS, J. A., COOKSON, P., GAY, G., HAWLEY, W. D., IRVINE, J. J., & NIETO, S., ET AL. (2005). Education and Diversity. *Social Education, 69* (1), 36–40.

BROPHY, J. (1990). Teaching social studies for understanding and higher-order applications. In M. Wittrock (Ed.), *The Elementary School Journal, 90* (4), 353–417.

CARNINE, D., CRAWFORD, D., HARNISS, M., & HOLLENBECK, K. (1994). *Understanding U.S. history: Volume 1—Through the Civil War*. Eugene, OR: University of Oregon.

ELLIS, E. S., & SABORNIE, E. J. (1990). Strategy-based adaptive instruction in content-area classes: Social validity of six options. *Teacher Education and Special Education, 13* (2) 133–144.

KAUFFMAN, D., JOHNSON, S. M., KARDOS, S. M., LIU, E., & PESKE, H. G. (2002). "Lost at Sea": New teachers' experiences with curriculum and assessment. *The Teachers College Record, 104* (2), 273–300.

LENZ, B. K., & ALLEY, G. R. (1983). *The effects of advance organizers on the learning and retention of learning disabled adolescents within the context of a cooperative planning model*. Final research report submitted to the U.S. Department of Education, Office of Special Education, Washington, DC.

McKEOWN, M. G., & BECK, I. L. (1990). The assessment and characterization of young learners' knowledge of a topic in history. *American Educational Research Journal, 27* (4), 688–726.

McKEOWN, M. G., BECK, I. L., SINATRA, G. M., & LOXTERMAN, A. (1992). The contribution of prior knowledge and coherent text to comprehension. *Reading Research Quarterly, 27* (4), 78–93.

McLUHAN, T. C. (1971). *Touch the earth: A self-portrait of Indian existence*. New York: Promontory Press.

NATIONAL CENTER FOR HISTORY IN THE SCHOOLS. (1992). *Lessons from history*. Los Angeles: The National Center for History in the Schools.

NATIONAL CENTER TO IMPROVE THE TOOLS OF EDUCATORS. (2001). Retrieved Aug. 10, 2001 from idea.uoregon.edu/~ncite/

NATIONAL COUNCIL FOR THE SOCIAL STUDIES. (1994). Ten thematic strands in social studies. *Social Education, 58* (6) 365–368.

O'NEIL, J. (1989). Social studies: Charting a course for a field adrift. *ASCD Curriculum Update,* 1–8.

PLACIER, M., WALKER, M., & FOSTER, B. (2002). Writing the "show-me" standards: Teacher professionalism and political control in U.S. state curriculum policy. *Curriculum Inquiry, 32* (3), 281–310.

RAVITCH, D. (2000). *Left back: A century of failed school reforms*. New York: Simon & Schuster.

SANDHOLTZ, J. H., OGAWA, R. T., & SCRIBNER, S. P. (2004). Standards Gaps: Unintended consequences of local standards-based reform. *Teachers College Record, 106* (6), 1177–1202.

TWYMAN, T., & TINDAL, G. (2005). Reaching all of your students in social studies. *Teaching Exceptional Children Plus, 1* (5) Article 1. Retrieved November 1, 2005 from http://escholarship.bc.edu/education/tecplus/voll/iss5/1

CHAPTER 9

Modulating Instruction for English Language Learners

Russell Gersten
Instructional Research Group

Lana Edwards Santoro
Instructional Research Group

Robert Jiménez
University of Illinois

THE CURRENT WAVE of immigration has drastically reshaped the nature of education in the United States with 5.5 million English language learners in the public school system. Over half, 52 percent, of English language learners are born in the United States. These students are not new arrivals, but rather are second or third generation students who have greater development in speaking, reading, and writing English than their parents. An additional 48 percent of English language learners come into the United States education system at various ages (Hubler, 2005). In California, one out of every four students comes from a home where English is not the primary language (Barringer, 1993). Overall, approximately 440 languages are spoken in the schools today; Spanish speakers are the majority at 80 percent (Hubler, 2005).

Providing quality instruction for English language learners has become a major educational issue. Until recently, there has been a limited amount of scientific research on the instructional needs of English language learners. With funding support for research from the National Institutes of Health (NIH) and Institute for Education Sciences (IES), along with higher accountability demands, there has been a dramatic increase in instructional research on English language learners. Knowledge of instructional strategies for these students is critical to being a successful educator in this country at the present time. As a result of the surge in immigration, many teachers have become, often by default, teachers of English language learners.

Teaching this group of students is a complex endeavor. A serious issue is the "double demands" (Gersten, 1996) required of English language learners: they need to acquire a second language and at the same time master traditional subject matter. Additionally, many teachers who are confronted with a struggling English language learner are baffled by the student's seemingly unpredictable rate of academic progress (Gersten, 1999). Most encouraging, however, is recent evidence suggesting that the rate of learning for English language learners can be the same as native English-speaking children. For example, some English language learners can learn to read as quickly, if not more quickly, than some English speakers (Chiappe, Siegel, Wade-Woolley, 2002). Some selected studies that have been widely referenced in the past indicated that it took approximately five to seven years for a non-English speaker to become fully comfortable with a new language. More recent findings refute these assumptions. We now know that the rate of progress in reading development for English language learners is *not* predetermined by lack of language proficiency in English upon entering school (Lesaux & Siegel, 2003).

The goal of this chapter is to present promising practices for teaching English language learners and to present a framework that can be used to better understand and analyze the quality of instruction provided. In particular, specific procedures are provided for adapting or adjusting teaching practices so that they are successful with students for whom English is a second language. As Gersten and Woodward (1985) noted, "bilingual education . . . (is) relatively easy to write about, yet difficult to implement sensitively on a day to day basis" (p. 78). This chapter highlights key findings from instructional research on English language learners that have relevance for teachers and curriculum developers.

Unlike the preceding chapters, this chapter deals less with curriculum design and more with how to *adapt* existing curricula in order to sensitively and effectively teach English language learners. Therefore, we explicitly touch upon only a few of the six core principles that are the foundation of this volume—*big ideas, conspicuous strategies, mediated scaffolding, primed background knowledge, strategic integration*, and *judicious review*. Rather, our goal is to begin to delineate instructional strategies that will help teachers perform the complex task of teaching academic content while developing students' English language abilities. The framework and strategies are based on contemporary research as well as our own ongoing research on the topic.

Throughout this chapter, we intentionally try to merge the findings from second-language acquisition research and bilingual education research with those on effective teaching, literacy instruction, and cognitive strategy instruction. These traditions have rarely been integrated in the past (Goldenberg, 1996).

We begin by sensitizing the reader to some common recurrent problems that have been documented by prior research. We then provide a framework for delineating productive instructional practice.

Because of the complexity of the issues and the extreme diversity of the population, we often point in directions that are likely to be productive, rather than toward a single methodology. All the examples in this chapter are taken from our observational field notes of actual classroom instruction (Gersten, 1999; Gersten & Jiménez, 1994; Jiménez & Gersten, 1999).

PROBLEMS IN CURRENT INSTRUCTION OF ENGLISH LANGUAGE LEARNERS

Until recently, much research has documented problems in the instruction of English language learners. There was a clear need for research documenting the need for improvement. When students are presented with conventional curriculum with no modifications, they tend to flounder, become overwhelmed, and mentally tune out or withdraw from active classroom participation (Gersten, 1999; Gersten & Woodward, 1994).

Over 20 years ago, the research of Moll, Estrada, Diaz, and Lopes (1980) poignantly delineated the pain and frustration that English language learners struggling to learn English sometimes feel when taught in all-English settings. Students may fail to understand what the teacher is talking about, and may become frustrated when they have an idea but cannot adequately express their thoughts in English. Moll et al. found that teachers tended to correct pronunciation errors (e.g., *seyd* for "said") or interrupt passage reading with attempts to define simple English words (e.g., "surprise", "guess"), thereby breaking the flow of the story. Moll et al. decried "the deliberate, slow pace of lessons with students in the low reading groups" (p. 305), and the lack of intellectual challenge and conceptual development provided to them.

This focus on the details of accurate English language production makes the students appear less competent than they really are. When Moll et al. (1980) followed the same students into a Spanish reading lesson, they observed that the students, although considered "low ability" by their teacher, were able to answer comprehension questions correctly on grade-level material, to develop and expand on ideas in the stories, and to process more complex text. Further, the students could read texts usually reserved for "high-ability" students.

Yates and Ortiz (1991) found that many teachers view language minority children as simply low-performing native English-speaking children. This tendency has led many to merely adopt a watered-down curriculum, including reading material well below the students' ability to comprehend. This recurrent problem denies language minority children access to the type of instructional material they need in order to make adequate academic progress. This curriculum mismatch, in all likelihood, is one reason for the extremely low academic performance levels of many English language learners.

According to Fradd (1987), teachers who work with English language learners often tend to use "brief utterances such as 'What is this?' or 'What color is that?'" (p. 146). Students learn to reply in like form, in one- or two-word utterances. Not surprisingly, little curriculum content or social expectation is communicated in this type of verbal exchange. In classroom observations of English language learners, Ramírez (1992) noted the same phenomenon *regardless of teachers' or districts' philosophy of bilingual education*.

For years, program evaluation research attempted to determine which model for educating English language learners produced the highest levels of student academic achievement (Baker & de Kanter, 1983; Danoff, Coles, McLaughlin, & Reynolds, 1977–1978; Gersten & Woodward, 1995; Ramírez, 1992; Willig, 1985). This research, as well as a series of research reviews and meta-analyses (Baker & de Kanter, 1981; Greene, 1998; Rossell & Baker, 1996; Willig, 1985) have often yielded differing conclusions. In a synthesis of almost 20 years of program evaluation research, Cziko (1992) concluded, "it may well be unlikely that this question [of which is the best approach for teaching English-language learners in the United States] will ever be satisfactorily answered regardless of the quantity and quality of additional evaluative research" (p. 15). The report by the National Academy of Sciences (August & Hakuta, 1997) concluded that "for numerous reasons, we see little value in conducting evaluations to determine which type of program is best" (p. 138).

Much of the early educational research on English language learners focused on determining the rate at which English language instruction should be introduced. These evaluation efforts were guided at times by theoretical issues, at other times by political issues involving bilingual education (August & Hakuta, 1998; Crawford, 1995).

The type of bilingual program model and the language of instruction employed, while important, have received far more attention in research and in public debate than the equally critical issue of how ideas and concepts are taught. Recently, however, the research focus has shifted away from searching for the "best" program model toward identifying useful and feasible instructional practices (August, 1999; August & Hakuta, 1998; Berman et al., 1992; Gersten & Baker, 2000; Tikunoff, 1985).

Differing Theories About and Approaches to Second Language Instruction

The goal of building competence in English without unduly frustrating students requires a complex balance between the utilization of the native language and the language to be acquired. In reality, many models of bilingual education exist (Ramírez, 1992; Rossell & Baker, 1996). For the purposes of this discussion, however, we will briefly describe two of the major approaches advocated for educating English language learners and the underlying rationales of each.

Native Language Emphasis. For Latino students, the most commonly utilized model of bilingual education has a strong native language component (Cummins, 1989; Hakuta & Snow, 1986; Troike, 1981; Wong-Fillmore & Valadez, 1986). We use the term "native language emphasis" to describe this approach.

Troike (1981) cogently presented the conceptual framework for native language emphasis:

1. People are more likely to learn anything, including English, if they understand what they are being taught.
2. Students with limited English ability will not fall behind their English-speaking peers if they can keep up with subject matter content through their native language while they are mastering English. (p. 498)

Wong-Fillmore and Valadez (1986) applied Troike's rationale for a native language emphasis to reading: "It is not possible to read in a language one does not know" (pp. 660–661).

In other words, until students obtain a reasonably good knowledge of English, particularly in conceptually complex areas such as reading/language arts and social studies, instruction should be in the native language. This approach ensures that students are not deprived of the experience of learning core concepts in the school curriculum during the years when their English language vocabulary is limited.

Theorists such as Cummins (1989) assert that once students succeed at comprehending complex academic material in their native language, they will transfer this knowledge to the same subjects taught in English. Although it may seem a belaboring process, it would seem more sensible to teach complex academic content to students in their native language first so that they can understand and discuss challenging material without the added demand of constantly translating or expressing ideas in a second language.

There remains great diversity in opinion and practice as to how rapidly students should be introduced to English language instruction and how long native language instruction should be maintained (August & Hakuta, 1998; Crawford, 1995; Gersten & Woodward, 1994; Ramírez, 1992).

Sheltered English/Structured Immersion: Merging English Language Instruction with Content Learning.   Contemporary conceptualizations of education for English language learners acknowledge the participation of many monolingual teachers. Newer approaches, often called sheltered instruction (Echevarria, Vogt, & Short, 2000) or structured immersion (Gersten & Woodward, 1985; Genesee, 1984) emphasize the merger of English language instruction with content-area instruction.

The approach is currently used most frequently with Southeast Asian students in the elementary grades, and it is being used increasingly with all types of English language learners, including Latino students, at all grade levels. This is particularly true since the passage of Proposition 227 in California in 1998.

According to contemporary theorists, understanding of English can be obtained through well-designed content area instruction where English is used, *but at a level that is constantly modulated*—that is, adjusted and adapted so that it is comprehensible (Anderson & Roit, 1996; Chamot & O'Malley, 1989). Teachers attempt to control their classroom vocabulary, avoid use of synonyms and idioms, and use concrete objects, gestures, and visuals such as story maps to enhance student understanding of the essential concepts in academic material.

Teachers using the sheltered English approach do not shy away from teaching age-appropriate concepts such as "migration" to third graders or "peninsula" and "compromise" to sixth or seventh graders. Consciously making instruction highly interactive affords students many opportunities to verbalize their thoughts (even if the grammar or syntax is imperfect), so that they are able to grasp age-appropriate material.

In an articulate plea for the integration of reading with English language development, Anderson and Roit (1996) note: "Spoken language is fleeting and inconsistent over time. Text is stable and does not pass the learner by. It allows one to reread and reconsider that which is to be learned in its original form" (p. 2). Anderson and Roit demonstrate how the "potential reciprocity between learning to read and reading to learn has strong implications for developing oral language in English language learners, even as early as first grade" (p. 1).

Less than a decade ago, there were fierce controversies between proponents of structured immersion/sheltered English (Baker & de Kanter, 1983) and proponents of bilingual approaches that emphasize development in a native language (Wong-Fillmore & Valadez, 1986). In recent years, however, research and thinking has moved away from this dichotomy towards a search for coherent programs that employ an optimal mix of instructional methods. Researchers such as Barrera (1984), Saville-Troike (1982), Anderson and Roit (1996), and Gersten and Jiménez (1994) have stressed consistently that the key problem and issue is not the determination of the exact age or grade level at which to introduce English language instruction, but rather how to merge English language acquisition with academic learning in a fashion that is stimulating and not overly frustrating to students. In the remainder of this chapter, we present examples of how teachers have succeeded in meeting this challenge. Before presenting the examples, we provide a framework for understanding aspects of effective instruction for students making the transition into English.

CONSTRUCTS FOR CONCEPTUALIZING EFFECTIVE INSTRUCTIONAL PRACTICE

In recent years, a growing consensus has begun to recognize that effective instruction for English language learners encompasses far more than knowledge of second-language acquisition (August & Hakuta, 1998; Chamot, Dale, O'Malley, & Spanos, 1993; Gersten & Baker, 2000; Gersten & Geva, 2003; Gersten & Jiménez, 1998). Relevant research on literacy instruction for diverse learners, including research on cognitive strategy instruction, must be incorporated.

In this section we describe constructs for promoting learning and language acquisition that can serve as a basis for assessing the extent to which instruction is appropriately modified or adapted for English language learners. These constructs, listed in Figure 9–1, were developed from extensive research syntheses (Garcia, Pearson, & Jiménez, 1990; Gersten & Baker, 2000) and extensive classroom observational research (Gersten, 1996; Gersten, Baker, Haager, & Graves, 2005; Gersten & Jiménez, 1994; Jiménez & Gersten, 1999). They embody underlying principles of effective instruction that cross a wide range of theoretical orientations.

In a sense, all of these constructs for promoting learning and language acquisition are meant to delineate actions teachers can take to scaffold students' learning experiences. The term *mediated scaffolding* embodies notions of ongoing teacher support and active teacher involvement in helping students express ideas in a new language.

Most of these practices and instructional strategies can be utilized by monolingual teachers for working successfully with English language learners (Gersten, 1996). These include:

1. Selection of key vocabulary that will enhance understanding
2. Provision of a range of activities involving these key vocabulary concepts
3. Provision of meaningful English language input to students by responding to the intent of their utterances rather than pedantically correcting their speech
4. Active encouragement of students to practice expressing ideas and concepts in English

Increasingly, the need for the systematic approach implied by the constructs for promoting learning and language acquisition in English language learners is recognized by researchers (Cazden, 1992; Goldenberg, 1992–1993; Reyes, 1992).

In the remainder of this section, a range of examples of effective instructional practices taken from naturalistic research is presented. They focus on the teaching of reading because of its centrality in the curriculum of most American schools, and because of its potential to serve as a vehicle for learning English (Anderson & Roit, 1993).

Another reason for stressing language arts/reading instruction is that this is the area in which English language learners tend to experience the most difficulty. English language learners often need more work in language development, vocabulary, and listening comprehension than native speakers. States such as California are aware that current reading curricula and classroom instruction do not include enough focus on language development and have adjusted state textbook adoption criteria to reflect this need. This was also revealed both in student interviews

1. Mediated Scaffolding
   a. Provide support to students by "thinking aloud." Build on and clarify input of students.
   b. Use visual organizers/story maps or other aids to help students organize and relate information.

2. Relevant Primed Background Knowledge and Key Vocabulary Concepts
   a. Provide adequate background knowledge to students and/or informally assess whether students have background knowledge.
   b. Focus on key vocabulary words.
   c. Use consistent language.
   d. Incorporate students' primary language meaningfully into instruction.

3. Mediation and Feedback
   a. Provide feedback that focuses on meaning, not grammar, syntax, or pronunciation.
   b. Provide mediation and feedback frequently.
   c. Provide mediation and feedback that is comprehensible.
   d. Provide prompts or strategies.
   e. Pose questions that encourage students to clarify or expand on their initial statements.
   f. Provide activities and tasks that students can complete.
   g. Indicate to students when they are successful.
   h. Assign activities that are reasonable to avoid undue frustration.
   i. Allow use of native language responses (when context is appropriate).
   j. Exhibit sensitivity to common problems in second-language acquisition.

4. Involvement
   a. Encourage active involvement.
   b. Encourage involvement of *all* students, including low-performing students.
   c. Foster extended discourse.

5. Challenge
   a. Ensure that instruction poses challenges that are implicit (cognitive challenge, use of higher-order questions).
   b. Ensure that instruction poses challenges that are explicit (high but with reasonable expectations).

6. Respect for and Responsiveness to Cultural and Personal Diversity
   a. Show respect for students as individuals and for students' cultures and families. Respond to things students say. Possess knowledge of cultural diversity.
   b. Incorporate students' experiences into writing and language arts activities.
   c. Attempt to link content to students' lives.
   d. Provide experiences that enhance understanding.
   e. View diversity as an asset. Reject notions of cultural deficit.

FIGURE 9–1
Constructs for Promoting Learning and Language Acquisition

(Gersten, 1999; Gersten & Woodward, 1994) and in patterns of achievement (de la Rosa & Maw, 1990; Ramírez, 1992). The following instructional techniques can be—and have been—used in other content areas, such as science and social studies (Chamot & O'Malley, 1989). As the scenarios illustrate, it's often more important to provide clear feedback and instructional models than spend time on extensive curriculum modifications, especially when students are having specific difficulty hearing and/or vocalizing particular sounds.

Scenario One: Merging Language Learning with Reading Instruction

The following example demonstrates how literature and language development can be merged for a group of third graders with very little English proficiency. Constructs 1, 2, and 3 described in Figure 9–1 are in evidence. These students also received native language instruction during a portion of their school day. The example comes from our observational research (Gersten & Jiménez, 1994).

The teacher began by reading a story to the class in the form of a big book, *Bringing the Rain to Kapiti Plain,* by Verna Aardema (1981). She spoke to the students in a clearer, less hurried pace than she used in normal conversation. She also intentionally avoided synonyms. Both of these strategies seemed to increase students' levels of involvement in the lesson (as judged by eye contact), and most importantly, their comprehension.

After reading two or three pages of the story, she paused to check the students' understanding:

> **TEACHER:**   What does the bow do?
> **SIPYANA:**   Shoots arrow.

Note that the question is intentionally literal, so that the teacher could assess whether students understood a crucial vocabulary word, *bow*. Because the protagonist of the story is portrayed as a hero who causes rain to fall by shooting a feather from his bow into a cloud, it made sense that some children might benefit from hearing an explanation of this key word (Construct 2: Relevant Background Knowledge and Key Vocabulary Concepts).

A second question called for a moderate inference. It elicited a correct but truncated answer from a student: teacher: What does he hope will happen when he shoots the arrow?

> **TRAN:**   The rain. (He motions rain falling.)
> **TEACHER:**   Right, the rain will fall down.

This student understood both the intent of the story and the question posed by his teacher, but was unable (or was afraid to) fully express his thoughts in English. The teacher extended and elaborated on the child's utterance. Her action had the dual effect of affirming the student's response and modeling a more complete English sentence structure for the others, *but without shaming the student* (Construct 1a: Provide support to students, and Construct 3: Mediation and Feedback). Note that this teacher speaks *none* of the five languages represented in her class (Lao, Cambodian, Thai, Spanish, and Vietnamese), yet her approach enables her to support students' understanding of the reading material.

Overall, oral language and vocabulary is the first step to building literacy skills (de Leon & Medina, 1998). August and Hakuta (1997) noted that vocabulary is the primary determinant of comprehension and Jiménez et al. (1996) identified vocabulary as the single greatest deterrent for comprehension for most English language learners. As presented in the previous scenario, general principles of language and vocabulary instruction for native English speakers also hold true for English language learners (Beck, McKeown, & Kucan, 2002; Carlo, Snow, & August, 2004). Using a contextual approach, like the discussion of words and concepts within the context of *Bringing the Rain to Kapiti Plain,* and making multiple semantic connections by *strategically integrating* learned words with new words in future lessons helps promote language development. Systematic and judicious review, multiple examples, and different media presentations with multiple modalities are other instructional principles that can be incorporated into language learning during reading instruction.

Scenario Two: Building Intellectual Accountability During Literacy Instruction

In this example, when a teacher found that her third-grade class could not come up with a complete description or analysis of a character in the story they were reading, she provided one. For example, none of the students could explain precisely why a character was disobedient. Partial responses, such as "She was dying for gum," were provided. Finally, the teacher integrated comments by several students into a full response: "She is disobedient because she eats gum despite what her mother tells her" (Construct 1a: Build on and clarify input of students).

However, providing students with a complete response was used only as a last resort. Typically the teacher elicited more elaborate and sophisticated responses from the students. She stressed words, such as *disobedient, generous, anxious*, that not only helped them understand the story, but also would be key words in an English language development or English as a second language (ESL) curriculum (Construct 2b: Focus on key vocabulary words).

The teacher used a bit of Spanish now and then to clarify complex concepts. For example, when she realized that students were not sure what the word *generous* meant, she used the Spanish word *generoso.* Most importantly, she spent a good deal of time framing a discussion of the generosity of a character by asking students to provide evidence located in the text. Because of the meaningful incorporation of students' primary language and the comprehensible support structures provided for locating needed information, this instructional activity exemplified Construct 3j: Exhibit sensitivity to common problems in second language learning.

Before reading, the teacher always asked students to generate predictions, which she placed on an overhead transparency. After reading the text, each prediction was evaluated by the class. The teacher explicitly pointed out that the main character was "nice and sweet" rather than the "troublemaker" that one student had predicted based on the title of the story. No negative value was placed on making predictions that were not validated, but the teacher made it clear that all predictions would always be taken seriously, reviewed, and evaluated. This sense of intellectual accountability not only facilitated students' ability to perform these same functions later, but also served as motivational devices: Students looked forward to seeing how closely their predictions actually matched the information they encountered in text (Construct 4: Involvement, and Construct 5: Challenge).

In addition to building intellectual accountability, this scenario also illustrates how the teacher used a structured form of classroom discourse and embedded authentic, language-focused conversations to provide a form of *mediated scaffolding* for student understanding (de Leon & Medina, 1998). Text-focused discourse can increase student comprehension by building on ideas and promoting meaningful connections between ideas. By anchoring comprehension in the context of text-focused discourse, teachers can clarify and substantiate students' understandings of concepts, vocabulary, and ideas (Gersten et al., 2001; Pressley & McCormick, 1995). Integrative dialogue, with a teacher's intentional strategic question-asking and prompts, requires a child to step back and reflect on the storyline or the story language. In the scenario just described, the teacher required students think about the character in the story and make story predictions by becoming part of an active teacher–student dialogue about the text. For English language learners, just like other native English speakers, this interactive dialogue leads to deep processing, repetition, and additional connections (Beck, McKeown, Hamilton, & Kucan, 1997; Whitehurst et al., 1994).

Scenario Three: Accessing First Language Knowledge During Literacy Instruction

A recent trend has been to develop strategies that teachers can use to activate the skills and strategies that students possess in Spanish and to encourage them to use this knowledge in their English language classrooms (Chamot, 1992). This section contains an example that illustrates the powerful role the use of children's native language can play in teaching and learning. The example is from a classroom in which students were beginning to make the transition from Spanish content instruction to English-language content instruction. Note that students who appeared incompetent in an all-English context actually could produce credible responses to teacher requests when given the chance to respond in their native language.

In the example, a teacher conducted a conversation with his fifth-grade students in preparation for a story they were about to read in English about cowboys and cowgirls. The teacher and his students collaboratively created a list of English vocabulary words related to this topic. This technique, checking for understanding, is simple but effective as the comment by one student, José, attests:

TEACHER: If you don't understand all those words, raise your hand.
CRISTINA: Holster
CHELI: Chaps
Teacher draws a picture of chaps and a holster.
JOSÉ: *O, sí, sí, sí. Ya sé que son.* (Oh, yes, yes, yes. Now I know what they are!)

Like the teacher in the preceding example, this teacher shows sensitivity to problems in second-language learning. Note that he intentionally used visual representations to assist children to think in English (Construct 1b: Use visual organizers to help students organize and relate information). José's comments indicate that he possessed the necessary information for comprehending the vocabulary presented, but without the proper mediation by the teacher (in this case, use of visuals), he might have been incapable of convincing either himself or his teacher that he did.

Scenario Four: Integrating Responsiveness to Cultural and Personal Diversity into Literacy Instruction

Listening to students is a distinguishing feature of this next example. The classroom observed was a fourth-grade "transition room"—that is, a class of students in their first year of virtually all-English language instruction. The teacher is monolingual and has no formal background in second language acquisition, but does have a real commitment to teaching minority students. This teacher utilizes a relatively pure process approach involving a writers' workshop students' selections of books that they will read (in English), and a heavy emphasis on projects and journal writing.

The teacher had just finished a conference with a student named Ruben. Ruben was a quiet, bookworm type of student. Ruben wanted to read a book about Michael Jordan. A boy in the room said, "Ruben has no business doing that. He doesn't know anything about sports." The teacher overheard this remark and intervened. He said, "That's not true. Ruben and his brother watch soccer and basketball games all the time. He knows a lot about basketball." This is an illustration of Construct 6: Respect for and Responsiveness to Cultural and Personal Diversity.

A minute later, another student, Cynthia, asked if it was all right to read a book about the Monitor and Merrimack again. She had read it in the fall, but felt her English was much better now than it had been at that time and she knew a lot more about history. The teacher said "Sure" and then described to the class what Cynthia was doing and told them that it was okay for anyone else in the class to do the same thing. The teacher suggested that because they had become much better readers, they may want to go back and reread something they had previously read.

These types of authentic interactions are interesting in that the students are treated like real people, with likes, dislikes, and idiosyncrasies. The teacher listened carefully to what they said, and usually found it interesting. Note how the teacher in the previous example used this strategy to directly draw students' attention to the benefits associated with rereading.

These techniques allow teachers to encourage and assist in oral English language development because:

1. Remarks and comments of students were taken seriously.
2. Students were provided with opportunities to engage in extended discourse in English, using complex concepts and attempting to explain concepts in their own words (Construct 4: Involvement).

As evidenced by the previous example, mere knowledge of Spanish is clearly not sufficient and not always necessary. Although teachers observed in this study who tended to really treat their students as individuals also tended to do more "thinking aloud" and modeling of cognitive processes, the correlation was far from perfect. The interplay of this human aspect of instruction and the more cognitively or behaviorally oriented aspects of effective teaching requires further investigation.

The teachers discussed in the preceding section achieved a delicate balance of high structure, clear focus, and rich objectives that was rare. In order to accomplish these goals with students with limited English-speaking ability, the teachers needed to utilize many of the effective teaching techniques: use of clear and consistent language to describe difficult concepts (Gersten & Jiménez, 1998; Gersten, Woodward, & Darch, 1986), clear statement of objectives, a range of activities to review and clarify applications of new concepts and material, and clear rules not only for social behavior in class, but for instructional conversations (Goldenberg, 1992–1993). Most importantly, high levels of teacher–student interaction were virtually always prevalent.

The most impressive strategy we observed—and it was rare—was for teachers to actually focus on a single aspect of written language for a short period of time, such as verbs, adjectives, or questions and question marks, and to essentially ignore other aspects of language during that time frame. This approach is akin to the focus on "big ideas" recommended throughout this book. For example, instruction for English language learners in kindergarten might focus on syntax and the use of abstract words like *will, can,* and *have,* while words like *because* and *however* might be the focus in the primary grades. Note, however, that the big ideas stressed for second language learners are geared toward helping students focus on critical aspects of English language production, both oral and written. Often referred to as "academic English," the language of school and the classroom becomes clearer and more meaningful to students when there is focus on only one or two abstract/foundational concepts or words (Echevarria, Vogt, & Short, 2004). In other words, teachers often impact language comprehension with more instructional depth when only one or two abstract words are introduced with a set of more concrete words. A word set with the abstract word, *which,* and more concrete words, *tunnel, fatigue,* and *superior* is an example of how words can be selected by following these instructional guidelines.

When teachers focus on only one critical aspect of language at a time, students know what is expected of them and can direct their energy and attention to that one aspect of the new language. For example, one teacher asked students to rewrite their story using several "words that describe" (adjectives). The teacher wrote a list of possible words that describe on the board, but students could not succeed by merely copying them; they had to know which words fit the context of their story (Construct 1b: Use aids to help students organize and relate information).

The teacher's feedback for that day focused solely on words that describe; no comments were made on spelling or punctuation (Construct 3a: Provide feedback that focuses on meaning). "Correcting" students' grammatical errors has a potentially negative effect on students' self-esteem. Instead, teachers should provide feedback that is based more on the content than on the form of the student's response, at least initially.

Teachers with expertise in more structured approaches such as direct instruction, active teaching, or any of the other approaches that have become so popular in the last decade have a battery of techniques, strategies, and ways of conceptualizing instruction that have the potential to be successful with English language learners. When students falter or flounder in their attempts to work out a solution, are unable collectively to articulate how they figured out a character's motive, or cannot draw an appropriate inference, our observations (Gersten, 1999; Jiménez & Gersten, 1999) consistently suggest that it is essential for the teacher to step in and provide a model (e.g., mediated scaffolding).

SUMMARY

Providing quality instruction for English language learners is of critical importance to educators across the nation. Educators need to be sensitive to the double demands placed on English language learners that include learning the English language while mastering challenging content. We believe that the guidelines presented in this chapter for modulating instruction will allow for more sensitive, cognitively challenging, and ultimately, more effective teaching of English language learners. These guidelines include providing students with:

1. Mediated scaffolding
2. Primed background knowledge
3. Mediation and feedback
4. Opportunities for active involvement
5. Challenging content
6. Respect for responsiveness to cultural and personal diversity

REFERENCES

AARDEMA, V. (1981). *Bringing the rain to Kapiti Plain*. New York: Dial Press.

ANDERSON, V., & ROIT, M. (1993). *Reading as a gateway to language for primary students of limited English proficiency*. Manuscript submitted for publication.

ANDERSON, V., & ROIT, M. (1996). Linking reading comprehension instruction to language development for language-minority students. *Elementary School Journal, 96*, 295–310.

AUGUST, D. (1999). *Vocabulary knowledge and reading comprehension in English language learners*. Presentation at 1999 American Educational Research Association, Montréal, Canada (with Barry McLaughlin, Catherine Snow, and Terri Lively).

AUGUST, D., & HAKUTA, K. (1997). *Improving schooling for language-minority children*. Washington, DC: National Academy Press.

AUGUST, D., & HAKUTA, K. (Eds.). (1998). *Educating language-minority children*. Washington, DC: National Academies Press.

BAKER, K. A., & DE KANTER, A. A. (1981). *Effectiveness of bilingual education: A review of the literature*. Washington, DC: U.S. Department of Education.

BAKER, K. A., & DE KANTER, A. A. (1983). *Bilingual education: A reappraisal of federal policy*. Lexington, MA: Lexington Books.

BARRERA, R. (1984). Bilingual reading in the primary grades: Some questions about questionable views and practices. In T. H. Escobar (Ed.), *Early childhood bilingual education* (pp. 164–183). New York: Teachers College Press.

BARRINGER, F. (1993, April 28). When English is foreign tongue: Census finds a sharp rise in '80s. *New York Times*, pp. 1, 10.

BECK, I. L., MCKEOWN, M. G., & KUCAN, L. (2002). *Bringing words to life: Robust vocabulary instruction*. New York: Guilford.

BECK, I. L., MCKEOWN, M. G., HAMILTON, R., & KUCAN, L. (1997). *Questioning the author: An approach for enhancing student engagement with text*. Newark, DE: International Reading Association.

BERMAN, P., CHAMBERS, J., GANDARA, P., MCLAUGHLIN, B., MINICUCCI, C., NELSON, B., et al. (1992). *Meeting the challenge of language diversity. Volume I: Executive summary*. Berkeley, CA: BW Associates.

CARLO, M. S., AUGUST, D., MCLAUGHLIN, B., SNOW, C. E., DRESSLER, C., LIPPMAN, D., LIVELY, T., & WHITE, C. (2004). Closing the gap: Addressing the vocabulary needs for English language learners in bilingual and mainstream classrooms. *Reading Research Quarterly, 39*, 188–215.

CAZDEN, C. B. (1992). *Whole language plus: Essays on literacy in the United States & New Zealand*. New York: Teachers College Press.

CHAMOT, A. U. (1992, August). *Changing instruction for language minority students to achieve national goals*. Paper presented at Third National Research Symposium on Limited English Proficient Students, Office of Bilingual Education and Minority Languages Affairs, Arlington, VA.

CHAMOT, A. U., DALE, M., O'MALLEY, J. M., & SPANOS, G. A. (1993). Learning and problem solving strategies of ESL students. *Bilingual Research Journal, 16*(3 & 4), 1–34.

CHAMOT, A. U., & O'MALLEY, J. M. (1989). The cognitive academic language learning approach. In P. Rigg & V. Allen (Eds.), *When they don't all speak English* (pp. 108–125). Urbana, IL: National Council of Teachers of English.

CHIAPPE, P., SIEGEL, L., & WADE-WOOLLEY, L. (2002). "Linguistic diversity and the development of reading skills: A longitudinal study." *Scientific Studies of Reading, 6*, 369–400.

CRAWFORD, J. (1995). *Bilingual education: History, politics, theory and practice*. Los Angeles: Bilingual Education Services.

CUMMINS, J. (1989). A theoretical framework for bilingual special education. *Exceptional Children, 56*(2), 111–119.

CZIKO, G. A. (1992). The evaluation of bilingual education. *Educational Researcher, 21*(2), 10–15.

DANOFF, M. N., COLES, G. J., MCLAUGHLIN, D. H., & REYNOLDS, D. J. (1977–1978). *Evaluation of the impact of ESEA Title VII Spanish/English Bilingual Education Program*. Palo Alto, CA: American Institutes for Research.

DE LA ROSA, D., & MAW, C. (1990). *Hispanic education: A statistical portrait*. Washington, DC: National Council of La Raza.

DE LEON, J., & MEDINA, C. (1998). Language and preliteracy development of English as a second language learners in early childhood special education. In R. Gersten & R. Jiménez (Eds.), *Promoting learning for culturally and linguistically diverse students: Classroom applications from contemporary research* (pp. 26–41). Belmont, CA: Wadsworth.

ECHEVARRIA, J., VOGT, M., & SHORT, D. J. (2000). *Making content comprehensible for English language learners: The SIOP model.* Boston, MA: Allyn and Bacon.

FRADD, S. H. (1987). Accommodating the needs of limited English proficient students in regular classrooms. In S. Fradd & W. Tikunoff (Eds.), *Bilingual education and special education: A guide for administrators* (pp. 133–182). Boston: Little, Brown.

GARCIA, G., PEARSON, P., & JIMÉNEZ, R. (1990). *The at-risk dilemma: A synthesis of reading research.* Champaign, IL: University of Illinois at Urbana-Champaign, Reading Research and Education Center.

GENESEE, F. (1984). Historical and theoretical foundations of immersion education. Studies on immersion education (pp. 32–57). Sacramento: California State Department of Education.

GERSTEN, R. (1996). Literacy instruction for language-minority students: The transition years. *Elementary School Journal, 96*(3), 227–244.

GERSTEN, R. (1999). Lost opportunities: Challenges confronting four teachers of English-language learners. *Elementary School Journal, 100*(1), 37–56.

GERSTEN, R., & BAKER, S. (2000). What we know about effective instructional practices for English-language learners. *Exceptional Children.*

GERSTEN, R., BAKER, S. K., HAAGER, D. & GRAVES, A. W. (2005). Exploring the role of teacher quality in predicting reading outcomes for first-grade English learners: An observational study. *Remedial & Special Education, 26,* 197–206.

GERSTEN, R., & JIMÉNEZ, R. (Eds.). (1998). *Promoting learning for culturally and linguistically diverse students: Classroom applications from contemporary research.* Belmont, CA: Wadsworth.

GERSTEN, R., & FUCHS, L. S, WILLIAMS, J. P., & BAKER, S. (2001). Teaching reading comprehension strategies to students with learning disabilities. *Review of Educational Research, 71,* 279–320.

GERSTEN, R., & GEVA, E. (2003). Teaching reading to early language learners. *Educational Leadership, 60,* 44–49.

GERSTEN, R., & JIMÉNEZ, R. (1994). A delicate balance: Enhancing literacy instruction for students of English as a second language. *The Reading Teacher, 47*(6), 438–449.

GERSTEN, R., & WOODWARD, J. (1985). A case for structured immersion. *Educational Leadership, 43*(1), 75–78.

GERSTEN, R., & WOODWARD, J. (1994). The language minority student and special education: Issues, themes and paradoxes. *Exceptional Children, 60*(4), 310–322.

GERSTEN, R., & WOODWARD, J. (1995). A longitudinal study of transitional and immersion bilingual education programs in one district. *Elementary School Journal, 95,* 223–240.

GERSTEN, R., WOODWARD, J., & DARCH, C. (1986). Direct instruction: A research-based approach for curriculum design and teaching. *Exceptional Children, 53*(1), 17–36.

GOLDENBERG, C. (1992–1993). Instructional conversations: Promoting comprehension through discussion. *The Reading Teacher, 46*(4), 316–326.

GOLDENBERG, C. (1996). The education of language-minority students: Where are we, and where do we need to go? *Elementary School Journal, 93,* 353–361.

GREENE, J. P. (1998). *A meta-analysis of the effectiveness of bilingual education.* Unpublished technical report. Austin: University of Texas & The Thomas Rivera Policy Institute.

HAKUTA, K., & SNOW, C. (1986). The role of research in policy decisions about bilingual education. *NABE News, 9*(3), 1, 18–21.

HUBLER, D. (2005, August 10). Task force to gauge progress of English-language learners. *Education Daily,* 1–2.

JIMENEZ, R., GARCIA, G. E., & PEARSON, P. D. (1996). The reading strategies of bilingual Latina/o students who are successful English readers: Opportunities and obstacles. *Reading Research Quarterly, 31,* 2–25.

JIMÉNEZ, R. T., & GERSTEN, R. (1999). Lessons and dilemmas derived from the literacy instruction of two Latina/o teachers. *American Educational Research Journal, 36* (2), 265–301.

LESAUX, N., & SIEGEL, L. (2003). The development of reading in children who speak English as a second language. *Developmental Psychology, 39,* 1005–1019.

MOLL, L. C., ESTRADA, E., DIAZ, E., & LOPES, L. M. (1980). The organization of bilingual lessons: Implications for schooling. *The Quarterly Newsletter of the Laboratory of Comparative Human Cognition, 2* (3), 53–58.

PRESSLEY, M., & MCCORMICK, C. B. (1995). *Advanced educational psychology for educators, researchers, and policymakers.* New York: HarperCollins.

RAMÍREZ, J. D. (1992). Executive summary of volumes I and II of the final report: Longitudinal study of structured English immersion strategy, early-exit and late-exit transitional bilingual education programs for language-minority children. *Bilingual Research Journal, 16* (1), 1–62.

REYES, M. DE LA LUZ (1992). Challenging venerable assumptions: Literacy instruction for linguistically different students. *Harvard Educational Review, 62* (4), 427–446.

ROSSELL, C. H., & BAKER, K. (1996). The educational effectiveness of bilingual education. *Research in the Teaching of English, 30* (1), 7–74.

SAVILLE-TROIKE, M. (1982). The development of bilingual and bicultural competence in young children. *Current topics in early childhood education.* Norwood, NJ: Ablex.

TIKUNOFF, W. J. (1985). *Applying significant bilingual instructional features in the classroom.* Rosslyn, VA: National Clearinghouse for Bilingual Education.

TROIKE, R. C. (1981). Synthesis of research on bilingual education. *Educational Leadership, 38* (6), 498–504.

WHITEHURST, G. J., ARNOLD, D. S., EPSTEIN, J. N., ANGELL, A. L., SMITH, M., FISCHEL, J. E. (1994). A picture book reading intervention in day care and homes for children from low-income families. *Developmental Psychology, 30,* 679–689.

WILLIG, A. C. (1985). A meta-analysis of selected studies on the effectiveness of bilingual education. *Review of Educational Research, 55* (3), 269–317.

WONG-FILLMORE, L., & VALADEZ, C. (1986). Teaching bilingual learners. In M. C. Wittrock (Ed.), *Handbook of research on teaching* (pp. 648–685). Upper Saddle River, NJ: Prentice Hall.

YATES, J. R., & ORTIZ, A. A. (1991). Professional development needs of teachers who serve exceptional language minorities in today's schools. *Teacher Education and Special Education, 14* (1), 11–18.

APPENDIX A
Answers to Content Questions

Chapter 3: Effective Strategies for Teaching Beginning Reading

Content Questions

1. What are two factors that could potentially help decrease the pervasiveness of reading difficulties in the United States?

    The first factor is an emerging coalition of support for research-based efforts directed at improving reading outcomes for all students, and especially students at risk of reading disability and reading failure. The second factor is the consolidation of a substantial knowledge base built on the sizable body of converging, multidisciplinary research evidence accumulated over the past 40 years. (pp. 46–47)

2. What was the conclusion of the National Academy of Sciences in the 1998 report of the National Research Council?

    The weight of empirical research evidence in beginning reading was sufficient to reach broad consensus within the field. (p. 47)

3. Name one important conclusion from the research on beginning reading.

    Conclusions include. (a) the importance of learning to read in the early grades, and (b) students disadvantaged in reading skills have an extremely difficult time catching up to their peers. (pp. 47–48)

4. What are the three big ideas in beginning reading instruction?

    Three big ideas in beginning reading instruction include

    a. phonological awareness
    b. alphabetic understanding
    c. automaticity with the code (p. 49)

5. Why do many children have difficulty developing phonological awareness?

    The understanding that language is made up of discrete sounds is an unnatural insight because words are pronounced as whole units in conversational language. Facilitating phonological awareness, therefore, requires directly teaching children strategies to "attend to that which we have learned not to attend to" (Adams, 1990, p. 66). (p. 54)

6. What are the alphabetic understanding strategies that should be taught conspicuously?

    Instruction that conspicuously teaches alphabetic understanding provides students with strategies for producing letter–sound correspondences and decoding words. (pp. 56–57)

7. Describe a sequence for scaffolding decoding instruction.

    a. Scaffold 1—Model. The teacher says the sounds in a word while touching under each letter.
    b. Scaffold 2—Overt Sound Out. The teacher touches under each letter while students say each sound.

    c. Scaffold 3—Internal Sound Out. The teacher touches under each letter while students say each sound in their head.

    d. Scaffold 4—Whole Word Reading. The teacher points to the word and students sound it out independently. (p. 59)

8. Name four task scaffolds in beginning reading instruction.

   Scaffolding in beginning reading instruction requires

   a. Beginning with easy tasks and systematically progressing to more difficult ones.
   b. Introducing a manageable amount of information in a lesson.
   c. Purposefully separating highly similar and potentially confusing concepts
   d. Scaffolding types of student responses. (pp. 59–60)

9. How should phonological awareness, alphabetic understanding, and automaticity with code be integrated strategically?

   Students who know some letter–sound correspondences and are able to orally blend and segment words should begin word reading. Similarly, students who are able to read simple words should move into reading connected, decodable texts to develop automaticity and fluency. (pp. 61–62)

Chapter 4: Effective Strategies for Teaching Reading Comprehension

Content Questions

1. Describe inside-out and outside-in components of literacy development.

   Inside-out components include phonological awareness, alphabetic understanding, and automaticity with the code. These code-based components require students to understand and use our complex alphabetic code to read words and connected text. Outside-in components relate to comprehending text. These meaning-based components skills require students to draw on their understanding of language, word meanings, prior knowledge, and strategies for extracting and constructing meaning. (p. 80)

2. List four big ideas in reading comprehension.

   Four big ideas in reading comprehension are (a) fluency, (b) vocabulary knowledge, (c) strategic processing, and (d) text features. (p. 82)

3. Describe two reasons why reading fluency is important to reading comprehension.

   First, fluent reading frees up attention for constructing and responding to the meaning of a text. Second, fluent readers are likely to read more than their peers who are not fluent. This results in benefits such as enhanced reading fluency, vocabulary, and background knowledge. (p. 83)

4. Name and briefly describe two dimensions of vocabulary knowledge that have implications for reading and listening comprehension.

   Breadth and depth of word knowledge both contribute to reading and listening comprehension: (a) breadth of word knowledge refers to the total number of word meanings that students possess, (b) depth of word knowledge refers to the different levels at which words may be understood (e.g., totally unknown, partially known, and fully known). (p. 84)

5. List eight reading comprehension strategies.

    Reading comprehension strategies include (a) identifying important information, (b) inferring/predicting, (c) monitoring/clarifying, (d) generating and answering questions, (e) visualizing, (f) summarizing, (g) synthesizing, and (h) evaluating. (p. 85)

6. Describe metacognition and explain why it is important to reading comprehension.

    Metacognition is the ability to manage and control cognitive activities in a reflective manner or to "think about one's thinking." Students with this ability monitor for understanding, apply strategies flexibly, and effectively combine strategies. (p. 86)

7. Describe why experiences with informational text might benefit young children.

    Students are increasingly expected to read expository or information books as reading development progresses. However, informational texts use text organizational patterns, or combinations of patterns, that are more difficult than narrative text structure. (p. 88)

8. List three strategies to promote strategic integration in reading comprehension.

    Strategies to promote strategic integration in reading comprehension include: (a) teaching the use of strategies in combination; (b) providing opportunities for practice with combined text structures/organizational patterns; (c) applying comprehension strategies across multiple content domains. (pp. 93–95)

Chapter 5: Effective Strategies for Teaching Writing

Content Questions

1. How does Smith (1982) characterize the writing processes?

    The writer works as both author and secretary. The writer-as-author concentrates on content and composition. Simultaneously, the author-as-secretary concentrates on the mechanics of writing. (p. 113)

2. What has been the predominant approach to writing instruction in American schools?

    Writing instruction has focused primarily on secretarial concerns, and composition activities have been minimal. The emphasis on skill-dominant approaches is even more prevalent for diverse learners. (p. 113)

3. Explain the authors' recommendation for resolving conflicts between skills-dominant and composition-dominant approaches for writing instruction.

    Parallel instruction is recommended involving both author and secretary roles for all aspects of writing throughout the entire process. (p. 114)

4. Identify and describe three big ideas of writing instruction.

    a. *The writing process involves planning, drafting, and revising written work.*
    b. *Text structures represent structural characteristics that are commonly recurring elements for each writing genre.*
    c. *Peer interaction involves all students in authoring, editing, and reading roles in cooperative work groups. (pp. 115–117)*

5. What are "planning strategies" in writing and why should these strategies be presented conspicuously?

Conspicuous "planning strategies" help students with the steps of starting and completing their planning for composition. The normally covert cognitive processes of writing experts are presented conspicuously to students. (pp. 117–118)

6. Briefly describe the conspicuous strategy that is recommended for addressing grammar problems in sentence writing.

Students are taught to decompose or simplify the original sentence in question, and then to revise the mechanics of the sentence accordingly. (p. 118)

7. Describe three conditions in which scaffolding can be provided to learners.

Scaffolding can be provided:

a. directly by teachers, through guidance and feedback.
b. by peers through collaboration.
c. through instructional materials. (p. 119)

8. Define the term "procedural facilitators" and describe how it is used for writing instruction. What is the most effective use of procedural facilitators?

The term "procedural facilitators" describes scaffolding that is built into tasks. It assumes that students have the underlying competencies necessary for writing, but provides students with additional assistance in implementing their skills due to the complexity of writing. The most effective use of procedural facilitators involves integration with other forms of support whenever the student is experiencing difficulty with a complex task. (pp. 119–120)

Chapter 6: Effective Strategies for Teaching Mathematics

Content Questions

1. Describe the challenge in providing students with useful strategies.

The major challenge of strategy instruction is to develop strategies with a good balance of broad and specific applications that are "intermediate in generality" (Prawat, 1989). Strategies that are too narrow encourage rote knowledge with little application or understanding. Strategies that are too broad are not dependable for solving problems. (p. 148)

2. What is the most valuable use of big ideas in mathematics instruction?

Big ideas that connect different problem types that seem unrelated to a single strategy are most valuable, especially to learners who have difficulty making such connections. (p. 149)

3. List seven applications of the proportions strategy.

Applications of the proportions strategy include

a. simple proportion problems
b. rate
c. measurement equivalence
d. percent
e. probability
f. the coordinate system
g. functions (p. 154)

4. What has been a problem with providing instructional feedback in traditional mathematics instruction?

   Feedback is given too late, after the problem is solved, and the grade is given too early, before the student has had adequate practice with solving the problem. (p. 155)

5. Explain the authors' suggestions for scaffolding mathematics problems.

   After modeling the formula, the teacher scaffolds the steps of the strategy, initially providing students with feedback at every step. (p. 155)

6. How can instruction prepare diverse learners for the challenges posed by the NCTM standards?

   Instruction should provide learners with necessary prior knowledge and flexible strategies based on big ideas. (p. 156)

7. What behaviors do must diverse learners perform in order to solve novel problems?

   For diverse learners to successfully engage in solving novel problems, they must be able to apply a strategy and know when not to apply it. (p. 157)

8. Name and describe two aspects necessary for the successful integration of problem-solving strategies.

   Advanced strategies are taught in order to accommodate more complex problem types. New strategies are assimilated with simpler strategies that handle fewer elements. (p. 158)

Chapter 7: Effective Strategies for Teaching Science

Content Questions

1. Describe the big ideas of science according to NRC standards.

   A big idea of science

   a. is representative of central scientific ideas and principles.
   b. has explanatory and predictive power.
   c. encourages the formulation of significant questions.
   d. is applicable to a variety of contexts and situations. (p. 172)

2. List four commonly cited criticisms of science texts.

   Science texts

   a. contain too many concepts.
   b. present ideas in lists rather than in an integrated format.
   c. have unclear prose and illustrations.
   d. are ineffective in affecting conceptual change for meaningful learning. (p. 173)

3. Name and describe the steps of the scientific method.

   The scientific method involves:

   a. forming hypotheses to explain observed patterns or discrepancies.
   b. controlling and manipulating variables.
   c. planning investigations to test hypotheses.
   d. interpreting the resulting data. (p. 174)

4. What have been the findings of research comparing nonexplicit inquiry strategies with explicit methods of instruction?

   Instruction, that makes the strategies of science inquiry explicit has resulted in better learning than nonexplicit, inquiry methods of instruction. (p. 176)

5. List five examples of significant big ideas in science subject matter.

   Big ideas in science subject matter include (a) the nature of science, (b) energy transformations, (c) forces of nature, (d) flow of matter and energy in ecosystems, and (e) the interdependence of life. (p. 178)

6. What are three benefits of presenting big ideas in science curriculum?

   Big ideas

   a. apply to other domains of science and everyday phenomena.
   b. use time efficiently by covering more content meaningfully with fewer principles.
   c. function as prior knowledge for new science learning. (pp. 178–179)

7. Provide three examples that contribute to the "considerate" quality of an instructional tool.

   Examples of "considerate" instructional tools include

   a. Visual maps (e.g., concept maps, pictures, and diagrams).
   b. Contextual cues and rhetoric (headings and signal words).
   c. Structure, coherence, unity, and audience appropriateness. (p. 182)

8. Describe the continuum of instructional, scaffolding in science.

   Instructional Scaffolding in Science progresses from

   a. overt descriptions of thinking strategies to covert thinking strategies.
   b. teacher-directed to student-directed activity.
   c. prompted to unprompted assistance.
   d. instruction in component concepts to integrated concepts into a whole.
   e. contrived examples to naturalistic examples. (p. 188)

9. List each of the four components of judicious review and their benefits for science students.

   The four components of judicious review and their benefits include

   a. Sufficient review, which provides ample opportunity to develop problem-solving abilities and to apply concepts for understanding of big ideas.
   b. Distributed review, which contributes to long-term retention and problem-solving abilities.
   c. Varied review, which encourages a deeper understanding of concepts and contributes to the development of problem-solving abilities.
   d. Cumulative review, which promotes the development of an integrated understanding of big ideas. (pp. 189–190, 193)

Chapter 8: Effective Strategies for Teaching Social Studies

Content Questions

1. Describe two different struggles over expectations for teaching social studies.

   a. Determining the relative weight to give the various disciplines and identifying the disciplines that should be included in the social studies curriculum.
   b. The level of competency expected for students of social studies. (p. 204)

2. What is the purpose of social studies education, according to the recommendations of the National Council for Social Studies (NCSS)?

   The purpose of social studies education is to develop well-educated citizens who share common knowledge drawn from a range of disciplines in a systematic way. The content knowledge is derived through exploring important questions, rather than memorizing knowledge. (pp. 204–205)

3. Identify the problems associated with the instructional materials of elementary and secondary level social studies.

   Elementary level social studies materials teach too little content, and secondary level materials present quick overviews of too much content that lack depth. (p. 205)

4. How are big ideas identified in social studies instruction?

   Instructionally effective big ideas enable the learner to organize, interrelate, and apply information so that meaningful connections are made within social studies and between social studies content and their own lives. "Big ideas," if carefully chosen, can bring order to social studies content. (pp. 207–208)

5. Identify three examples of big ideas for social studies curriculum.

   Big ideas for social studies include

   a. problem–solution–effect
   b. multiple perspectives
   c. factors of group success (pp. 208–213)

6. Describe the components of problem–solution–effect as a big idea in social studies.

   a. Problems are attributed to economic or human rights issues.
   b. Solutions refer to the recurring actions that people implement to solve problems.
   - Move: *People move in order to solve a problem, hoping to find a place where the problem does not exist.*
   - Invent: *People invent new ways of accomplishing things that they could not do before.*
   - Dominate: *People control or dominate others as an attempt to solve problems.*
   - Accommodate: *People adjust or adapt in order to solve a problem.*
   - Tolerate: *When people decide not to move, invent, dominate, or accommodate, they tolerate the problem.*
   c. Effects: Solutions to problems cause consequences or effects. Problems may cease to exist or new problems are created. (pp. 208–210)

7. Define what is meant by a strategy and provide an example of a conspicuous strategy.

   A strategy is a general set of steps used to solve a problem or analyze content. An example of a conspicuous strategy in social studies would be application of the big idea of problem–solution–effect when examining group behavior. (p. 214)

8. Provide three examples of content organizers that can be used to scaffold social studies instruction.

   Three examples of content organizers that can be used to scaffold social studies instruction include maps, time lines, and study guides. (p. 215)

APPENDIX B
Curriculum Maps for Grades K–3 for Phonological Awareness, Alphabetic Principle, and Spelling

Mapping of Instruction to Achieve Instructional Priorities
Kindergarten

Instructional Priority: Phonological Awareness	1	2	3	4	5	6	7	8	9
Focus 1: Sound and Word Discrimination									
1a: Tells whether words and sounds are the same or different	X	X							
1b: Identifies which word is different	X	X							
1c: Identifies different speech sound			X	X					
Focus 2: Rhyming†									
2a: Identifies whether words rhyme	X								
2b: Produces a word that rhymes		X	X						
Focus 3: Blending									
3a: Orally blends syllables or onset-rimes			X	X					
*3b: Orally blends separate phonemes					X	X	X		
Focus 4: Segmentation									
4a: Claps words in sentences		X	X						
4b: Claps syllables in words			X	X					
4c: Says syllables			X	X					
*4d: Identifies initial sound in 1-syllable words				10	25				
*4e: Segments individual sounds in words							10	20	35‡

*High-priority skill

†Optimal time for rhyme instruction not established

‡Sounds per minute

257

Mapping of Instruction to Achieve instructional Priorities
Grade 1

Instructional Priority: Phonological Awareness	1	2	3	4	5	6	7	8	9
Focus 1: Sound Isolation									
1a: Identifies initial sound in 1-syllable words	X	X							
1b: Identifies final sound in 1-syllable words	X	X	X						
1c: Identifies medial sound in 1-syllable words	X	X	X	X					
Focus 2: Sound Blending									
*2a: Blends 3–4 phonemes into a whole word	X	X	X	X	X				
Focus 3: Sound Segmentation									
*3a: Segments 3- and 4-phoneme, 1-syllable words	35	38	41[†]						

*High-priority skill
[†]Number of phoneme segments per minute

258

Mapping of Instruction to Achieve Instructional Priorities
Kindergarten

Instructional Priority: Alphabetic Principle	1	2	3	4	5	6	7	8	9
Focus 1: Letter-Sound Correspondence									
1a: Identifies letter matched to a sound	X	X	X	X	X	X			
*1b: Says the most common sound associated with individual letters			4	8	12	16	20	24	24[†]
Focus 2: Decoding (Sounding Out Words)									
*2a: Blends letter sounds in 1-syllable words					12	16	20	24	24[†]
Focus 3: Sight-Word Reading									
3a: Recognizes some words by sight						X	X	X	X

*High-priority skill

[†]Sounds per minute

Mapping of Instruction to Achieve Instructional Priorities
Grade 1

Instructional Priority: Alphabetic Principle	1	2	3	4	5	6	7	8	9
Focus 1: Letter and Letter Combinations									
*1a: Produces L–S correspondences (1/sec)	X	X							
*1b: Produces sounds to common letter combinations			X	X	X	X			
Focus 2: Decoding (Sounding Out)									
*2a: Decodes words with consonant blends		X	X	X					
*2b: Decodes words with letter combinations			X	X	X	X	X		
*2c: Reads regular 1-syllable words fluently			X	X	X	X	X	X	
*2d: Reads words with common parts				X	X	X	X		
Focus 3: Sight-Word Reading									
*3a: Reads common sight words automatically	X	X	X	X	X	X	X	X	X
Focus 4: Reading Connected Text									
*4a: Read accurately (1 error in 20 words)			X	X	X	X	X	X	X
*4b: Reads fluently (1 words per 2–3 sec mid year; 1 word per sec end of year	8	16	24	30	36	42	48	54	60
4c: Phrasing attending to ending punctuation						X	X	X	X
4d: Reads and rereads to increase familiarity						X	X	X	X
4e: Rereads and self-corrects while reading		X	X	X	X				

*High-priority skill

Mapping of Instruction to Achieve Instructional Priorities
Grade 1

Instructional Priority: Spelling[†]

Focus 1: Word Spelling

	1	2	3	4	5	6	7	8	9
*1a: Writes letter associated with each sound in 1-syllable, phonetically regular words	X	X	X						
*1b: Spells single-syllable regular words correctly and independently		X	X	X	X				
*1c: Spells studied sight words accurately	X	X	X	X	X	X	X	X	X

*High-priority skill

[†]Once students can read phonetically regular words, they should be taught how to spell those words.

Mapping of Instruction to Achieve Instructional Priorities
Grade 2

Instructional Priority: Alphabetic Principle	1	2	3	4	5	6	7	8	9
Focus 1: Letter-Sound Knowledge									
*1a: Produces diphthongs and digraphs	X	X							
Focus 2: Decoding and Word Recognition									
*2a: Uses advanced phonic elements to recognize words	X	X	X	X					
2b: Reads compound words, contractions, possessives, inflectional endings			X	X	X	X			
2c: Reads multisyllabic words					X	X	X		
Focus 3: Sight-Word Reading									
*3a: Reads more sight words accurately	X	X	X	X	X	X	X	X	X
Focus 4: Reading Connected Text									
*4a: Reads 90–100 wpm	60	65	70	75	80	85	90	95	100
*4b: Reads with phrasing and expression			X	X	X				
4c: Listens to fluent oral reading and practices increasing oral reading fluency	10†	10	10	15	15	20	20	20	20
4d: Reads and rereads to increase familiarity	X	X	X	X	X	X	X	X	X
4e: Self-corrects word recognition errors	X	X							

*High-priority skill

†Minutes of practice per day

Mapping of Instruction to Achieve Instructional Priorities
Grade 2

Instructional Priority: Spelling	1	2	3	4	5	6	7	8	9
Focus 1: Word Spelling									
*1a: Spells previously studied phonetically regular words correctly	X	X	X	X	X	X	X	X	X
*1b: Uses phonetic strategies to spell unfamiliar words		X	X	X	X	X	X	X	X
1c: Spells frequently used sight words accurately		X	X	X	X	X	X	X	X
1d: Uses dictionary to check spellings					X	X	X	X	X

*High-priority skill

263

Mapping of Instruction to Achieve Instructional Priorities
Grade 3

Instructional Priority: Alphabetic Principle	1	2	3	4	5	6	7	8	9
Focus 1: Decoding and Word Recognition									
*1a: Produces common word parts	X								
*1b: Reads regular multisyllabic words		X	X	X	X				
1c: Reads compound words, contractions, possessives, inflectional endings		X	X	X	X	X			
1d: Uses word meaning and order in the sentence to confirm decoding efforts		X	X	X					
1e: Uses word structure knowledge to recognize multisyllabic words		X	X	X					
Focus 2: Sight-Word Reading									
*2a: Increases sight words read fluently	X	X	X	X	X	X	X	X	X
Focus 3: Reading Connected Text									
*3a: Reads 120 wpm	90	94	98	102	106	110	112	116	120
3b: Reads with phrasing, expression, inflection	X	X	X						
3c: Increases independent reading	5	10	10	15	15	20	20	25	30 minutes per day

*High-priority skill

Mapping of Instruction to Achieve Instructional Priorities
Grade 3

Instructional Priority: Spelling

	1	2	3	4	5	6	7	8	9
Focus 1: Word Spelling									
*1a: Spells phonetically regular words correctly	X								
*1b: Spells previously studied contractions, possessives, compound words, and words with inflectional endings		X	X	X	X	X			
1c: Organizes words in alphabetical order			X	X	X				
1d: Uses the dictionary or glossary to confirm and correct uncertain spellings					X	X	X		

*High-priority skill

265

A P P E N D I X   C
Author Note

Preparation of the chapters in this book was supported in part by The National Center to Improve the Tools of Educators, funded by the Office of Special Education Programs, U.S. Department of Education under Contract Number HS96013001.

Preparation of Chapter 9 was supported in part by the Division of Innovation and Development (HO23H00014), U.S. Department of Education, Office of Special Education Programs. Preparation of Chapter 3 was supported in part by Project Optimize, Grant Number H324C980156 funded by the Office of Special Education Programs, U.S. Department of Education.

The material in this book does not necessarily represent the policy of the U.S. Department of Education, nor is the material necessarily endorsed by the federal government.

Correspondence concerning this book should be addressed to Michael D. Coyne, Neag School of Education, University of Connecticut, Storrs, CT 06269-6024. Electronic mail may be sent to mike.coyne@uconn.edu.

NAME INDEX

SUBJECT INDEX